The History of the Green Bay Packers
Book III
The Lambeau Years
Part Three

by

Larry D. Names

Angel Press of WI

Wautoma, Wisconsin

1990

Angel Press of WI
P.O. Box 643
Wautoma, WI 54982

Copyright © 1990 by Larry D. Names
ISBN: 0-939995-02-6

All rights reserved, including the right
to reproduce this book or any portion thereof in
any form whatsoever. For information,
address inquiries to:
Angel Press of WI
P.O. Box 643
Wautoma, WI 54982

First Printing October 1990

Printed by
Bookcrafters
Chelsea, Michigan

Photographs courtesy of
The Green Bay Packers Hall of Fame
Pro Football Hall of Fame

Front cover photograph courtesy of
Tony Canadeo

Publisher............................Joseph H. Schlaefer

TABLE OF CONTENTS

Acknowledgements 9

Preface 11

Introduction 14

Chapter 1
    Another War Begins 21
        World War II and the NFL. Expansion during the war. New pro leagues on the drawing board. Red Grange accepts presidency of new USFL. Another AFL formed on West Coast. All-America Conference formed in '44 in Chicago. NFL Commissioner Elmer Layden snubs new leagues. Grange gives warning about football war. AAC Commissioner Jim Crowley leads fight for recognition of new league. Brooklyn team jumps to AAC. Grange offers another warning to owners. NFL starts working agreements with minor leagues. George Marshall berates AAC. Layden fired by NFL. Bert Bell made NFL commissioner. Cleveland Rams move to Los Angeles. 1946 football season ready to begin.

Chapter 2
    No Hutson, No Panache 33
        Review of 1945 NFL season. Review of Don Hutson's career with Packers. Comparison of Hutson's records to other NFL greats throughout the years. Hutson compared to Babe Ruth. Joe Laws retires. Bernie Crimmins retires. Winter meetings in New York. Packers make working agreement with San Diego Bombers of PCL. John Strzykalski is Green Bay's first pick in draft. Packers pressured to move to San Francisco. Seating capacity increased at State Fair Park in Milwaukee. Rumor that AAC Chicago Rockets to play some games in Milwaukee. Packers only lose one player to AAC. Rams break invisible color barrier by hiring Kenny Washington. Packers buy Rockwood Lodge. Training camp roster for '46. Packers open exhibition season in Milwaukee. Packers open regular season with loss to Bears. Commissioner Bert Bell cites attendance figures that really make NFL look bad. Packers lose second game to Bears. George Whitney Calhoun's attendance streak comes to an end in Chicago. Packers lose two of last three games to finish with worst record since 1934.

Chapter 3
    The AAC Challenge 46

Clark Hinkle's speech berating local interests in Green Bay. Bert Bell dispells rumors about Packers moving. Statistics show Green Bay not holding up NFL but NFL is holding up Packers. Rumor that AAC Miami franchise moving to Baltimore in order to keep Packers out of Maryland city. Gambling scandal over NFL title game in '46. Lambeau makes foolish statement to press on secrecy of NFL draft. Bears use first Bonus Pick in draft to take Bob Fennimore. Crowley resigns post as AAC commissioner to become part owner and coach of Chicago Rockets. Rumor that Rockets planning to move to Milwaukee. NFL talking about expansion for '47. Chicago Cards owner Charlie Bidwill dies. New AAC Commissioner Adm. Jonas Ingram calls for cease-fire in football war. Bert Bell ignores Ingram. AAC challenges NFL to title game. Bell says no. Rumor that Packers would never survive football war.

Chapter 4
Turning Back Time 56

Lambeau looking to improve passing attack. Green Bay's draft list for '47. Lambeau trades for Jack Jacobs. Lambeau replaces Calhoun with George Strickler as publicity man. Packers lose Cliff Aberson to baseball. Lambeau picks up Ward Cuff, Damon Tassos, and Bob McDougal in trades. Bo Molenda hired as backfield coach. Lee Joannes retires as president of Packers. Emil Fischer replaces Joannes. Executive committee expanded to 12 members. Packer board increased to 25 members. Lambeau making excuses for having only 42 men in training camp. Lambeau's power shifted to committees. Andy Uram tries a comeback with Packers. Rash of injuries strike Packers. Roster for '47. Packers open season on high note beating Bears and Rams. Cardinals down Packers in Green Bay. Beat Redskins and Lions before losing to Steelers for first time in history. Loss to Bears in Chicago. Art Daley makes comparison of Cuff and Fritsch as placekickers. Packers finish last winning season of the decade.

Chapter 5
The First Winter of Lambeau's Discontent 75

Lambeau weighing decision to quit Packers. Radio and the Packers. Lloyd Larson on sports and television. Rumors that Lambeau talking with other teams. Passing stats show Packers better through the air in '47 but worse on ground. Age and injuries taking toll on Packers. Draft list for '48. Signing of Jug Girard. Rumor that Bruce Smith to quit playing and take up coaching. Strickler causing problems for Lambeau. Charley Brock retires.

Chapter 6
Onward Football Soldiers 83

Philadelphia owner Alexis Thompson calls for cease-fire in pro football war. Bell and NFL owners ignore Thompson. Chicago Rockets in deep financial trouble. Cecil Isbell takes slap at Green Bay. Art Daley compares Packers to Baltimore Colts and comes up short. George Marshall feuds with Arch Ward over College All-Star game. Rest of NFL backs away from Marshall's stance on Ward. AAC awards franchise to Brooklyn. NFL winter meetings. Lions sold. NFL tables expansion. AAC moves to bolster Rockets and stay in Chicago. Comparison of NFL teams by city size. Financial strength of NFL teams. Jock Sutherland dies

Chapter 7
Once More into the Line 90

Lambeau having trouble signing draftees. Tony Canadeo holdouts. Lambeau threatens to trade Canadeo. Lambeau makes conflicting statements on player salaries, team profits, and financial history of NFL. List of returning veterans. Rest of roster for '48. John Torinus, Sr., elected to board of directors. Five veterans officially retire. Green Bay draftee, Jay Rhodemyre, voted top performer in College All-Star game. Injuries begin plaguing Packers in training camp. Lambeau making panicky trades in order to bolster line. Flap over Washington's Harry Gilmer. More injuries. Packers open season on positive note, downing Boston. Bears wallop Packers. Packers beat Lions, then lose to Cards. Lambeau fines several players for lackadaisical play, releases Bruce Smith. Packers defeat Rams for last win of '48. Rams sign Bruce Smith. Press-Gazette makes excuses for Packer loss to Washington. Packers continue to lose despite solid play of some players. Clyde Goodnight suffers season-ending injury. Lambeau says wait until next year.

Chapter 8
The War Drags On 108

Chicago Rockets change owners again. Attendance marks for '48 season. Comparison of Green Bay versus Milwaukee as playing site for Packers. History of big league sports in Milwaukee. Bert Bell eats words about success of NFL in '48. Alexis Thompson and Jonas Ingram trying to find peace. Thompson says Green Bay should be dumped from NFL. Lambeau launches counterattack with figures that only tell half the truth. Majority of players want merger of two leagues. NFL remaining adamant about a merger. Secret meetings between officials from both leagues. Owners fail to reach accord on merger. NFL owners holding out for Cleveland and San Francisco to join them. Cleveland and San Francisco owners refused to jump leagues. Bell's lack of vision forces war into another year.

Chapter 9
   The Second Winter of Lambeau's Discontent 116
   Fans begin to question Lambeau's coaching. Lloyd Larson attacks use of Rockwood Lodge. George Strickler writes inane defense of Rockwood Lodge. Buckets Goldenberg defends Lodge. Larson counterpunches. Controversy over Stan Heath. Draft list for '49 short and spotty. Lambeau nudges Walt Kiesling aside. Packers' draft list for '49. Lambeau hires Bob Snyder, Charley Brock, and Tom Stidham as assistant coaches.

Chapter 10
   Who's On First? 124
   Packer passing attack again anemic in '48. Packers land Stan Heath. Lambeau tries to sign Elroy Hirsch. List of Packers' rookies for '49. List of veterans for '49. Baby Ray and Don Deeks retire. John Torinus, Sr., replaces Andy Turnbull on executive committee. Margaret O'Brien becomes Packers' mascot. Canadeo breaks wrist in practice. Girard hurt in exhibition game against Eagles. Lambeau trades for Bob Cifers. More injuries in second exhibition game. Packers look pathetic in pre-season. Sell-out crowd watches Bears shoutout Packers in opener. Lambeau shocks football world by stepping down as field coach. More injuries foretell of Packers' worst season ever. Lambeau releases injured players, including Clyde Goodnight. Rams crush Packers before Green Bay manages to down hapless Yanks. Packers lose to Cards then slip by Detroit for last win of '49. Canadeo only bright spot for Packers.

Chapter 11
   Peace At Last 136
   AAC hires new commissioner, O.O. "Scrappy" Kessing. Rumor that settlement reached between the two leagues. Question about Lambeau's importance in NFL. One more flap over rights to a player, then peace comes. Outline of merger. More rumors about merger. New league to be called National American Football League. Questions over alignment of new league.

10**Chapter 12**
   Humpty Dumpty Sat on a Wall 142
   Losing record just tip of Green Bay's iceberg of problems. July 28, 1947 very important date in Packer history. Review of how the Packers were saved from bankruptcy by Jerry Clifford and Frank Jonet. Review of Lambeau's affairs off the field that affected his position with the organization. Lambeau's ex-wife and the Herbers. Disputes between Lambeau and Joannes. Lambeau's highhanded methods concerning Dr. Kelly and

The Lambeau Years — Part Three 7

G.W. Calhoun. Clifford investigates Lambeaus activities. Joannes steps down as president of Packers. Fischer takes up the fight where Joannes left off. Increase of board of directors and executive committee. Authority for running team handed over to various committees. Lambeau more or less stripped of power.

Chapter 13
Humpty Dumpty Started to Fall 150
Rockwood Lodge was the beginning of Lambeau's downfall. Lambeau blamed assistants for defeats. R.G. Lynch writes about sports fans in Milwaukee. Art Daley joins Lynch in crusading for more fan support in Milwaukee. Rumor that group of Texas oilmen plan to buy Packers and move them to Texas. Rumor that Packers would fold before 1950 season.

Chapter 14
All the King's Horses and All the King's Men 158
Rumors surrounding Lambeau's status in Green Bay.

Chapter 15
. . . Kept Humpty Around to Play Again 165
Rumors about Lambeau moving to other organizations. Emil Fischer denies Lambeau is leaving Green Bay. Thanksgiving Day fund-raiser. Lambeau making excuses for lousy season. Art Daley defending Lambeau. John Torinus, Sr., story about Lambeau and Clifford meeting on the courthouse steps before the board of directors meeting. Board passes resolution to renew Lambeau's contract for two years. Board to offer new stock to raise money to operate franchise. Packers announce that only two games would be played in Milwaukee in 1950. Cardinals looking for a new coach. Dr. Kelly resigns from board of directors. Rumor that Gene Ronzani would replace Lambeau as coach of the Packers. Winter meetings in Philadelphia. Lambeau calls for profit sharing for Packers stockholders. Newspapers support Lambeau. Rockwood Lodge burns. Lambeau quits to coach Cardinals.

Chapter 16
Let The Truth Be Known 179
Aftershock of Lambeau's resignation. The problems with Lambeau spending his winters in California. Ollie Kuechle defends Lambeau. George Strickler sent packing with Lambeau. Los Angeles columnist tells truth about Lambeau and the Los Angeles Dons. Clifford threatened to sue Lambeau if he walked out on his contract in '47.

Summary 189

Appendix A
The All-Time Packers of '46 195

Appendix B
A Picture Is Worth A thousand Words —
    Sometimes 200

Appendix C
A Good Yarn 204

Appendix D
The Packers' First Coach 205

Appendix E
"The Green Bay Story" 209

Appendix F
The Alumni Association 211

Appendix G
The Fans to the Rescue 214

Appendix H
Who Really Owned the Packers? 220

Index 228

Bibliography 236

§ § §

Acknowledgements

The first person I wish to thank is my wife Peggy who isn't a football fan. She displayed the patience of a saint for several months as I bombarded her with every little bit of information about the Green Bay Packers I gleaned from various sources. Also, she was an invaluable research assistant. I couldn't have done this book without her.

This book may never have gotten off the ground if my close friend and confidant Fr. Joesph Schlaefer hadn't given me the confidence to write it. He knows how grateful I am for this opportunity, but I would like the whole world to know what a truly remarkable man he is. It's a great honor to be his friend.

My friend Greg Scott provided some invaluable editorial assistance. His suggestions and prodding kept me digging for the facts.

Craig Cramer at the Wisconsin State Historical Society in Madison put me on the right track in researching the old newspapers.

The librarians at the Brown County Public Library and the Berlin (Wisconsin) Public Library were very kind and helpful to me when I used their excellent facilities.

Abe Abrohams was a fountain of information about Nate Abrams and his family's contribution to Packers history.

Many thanks to the staff of the Green Bay Packers Hall of Fame for their assistance and cooperation.

Also many thanks to Joe Horrigan and Sandy Self at the Pro Football Hall of Fame in Canton, Ohio. Joe gave me some incredible insights into the overall history of the NFL, and Sandy made my visit to the Hall's library just about perfect.

Of course, I can never say enough about my good friend Jim Ford for his research assistance, advice, encouragement, and compliments on this book. So often Jim pointed me in the right direction to find some detail or he confirmed information I had uncovered through another source. Jim also talked to several people who provided answers to a myriad of questions about the Packers and Curly Lambeau in the early years. Without his contacts in Green Bay, this book wouldn't have all those little known details that separate it from others publications. Jim is a wonderful person, but if you've met Jim, then you already knew that.

One person that Jim Ford did introduce me to and who gave me some invaluable information was the Honorable William J. Duffy of Green Bay. Judge Duffy provided me with some stories about Jerry Clifford and Curly Lambeau that I'd never heard before, stories which made a lot of bits and pieces of Packer history fall together and make sense finally. It was primarily through Judge Duffy's efforts that Jerry Clifford finally received the recognition that has been denied him for too many years. Judge Duffy is one of those tireless people who make what they consider to be modest contributions to the history of the Packers which are actually as vital to the overall story as a sparkplug is to an Indy 500 race car. Thanks to him this book took on special meaning for me.

§ § §

PREFACE

When I began this series on the history of the Green Bay Packers, I thought the project would be quite simple. After all, several other writers had authored books on the Packers without much trouble, and although those tomes weren't written with the depth and detail that I intended to employ, I figured those predecessors would make decent research sources and I could draw on them considerably. I was wrong.

All earlier so-called chroniclers of Packer history failed to do justice to their subject, but that's just as well. Actually, I'm grateful that they didn't do a thorough job of reporting history because their ineptitude forced me to dig deeper for the truth.

Of course, I'm not perfect either. I've made a few mistakes, but I readily admit them because it's my intention to achieve as much of the truth about the Packers' past as possible.

As previously stated, I thought this series would be simple, a mere exercise in writing non-fiction. I was wrong about that, too. The original intent was to break down the Packers' history into three volumes. The first would cover the Lambeau years; the second from Lambeau thru Lombardi's last year as general manager of the Packers; and the third would go up to the end of Forrest Gregg's coaching contract which would have been 1988 had he stayed with the Packers. My plan was ill-conceived because I hadn't done any preliminary research other than to inspect the few books that had already been written about the Packers. I knew the Packers had a rich history, but I just didn't know how rich it was. I was like one of those blind men who were asked to examine a part of an elephant then describe the beast; I'm the guy who felt the pachyderm's tail then said it was a skinny, little animal.

As you know already, this is the third volume in the series and it only goes to the end of Lambeau's tenure with the Packers. I suppose the publisher could have squeezed all three of these books between one set of covers, but if he had, he would have been forced to eliminate much of the detail for which I have received so much praise from you, my readers. Then this history wouldn't have been any different than those that had come before it. Therefore, we chose to go this route, and I am glad we did because instead of writing what is called "a puff book" in the publishing industry in which only the good things that the Packers ever did would be mentioned I have been permitted to re-animate the real history of the Packers.

As previously stated, I have made a few mistakes in telling the earliest years of the Packers' history. In Part Two, I mentioned that Mrs. Colleen Barnett, daughter of the Packers' attorney Gerald Clifford, objected to my describing her father as diminutive when he was actually slightly larger than average in size. In this book, I've corrected a glaring mistake on page 78 of Part One. The mistake was the name of one of the incorporators of the Green Bay Football Club, Inc. Instead of Nathan Andrews, it should read Nathan Abrams. Where I got Nathan Andrews from I can't recall, but it makes no difference, anyway. The error was made, but now it's corrected in the appendices of this volume.

Also, much additional information concerning those earliest days of the Packers has been included in the appendices. I wish that I had come across this information at the time that I was researching and writing Part One because it would have gone a long way in further supporting the contentions of that book that Curly Lambeau was not the founder of the Green Bay Packers and that the team did not suddenly appear on the football horizon in 1919.

In Part One, I complained that memories were "often very short and far too convenient" to be considered as the sole or major source of information for a history book. That principle still applies, despite the fact that many people who lived during the period covered in this book are alive at this writing and still have complete control of their mental faculties. I have interviewed several people who fit this description. I have usually done so in order to corroborate information found in some of the printed material that I have studied, or vice versa. More often than not, I have relied on the written words of the journalists of the time.

The Lambeau Years — Part Three

Most prominent among the newspapermen is Art Daley who was sports editor of *The Green Bay Press-Gazette* for so many years, including those covered in this book. Daley is semi-retired now, continuing to write a column for *The Packer Report*, a fine periodical devoted exclusively to the Packers. I have quoted Daley extensively because he wrote extensively about the Packers during the time of this book, and occasionally, I have criticized his writing rather severely. Please do not misconstrue such commentary on his journalism as anything derogatory about the person who wrote the words. Writers are people, too, and we don't create masterpieces every time we strike the keys or stroke the pen, anymore than Don Majkowski hits his receivers with every pass or Sterling Sharpe holds on to every pass that's laid in his hands. Having read and studied more of Daley's words than most people and being a professional author of 10 books currently in print and five more already written but not yet released, I can say unequivocally that Art Daley is a writer of superior merit.

Although it may seem that I have batted Daley repeatedly about the head and shoulders with an inflated pig bladder, I reiterate to the reader that it was not my intent at any time to cast a shadow over the integrity of this fine gentleman. I also request the reader to understand that the information that a journalist imparts to his readership is usually only as good as the sources from whom it comes, which explains why Daley was sometime faulty in reporting in the facts. Finally, remember that Daley and his staff were working for people who were directly involved with the Packers and who were graduates of the old school of journalistic thought in which editors and reporters were taught that one does not relate the bad things that happen in your home town, especially if it affects the paper's advertisers. In other words, you don't bite the hand that feeds you, whether you're the publisher of the newspaper or merely an editor or reporter with a family to support.

Now with all that in mind, have a nice read.

§ § §

INTRODUCTION

"The world stops for no man." This was an adage that Curly Lambeau should have tattooed inside his skull, and he should have lived by it.

But he didn't, making his demise as the head coach of the Green Bay Packers inevitable.

John Torinus, Sr., wrote in his book, *The Packer Legend: An Inside Look*, that everything was all right in Green Bay "until Lambeau went Hollywood." Torinus insinuated that Lambeau took on a new attitude in the 1940s toward his home town and his friends and neighbors; simply, Torinus indicated that Lambeau began to think of himself as being too sophisticated for the people of Green Bay.

It was true that Lambeau had developed a new attitude toward the folks in his home town, but this change in Lambeau began in 1932, not the 1940s. The facts were simple: the people of Green Bay were willing to let Curly be whatever he wanted to be, and they were willing to let him do whatever he wanted to do – just as long as he kept putting winners on *their* football field.

After that initial losing season of 1933, Lambeau's squads posted winning records for the next 14 years, and the Packers won the National Football League title three times during that span, taking top honors in 1936, 1939, and 1944. From 1935 thru 1944, the Packers finished no lower than second place in the Western Division, tying for first in 1941 (but losing in a playoff with the Bears) and winning an additional division crown in 1938. Green Bay was also considered to be one of the NFL's "Big Four", a so-called elite group of dominant teams that included the Chicago Bears, New York Giants, and Washington Redskins.

During this same era, Hollywood was churning out several sports movies, a few of which had stories about pro football teams and players. In most of these, the Packers were mentioned as being a top team, whether the screenwriters had them playing in Green Bay or Chicago as the author of *The Cowboy Quarterback* did.

All of this was pretty heady stuff for the gentle people of Wisconsin, but despite the reality of the Packers' records in the NFL and the fantasies fed them by the dream makers of Tinseltown, the Packers and their fans remained Smalltown, U.S.A. This was their right because they owned the Packers. Of course, the actual number of legal owners of stock in the Green Bay Football Corporation was less than the population of most of the towns around Green Bay, but each one of those stockholders had families, large families, extended families. Everyone who was related to a stockholder or who was married to someone who was related to a stockholder or who had a relative who was married to someone who was related to a stockholder – and this pretty well covered the entire population of the Upper Midwest – all of these people considered themselves to be owners of the Green Bay Packers. When speaking of the Packers, they would use first person pronouns, such as we, us, or our. Packer fans weren't just fans; they were owners, part of the organization. That set them apart from fans of every other team in sports.

That was the only thing that set them apart from other fans. Like fans elsewhere, they were just as fickle, just as petty, just as mean and unforgiving when their team failed to win. And like other fans, they wanted someone to pay in blood for their team's lack of success on the field, and this meant the coach. Or did it?

The first individual to feel the wrath of Green Bay's fans was Curly Lambeau, the favorite son who had turned on them first. At least, that was how they, the fans, perceived matters to have unfolded. It never crossed their minds that Lambeau might have been trying to lead the Packers – and their fans – into the real Big Time of professional sports, something they had resisted successfully for two and a half decades by the end of the World War II. The key word here is "individual". Before Lambeau became the object of their disaffection, Packer fans had already become venomous toward the corporation's executive committee.

But that's getting ahead of the story.

At the end of 1945, no one suspected the turmoil that was ahead for Curly Lambeau, the Packers, and the stockholders of the Green Bay Packers, Inc. The Packers had just completed a decent season, finishing third in their division with a 6-4 mark, and they had a host of reasons to be optimistic that 1946 and the rest of the decade would be just as fruitful as the first five years had been.

During the war years, most of America's collegians marched off to serve in the armed forces immediately after graduation. Either as volunteers or as draftees, athletes were considered to be especially prime specimens for duty in the army and navy. This manpower drain left professional sports teams a little short on talent, but it didn't deter the teams of the NFL from drafting for the future. Each team staked claims on various players who were in the service with the hopes that these men would be able and willing to play in the NFL when and if the war was concluded successfully. When the Japanese surrendered in August 1945, every NFL coach began drooling over the talent that would soon be made available to him. The proverbial fly in the ointment was the lack of interest in playing pro football that so many of these men displayed upon being discharged from the armed forces.

But again, that's getting ahead of the story.

In the first two books in this series on the history of the Green Bay Packers, the myths about the origins of the team, the ownership of the franchise in the NFL, and much of Curly Lambeau's early involvement with the team were shown to be exactly that: myths. The real facts were given the reader, and in some cases, they were refused as evidenced by some of the mail received by this author over the years. On the other hand, a majority of readers were grateful to this author for finally telling the real story behind the founding of the Packers as a football team, the real story of how Lambeau came to be part of the organization, the real story of how the team got into the NFL twice, the truth behind the first bankruptcy, the truth behind the second bankruptcy, and the truth behind Don Hutson's records.

In this third volume on the Packers and the final episode in Curly Lambeau's tenure with the team, the reader will discover the truth about Lambeau's activities off the field that affected his conduct within the organization and that eventually led to his demise as the head coach of the Packers. It's not exactly a pretty picture, but it does prove that Earl L. "Curly" Lambeau was human after all.

§ § §

*This book is dedicated to
Larry Seiferth, Randy Lucas, Pat McGuire,
Ken Stone, Anjie Harris, Bill Phillips,
Mark Randall, Don Duquette, Mike Pyritz,
and Dave Duncan,*

*the DJs of radio station WOLX in Madison, Wisconsin.
Thanks for keeping me company while I wrote this book.*

The History of the Green Bay Packers

Book III
The Lambeau Years
Part Three

1
Another War Begins

If not for World War II, the second American Football League probably would have survived beyond the '41 season and quite likely would have become an intense rival of the National Football League. Inevitably, a war between the two leagues would have erupted, and it would have led to the demise of one circuit or a merger of the two. History has borne out this theorem of sports competition.

With the AFL dead, killed by the bombing of Pearl Harbor, many of the wealthy men in the country who wanted to own a professional football team all their own were forced to turn to the NFL for a franchise. They approached the league magnates in '42 but were repulsed with the explanation that expansion of the NFL would have to wait until after the war was over. Applicants came to the league meetings in '43, and all but one was repulsed again. Ted Collins was granted a franchise for Boston but wasn't given a definite date when he could begin play. In 1944, for the third year in a row, several applicants went to the league meetings and requested a franchise, only to be brushed off with the explanation that expansion would be delayed until after the war.*

Enough was enough. The applicants tired of being excluded from pro football. If the NFL wouldn't take them in, then they would start their own league.

One group of entrepeneurs rallied behind Roland Donald Payne, a Pittsburgh industrialist who put together the plans for the United States Football League. It was announced in July of '44 that the USFL would have franchises in Boston, New York, Philadelphia, Baltimore, and Pittsburgh for its Eastern Division

---

* See Chapter 17, pages 205-207, of *The History of the Green Bay Packers: The Lambeau Years – Part Two*.

and in Akron, Cincinnati, Chicago, St. Louis, and Honolulu for its Western Division. Two more franchises would be chosen from Seattle, Portland, Buffalo, Detroit, San Francisco, Los Angeles, New Orleans, Fort Worth, and Dallas. Payne said each team had capital ranging from $60,000 to $250,000. The new owners would meet in December to draft players and draw up a schedule of 20 games. One club, the Honolulu Bears, had already hired a coach and general manager, F.J. Brickner. The Hawaiian squad would establish a camp in California in the summer, train there, then use it as a return base while it played the first half of its schedule in mainland cities. Then it would travel to Hawaii and play each team in Honolulu over the second half of the season.

In November, Red Grange accepted the job of president for the USFL. He vigorously went about his job for six months, then abruptly quit the first of June the following year. A few days later the whole league folded up before playing a single game.

Another promoter who had dreams of starting a new professional football league was Chick Meehan, the former coach at Manhattan College. In a way, Meehan was like C.C. Pyle, the man who started the first American Football League back in '26 with Red Grange as his star attraction. Meehan had all the hype but none of the action that it took to start a league. When the USFL decided to fold, he did likewise with his Trans-America Football League, stating he couldn't get a playing site in New York and without a team in New York a league simply couldn't exist.

At this same time, plans for another new league were made by several West Coast businessmen. The fourth circuit to be called the American Football League would have teams up and down the Pacific Coast from Seattle to San Diego. Famed criminal attorney Jerry Giesler was elected president of the league, and it was hoped play could begin in the fall of '44. Giesler and the owners were also hoping to merge with the NFL after the war.

The NFL ignored the development of these three organizations until volatile George Marshall, the Redskins owner, informed the new American League that Dean McAdams belonged to Washington as a result of a trade with Brooklyn.

McAdams had signed to play with the AFL's Seattle Bombers and had politely told Marshall that he wasn't interested in playing for the Redskins, saying he owed nothing to them. Marshall then threatened to ban McAdams from the NFL for five years for jumping his contract. McAdams said he hadn't signed a contract with Washington, therefore, he wasn't jumping anything.

McAdams made a poor decision because the fourth AFL folded half way through its first and only season.

Yet another new organization was the All-America Football Conference, created in Chicago in September of '44. This group was made up primarily of those entrepeneurs who had tried to get into the NFL but had been rejected as being premature with their attempts. Instead of limiting their sphere of play to the West Coast like the AFL, they opted for the whole country from New York to Florida to California. Jimmy Crowley, the Green Bay boy who grew up to play for Notre Dame and the Packers then coach at Fordham, was named as the league's first president.

On St. Valentine's Day of '45, John L. Keeshin, the trucking magnate who owned the Chicago franchise in the untested AAC, announced he had reached agreement with the city of Chicago on a 10-year lease for Soldier Field. Keeshin revealed that the AAC owners had already invested $2,150,000 in talent, franchises, playing plants, and equipment. This was amazing information, but more amazing was the hiring of former Ohio State coach Paul Brown by the Cleveland Panthers at a salary of $25,000 a year.

A few weeks later Keeshin announced the signing of his own coach. Dick Hanley, the former Northwestern coach, agreed to be the head mentor of the Chicago Rockets, and the immortal Ernie Nevers signed on as Hanley's assistant.

The San Francisco 49ers signed former Santa Clara coach Buck Shaw as their top man, and the Miami Seahawks contracted former Alabama Poly coach Jack Meagher. Buffalo Bisons co-owner Sam Cordovano, having coached at Columbia, decided to take the reins of the team himself.

Some of the owners in the AAC were still willing to forego any plans for their own league if the NFL magnates would accept them into their circuit. Any hope of that happening was dashed by the NFL moguls in the April meetings of '45. The NFL changed its constitution to read that it would play the '46 season with "not less than 10 clubs nor more than 12." This effectively eliminated any possibility of a huge post-war expansion, meaning the AAC was on its own.

The AAC magnates held their constitutional convention in Chicago on April 18-20, 1945, announcing that Tom Gallery, the vice-president and general manager of the Brooklyn Tigers, would be attending all the meetings as the eighth member of the new circuit. Gallery denied that he was in Chicago for anything of the kind, saying he just happened to have business in the same neighborhood by coincidence. The NFL crowed over the AAC's embarrassment, but the AAC had the last laugh.

Meeting in Chicago were AAC owners Keeshin of Chicago, Sam Cordovano of Buffalo, Arthur McBride of Cleveland, Harvey Hester and William Bentley of Miami, Mal Stevens and Charles Grimes of New York, Tony Morabito of San Francisco, and Christy Walsh and Don Ameche of Los Angeles. These men delegated Keeshin and Cleveland coach Paul Brown to seek a meeting with NFL Commissioner Elmer Layden with the purpose of reaching an accord on drafting college players, setting up a mutually agreeable schedule, and a title game at the end of the season. Layden snubbed the AAC emissaries and issued a statement to the press that read:

"All I know of new leagues is what I read in the newspapers. There is nothing for the National league to talk about as far as new leagues are concerned until someone gets a football and plays a game."

Layden's attitude toward the new league was nothing new. He was merely expressing what the NFL owners had been saying for two decades: the National Football League was the only big-time pro football league and that was that. At the same time, he warned players in the armed forces not to listen to the siren calls of the new leagues. George Marshall told them the same thing but in blunter terms. Whereas Layden couched his ultimatum in diplomatic language in *The Touchback*, a newsletter to players in the services, Marshall came right out and told them through the newspapers that if they signed a contract with any of the new leagues they would be subject to five-year suspensions from the NFL.

When Red Grange resigned from the USFL, he issued a warning to the warring magnates:

"Professional football can never be on a sound basis until it owns its own parks or until baseball club owners organize their own football league and thereby use their own parks.

"The National Football league is using baseball parks. All they really have are contracts and uniforms and if ever baseball decides to forbid football teams to play in its parks, the National league – or any league – is ruined.

"The competition for players is becoming too stiff. The various leagues are bidding against each other for players and the salaries are getting too high. Players who should receive only $150 a week are signing contracts for $500 and that can only lead to trouble."

No one in 1945 realized how prophetic Grange was.

While Grange was hanging it up with the USFL, the NFL magnates were meeting in what was supposed to be a secret conference in New York. Their purpose was to decide what to do about the Brooklyn Tigers for '46. Over Tim Mara's protests, it was decided that it was essential for the Tigers to play in Yankee Stadium, if for no other reason than to keep the USFL and the AAC out of New York.

When the announcement came that the Tigers would be playing in Yankee Stadium in '46, Chick Meehan of the Trans-America League was quoted as saying: "With Yankee Stadium I had plenty of ammunition; without it I just had conversation."

The AAC was undaunted by the NFL's announcement. Its New York team announced that it would use the 30,000-seat Triboro Municipal Stadium since it couldn't get Yankee Stadium now.

In August, the Cleveland Panthers changed their nickname to the Browns. The management didn't want to be associated with a former Cleveland team of a decade earlier which was known as the Panthers. A contest was held to rename the franchise, and most of the entries suggested something that would identify the team with its coach, Paul Brown. Thus, the name Browns was chosen.

At this same time, the Browns signed Chicago Bears halfback Bob Steuber, the first player to jump from the NFL to the new AAC. Three weeks later Lou Rymkus, a tackle with the Redskins in '43, decided to try his luck with the Browns. Hampton Pool, formerly of the Bears, and Jim Poole, formerly of the Giants, signed on with the Miami Seahawks. This was an open declaration of war by the AAC on the NFL, but the formal announcement was still to come.

On September 1, after two days of meetings in Chicago, AAC Commissioner Jim Crowley said:

"We originally resolved not to tamper with the National league players, but since the NFL snubbed us we see no reason why we can't hire their players. Mr. Layden knows by now, no doubt, that we have a football."

In October, Don Ameche's partner, Christy Walsh, sold his interest in the Los Angeles franchise, and Ameche incorporated the club, selling shares to motion picture magnate Louis B. Mayer, singer-actor Bing Crosby, actor Pat O'Brien, horse racing park executive Ben Lindheimer, California sportsman Norman W. Church, motion picture magnate Leo Spitz, and investment banker Daniel F. Rice. The LA team, to be known as the Dons, had signed only one star player, former Notre Dame quarterback and Heisman Trophy recipient Angelo Bertelli, but Ameche said Bertelli was enough to build a team around.

On November 28, Oscar Fraley of *United Press International* wrote a column on Crowley as the commissioner of the AAC. In the story, Crowley took his best shots at Elmer Layden and the NFL, especially taking to task, without naming him, Detroit owner Fred Mandel who had blasted the AAC for raiding the colleges for returning players who still had eligibility left after serving in the armed forces. As Crowley so aptly put it, that was a case of the pot calling the kettle black. Crowley might have been referring to the incident where Mandel had tried to lure Clyde "Bulldog" Turner away from Hardin-Simmons before he could sign with the Bears. For this little bit of tampering, Mandel was fined $5,000 by the league.

Fraley also mentioned that it was still a possibility that Dan

Topping's Brooklyn Tigers could still jump to the AAC. He wrote that as he was leaving Crowley's office he passed a man coming in who looked suspiciously like Ray Flaherty, Topping's coach. Then Fraley came right out and stated it was Flaherty.

A week later Topping, a one-third owner of the New York Yankees baseball team which owned Yankee Stadium, announced his team was moving to the AAC because Tim Mara declined to agree on playing dates for the '46 season. In retaliation, Layden declared all Brooklyn players to be the property of the Boston Yanks and Topping's NFL franchise to be forfeit. Topping laughed and said Layden's decree didn't carry any weight in the AAC; he was taking his players with him and Ray Flaherty would be his coach.

With Topping's move, the AAC had a little more substance to it. The AAC now had eight teams, but two were in New York. The solution to this problem was to move the original Big Apple franchise to Brooklyn.

At its first winter meeting ever in Chicago in early January, the AAC decided not to buck the NFL if it didn't have to. Instead of playing games on Sundays in opposition to the NFL, the AAC opted to schedule most of its contests on Friday nights. The new league also approved a franchise for Baltimore that would be inactive for '46 but would begin play in '47 when the league planned to expand to 10 teams to match the NFL.

Red Grange again warned the owners of both leagues that if they engaged in a "battle of bucks" it could prove ruinous to pro football. At the same time, he cautioned the players not to go overboard making personal gains out of the situation.

"Of course, the players deserve all the money they can get," said Grange. "It's the first time pros really have been in a position to dicker. But it may turn out to be simply another case of killing the goose that lays the golden egg."

Grange further stated that cordial relations between the two leagues and a championship game at the end of the season would be beneficial to pro football. Title games in each league would be meaningless until the AAC and NFL champs squared off to determine which team really was the best that year.

Grange's warning went unheeded by most. The players grabbed every penny they could, and the owners risked millions, more out of spite than good business sense. America wanted pro sports, and entrepeneurs of all sorts thought they were seeing an opportunity to cash in on the new "Golden Era" of sports. Already by the end of '45, plans were being made and dollars spent to form a new football minor league in Texas, a third pro basketball league, and a pro soccer league. Boxing was on the rise all across the nation, and sportsmen were signing up any kid who was willing to step into a ring. The money was flowing, and all an athlete had to do was sign a contract to get some of it.

At this same time, Joseph Rosentover, the president of the dormant American Football Association, the eastern minor league, announced the AFA would resume play in '46 in eight cities. The AFA had a working agreement with the NFL before the war, and it was hoped by both sides that it would be resumed now that peace had been restored.

The revival of the AFA gave the NFL moguls an idea, one they had thought of before but prematurely. For years, the NFL owners had been trying to develop a farm system for their league, much the same as professional baseball had. Roster limits kept teams from stockpiling players, but there came times when replacements were necessary for injured personnel in the middle of the season. Signing a free agent was the only way of getting a new man, but the drawback was the player was usually out of shape. By the time he worked himself into condition and into the team's system, the man he was signed to replace was healthy again. The coaches wanted a system where they could pluck a guy off a farm team at a moment's notice to fill a spot on the big team's roster.

Before the war, the AFA and the minor AFL had given the NFL the semblance of a farm system, but the working agreements with the two organizations weren't exactly what the NFL wanted. Too many of the minor league franchises were financial losers that needed NFL help to survive. This was partially

The Lambeau Years — Part Three

due to the playing arenas the minor league teams had to use. They were usually parks with a few sections of bleachers for some fans to sit on, while most spectators stood around the edge of the playing field just as fans in Green Bay had done at Hagemeister Park before the building of Bellevue Park back in the '20s.

Also prior to the war, the NFL owners had tried to reach an agreement with the American Association of baseball on the establishment of a new minor league that would play in that organization's spacious stadiums. The AA magnates were all for having football in their stadiums in the fall, but they didn't want to be *owners* of the teams; they wanted to be *landlords*. They wanted the NFL or someone else to own the franchises and rent the stadiums from the AA. In other words, they wanted a piece of the pie without having to make the dough for the crust. Negotiations broke down, and nothing came of the idea.

With the war over now, the plan for a minor league in AA baseball parks was given new life at the annual winter meetings of the NFL in New York, but it died quickly when the AA leaders took the same stand as they had before the war. They were more than willing to rent out their stadiums, but they didn't want to have the financial responsibilities as owners of the teams.

When the AA shot down their proposal, Marshall, George Halas, and Bert Bell put their heads together and came up with a new plan. Instead of trying to form a new league, why not get working agreements with the established minor leagues and any new ones that were in the offing? The NFL began working toward that end immediately.

With the AFA already lined up on their side, the NFL owners coaxed and cajoled the Pacific Coast League and the Dixie League to join them in the battle against the now "outlaw" AAC. The NFL argued that the AAC magnates would be raiding their leagues for players as well as the NFL, and they would take them without giving anything back. The PCL and DL owners reacted out of fear and signed an agreement recognizing the NFL as the only major league in pro football.

While Marshall was barking out some of his usually very quotable insults aimed at the AAC during the meetings, Halas was taking a surprisingly different tack. Papa Bear was almost benevolent toward the new league. He said there were plenty of players to stock all the clubs in both leagues. By his estimations, colleges around the country graduated 9,000 football players every year. The NFL drafted 300 of them, signed up a few hundred more, but less than 25% of those drafted and signed ever played for an NFL team. This meant there was plenty of talent available for a new league. Halas even said it was okay for the NFL to lose a few of its established players to the AAC because this left room on their rosters for new men who could make their own marks in the league. This was an amazing statement coming from the owner of the team that had been hit the hardest by AAC raiders.

"Why should we worry about Topping or the rest of the All–America?" said Marshall to reporters in an interview during the meetings. He brought in NFL treasurer Dinny Shea who was once general manager of the Brooklyn club. Shea told how Topping's team had lost some $238,000 over an eight- or nine-year period. "See what I mean?" Marshall boomed. "We've just gotten rid of the most outstanding failure our league ever had. Why should we feel bad?"

Although the NFL owners were taking a seemingly mild attitude toward the AAC, they didn't exactly lay down and play dead for the new group. Just as the AAC had done a few weeks earlier in Chicago, the NFL owners conducted their annual college player draft in secrecy. At the same time, the Detroit Lions threatened to file a suit against Topping for signing their star player, Frankie Sinkwich, for the '46 season. When Marshall heard about it, he gave the newsmen a little rhyme that made reference to Sinkwich and his home state of Georgia:

> "If you want a football Peachie,
> "Go and see the All–Ameche."

Another Marshall dig at the AAC and Ameche referred to the size of the contracts the outlaw league was offering players.

"The trouble with that All–America league is that since Don Ameche played Alexander Graham Bell in the movies they've done nothing but talk in telephone numbers."

The biggest news to come out of the NFL winter meeting was

the "resignation" of Commissioner Elmer Layden. Rumors ran rampant throughout the football community about why Layden "resigned" before his contract was up in March. Some were saying that a group of five owners had come to the meeting with the express intent of deposing Layden and replacing him with Bert Bell because Layden had allowed the AAC to get a foothold in the pro football world. Others said Layden wanted more power, but when the owners were reluctant to give him any more, he quit.

The bottom line to Layden's resignation was some of the owners felt Layden was responsible for the present situation with the AAC. Some of them thought he could have handled matters involving the AAC with a little more tact and avoided the raiding of their rosters by the new league. Layden did bungle things with the AAC, but the owners were only using him as a scapegoat to hide their own shortcomings. Their greed brought about the AAC when they denied franchises to some of the men who started up the rival organization, and they brought on the raiding when they turned their noses up at the AAC instead of recognizing it as a junior partner in pro football and working with its organizers to avoid the very thing that was happening.

Now that they had gone beyond the point of no return in their competition with the AAC the NFL owners felt they had to do everything in their power to crush the opposition. To vanguard their forces, they elected Bert Bell as their new commissioner. It was felt around the league that Bell was a fighter, having brought the Eagles through *The Great Depression* and the Steelers through World War II.

The NFL won the first "Battle of New York" when Mara agreed to let Dan Topping's Brooklyn team move into Yankee Stadium. Then Topping pulled a "Benedict Arnold" and changed sides, giving the AAC a strong foothold in the nation's media capital. To add insult to injury, the AAC moved its original New York franchise to Brooklyn, giving it two teams in the Big Apple to the NFL's one. The NFL owners weren't too concerned because they still had two Chicago teams to one for the AAC.

Even so, Bell wasn't about to let Topping and the AAC get

away with this maneuver. The NFL countered by giving Dan Reeves, the owner of the champion Cleveland Rams, permission to move his club to Los Angeles and go into direct competition with Don Ameche's LA Dons. But moving to LA wasn't enough. The Rams had to have a playing field, and the best available was the Coliseum that seated over 100,000. Both pro teams applied for a lease on the stadium. The Rams were awarded the contract, and the NFL began crowing over its West Coast victory.

Bell and the NFL tried to follow up their win in LA by placing a team in San Francisco. Instead of granting a new franchise to an inexperienced owner, the commissioner wanted an established team to move to the "City by the Bay" and play in spacious Kezar Stadium. The first choice of Bell and the owners who supported his idea was the Green Bay Packers, but when Leland Joannes flatly said no and promised a battle if the league made any kind of move on the Packers, Bell looked to Charlie Bidwill to move the Cardinals to the West Coast. Bidwill took the same stand. Chicago was his home, and the Cards were there to stay.

The battle lines were now drawn. The NFL camp included teams in New York, Boston, Philadelphia, Washington, Pittsburgh, Detroit, Chicago, Green Bay, and Los Angeles; and the AAC forces counted New York, Brooklyn, Cleveland, Chicago, Miami, Buffalo, San Francisco, and Los Angeles. Both sides were determined to win an all-out football war, but neither knew how long it would last or how bitter it would get.

§ § §

2
No Hutson, No Panache

1945 was a year of enormous change throughout the whole world. In some respects, life returned to normal. In others, it would never be the same again.

For the National Football League, 1945 marked the end of two eras and the beginning of several new ones.

The Cleveland Rams won the Western Division title in '45, making them the first team other than the Green Bay Packers and the Chicago Bears to wear the crown since '35 when the Detroit Lions ascended to the top of the division. Furthermore, the Rams won the NFL championship, breaking the stranglehold the "Big Four" had had on it since '36. During those nine years (1936-44), the Bears and Packers each won three NFL titles; the Washington Redskins two; and the New York Giants one. Also, either the Giants or Redskins won the Eastern Division title in each of those nine years.

1945 was also the year Don Hutson played his last game for the Green Bay Packers. His retirement left such a gaping hole in Green Bay's offense that it wouldn't be filled by any one man for some years to come.

When Hutson hung up his cleats for good, he was the possessor of every Green Bay and nearly every NFL pass receiving and scoring record extent, whether the mark was for one quarter, one game, one season, or a career. In 11 years, he played in 117 of 120 regular season games, four NFL title games, and one divisional playoff game. Two of the contests he missed were the last two tilts of the '35 season when he was sidelined with appendicitis.

Hutson's most astounding marks for one quarter were those he set against the Lions in Green Bay in '45 when he caught four TD passes and booted five PATs for a total of 29 points in the second period of that game. Even in a later age when passing yards and 99 touchdowns. Per season, those numbers average out to 44.36 receptions for 726.45 yards and 9 TDs. Per game, he averaged 4.17 catches for 68.30 yards and 0.85 touchdowns. Hutson's averages per season were all beaten in succeeding years, but his averages per game still hadn't been bested at the time of this writing.

Carried one step further by taking the averages of Hutson's best season, 1942, and carrying them out to 16 games in a season, Don Hutson would have caught 107 passes for 1,761 yards and 24 touchdowns. The records for those three one-season categories as of this writing were 106 receptions by Art Monk, Washington Redskins, 1984, in 16 games; 1,746 yards by Charley Hennigan, Houston Oilers, 1961, in 14 games; and 22 TDs by Jerry Rice, San Francisco 49ers, 1987, in 15 games. Hennigan's yardage record deserves an asterisk in that he achieved it against inferior competition in the fourth American Football League's second season. He came close to that mark once more in '64, but again he was playing against inferior competition in the AFL.

The most incredible aspect of Hutson's career was his statistics for '43 thru '45. Even so, his numbers could have been much greater than they were, considering the quality of competition he faced in those years; and if they had been, the Packers in those years could have been more awesome than the Bears were from '40 thru '43. If Cecil Isbell had stayed in the game instead of turning to coaching, he and Hutson would have had one field day after another against the war time replacement players of the NFL. Unfortunately, Isbell quit the league, and Hutson was left with passers that he made look good.

Put as simply as possible, Don Hutson was to professional football what Babe Ruth was to Major League baseball. When Hutson quit playing, the Packers were virtually left without a passing attack because Lambeau had no receivers that came anywhere near the best of the rest in the NFL. To make matters worse, Green Bay had no passer like a Sid Luckman or a Sammy Baugh to compensate for the lack of pass-catchers.

Realizing what a gap he had to fill with Hutson's retirement at the conclusion of the '45 season, Lambeau was hoping to fill became much more dominant in the pro game, no one would catch four touchdown passes or score 29 points in a single quarter.

It must be remembered that Hutson played in an era when passing was an alternative to running, not the other way around. If a team threw over 20 passes in a game, it was usually because their opponent had a lead of eight points or more in the fourth quarter and the need to score quickly was urgent. Although the Packers routinely threw 20-25 passes in games in which they usually held the upper hand, not all of the aerials were aimed in Hutson's direction. Milt Gantenbein, Harry Jacunski, Carl Mulleneaux, and a host of good pass-catching backs were around to take the pressure off Hutson during his career.

Also, it must be noted that because he was the premier receiver of his time Hutson was double-teamed or triple-teamed by every defense he went up against after his first year in the league. That made his single-game record of 14 catches against the New York Giants in '42 all the more remarkable. By the way, the previous mark was 13 catches in one game, and Hutson set that record earlier in '42 against the Rams.

Oddly, Hutson didn't set a single-game yardage mark against the Giants, but he did set one against the Rams when he caught 13 passes for 209 yards. This broke the mark he had set just 10 days earlier against the Cards when he gained 207 yards on five catches. His best game was against Brooklyn in '43 when he racked up 237 yards on eight receptions.

His single-season marks were all eventually beaten, but only a few of them were broken within the number of games he played each year. In the years that Hutson played, the seasons were only 12 games long in '35 and '36, 11 games from '37 thru '42, and 10 games from '43 thru '45. His single-season marks included most catches, 74 in '42; most yards, 1,211 in '42; and most TDs, 17 in '42. Broken down to averages, that year Hutson caught 6.73 passes for 110.1 yards and 1.55 TDs per game. Those real season numbers stood as the best ever for decades, but his averages had yet to be topped at the time of this writing.

For his career, Hutson retired with 488 catches for 7,991

some of the void with players that he had drafted during the war and those who had just become available at the end of the '45 collegiate season.

Joe Laws was one of the most versatile backs to ever wear a Packer uniform. He played both halfback positions, fullback, and occasionally quarterback in Lambeau's version of the Notre Dame box offense. On defense, Laws was known as "Tiger" to his teammates, and he also handled punt returns when he was in the lineup.

In January of '46, Laws announced his retirement from the game, and the Packers had another hole to fill.

Besides Laws and Hutson retiring, Lambeau lost guard Bernie Crimmins to the college coaching ranks. Crimmins was an All–American at Notre Dame in '41, then he went into the Navy at the beginning of World War II. During the war, he was decorated with the Silver Star for gallantry in action.

Going into the draft meeting in New York, Lambeau told the press that he thought all returning war veterans who still had college eligibility remaining should resume pursuing their education. It was his opinion that they owed it to themselves to graduate from college before pursuing a career in pro football. Of course, he didn't believe that himself, at least not for the players that were on his wish list; but he was quite sincere about his statement when it came to players on other teams' lists, especially the Bears' list.

At the winter meeting in '46, the Packers came to a working agreement with the San Diego Bombers of the Pacific Coast League. As part of the deal, the Green Bay Packers, Inc., agreed to pay some of the salaries of the players the Packers sent down to them for seasoning. This was the first time Green Bay picked up part of the tab of a minor league organization. Lambeau and Lee Joannes felt it was a good thing for the club and the NFL to have this relationship with the PCL team. A few years later they weren't so sure that they had made the right move.

Lambeau's first draft choice was John Strzykalski, a back out of Marquette; but before the NFL meetings were finished, the Cleveland Browns had Strzykalski under contract. Lambeau didn't have much better luck with his other top choices. They either signed with the AAC or passed up playing pro ball altogether.

During the meetings, Joannes and Lambeau received a lot of pressure from the other NFL magnates to move the Packers to another city, preferably San Francisco where they could compete with the AAC's 49ers. The Green Bay executives refused to make any such move, saying the stockholders would never go for it because the corporation was structured as a non-profit organization that couldn't pay dividends and any proceeds from the sale of the team had to go to the American Legion post in Green Bay, meaning the stockholders had nothing to gain by the sale or transfer of the franchise. It was suggested that this could be changed, but Joannes and Lambeau were adamant about moving the team anywhere.

As a way of getting the other magnates off their backs, Joannes announced that the seating capacity of State Fair Park in Milwaukee and City Stadium in Green Bay would be increased. Bleachers for 13,000 customers were being purchased by the State Fair managers from the University of Chicago. The new seats would be erected on the east side of the field opposite the grandstand. This would raise the capacity to 34,000. At the same time, Joannes said the Packers planned to increase City Stadium to 30,000 seats from its current 22,500. Many wondered if the Packers could fill any more seats than they already were filling, considering the limited population of their drawing area. Only time would tell, but for the moment, the Packers were still safely based in Green Bay.

When rumors that the AAC's Chicago Rockets were planning to play some of their games in Milwaukee began surfacing, State Fair Park director Ralph E. Ammon denied the tale, saying nothing of the sort was in the works. But just in case Ammon wasn't telling the whole truth – which he was – the Packers negotiated an "exclusive use" contract with Ammon for the privilege of being the only professional football team allowed to play at State Fair Park.

With those matters out of the way, Lambeau went about the

business of lining up a team for the '46 season. Unlike years gone by, especially those before the war, this was no easy task. Green Bay had the NFL rights to 192 players, and Lambeau was certain he could find 35 good men in that group to fill up his roster for the coming campaign. He sent out over 100 contracts to veterans and draftees who had yet to play a single down of pro ball. Much to his chagrin, they didn't come back very rapidly or in any great quantity.

Unlike the other NFL clubs, the Packers lost only one player to the ACC. Bob Frankowski, the guard from Washington, preferred the West Coast to Green Bay, so he signed with the LA Dons. The Browns signed Ted Fritsch to a contract, then let him out of it when the Wisconsin native had a change of heart. Irv Comp admitted he was offered several contracts by AAC teams but had rejected them to return to the Packers.

Although the NFL had no formal ethnic barriers, the use of minority players was limited and sometimes confined to sideshows like Jim Thorpe's Oorang Indians of 1922-23. More than a half dozen men with African ancestors had played for several league teams in the '20s, but no great move to integrate the circuit was made until after World War II. The Rams general manager, Charles "Chili" Walsh, brought pro football into a new era when he signed Kenny Washington, the star back out of UCLA, to a playing contract for '46. A few other teams were quick to follow Walsh's example, but some would resist employing African-Americans for several years to come. Among the latter were the Green Bay Packers under Curly Lambeau.

As spring blossomed, Lambeau continued to tell reporters that no shortage of good players for the Packers existed. He expected a good five dozen of them to be in camp that summer, but he worried that they had no place to stay because there was a very severe housing shortage in the Green Bay area. To fix that problem, Lambeau convinced the executive committee to buy Rockwood Lodge, a former religious retreat built by the Norbertine Brothers in 1937. The pseudo-Tudor style home was located 15 miles northeast of the city on the bluff overlooking Green Bay. Plans were immediately made to remodel the lodge to house the entire team if necessary. A practice field was marked out on the lawn in front of the building, and five prefabricated houses for married players unable to find homes in Green Bay were brought in and set up on the property. At the time, it looked like a brilliant move on Lambeau's part as it gave the Packers that touch of class which he felt was lacking in Green Bay.

Lambeau was now spending most of the off season in sunny, warm southern California and was only returning to Green Bay when team or corporate matters demanded him to be there in person. Before returning from his last stay on the West Coast just prior to the opening of training camp, he hired former Packer Ernie Smith as a scout because it was becoming more and more important to have reliable first hand knowledge of college players and the best way to get it was through the use of a team's own scouts.

Times were certainly changing in '46, especially in the ticket office. New ticket sales director Carl Mraz reported in July that season ticket sales were up 20% already and this was only from the reminders that were sent out to the previous year's buyers. The office hadn't yet opened to the general public.

When camp opened in August, Lambeau had 57 players on hand; 27 veterans and 30 rookies. His assistant coaches included Don Hutson and Walt Kiesling. Seven veteran players were men who didn't get their discharges from the armed forces until it was too late to participate in the '45 season. During the coming '46 campaign, Lambeau would use a total of 39 men; 25 with pro experience and 14 rookies. The first year players were Dick Wildung, tackle, Minnesota; Buddy Gatewood, center, Baylor; Merv Pregulman, center, Michigan; Al Sparlis, guard, UCLA; Jug Bennett, guard, Hardin–Simmons; Urban Odson, tackle, Minnesota; Hal Prescott, end, Hardin–Simmons; Hank Miller, end, Iowa; Don Wells, end, Georgia; Bob Forte, back, Arkansas; Cliff Aberson, back, Chicago; Bob Nussbaumer, back, Michigan; Walt Schlinkman, back, Texas Tech; and Al Zupek, back, Lawrence. Coming back from the war and making the team were Ray Riddick, Russ Letlow, Bill Lee, Tony Canadeo, and Herm Rohrig. The Packers picked up Charley Mitchell, a back from Tulsa who had played the '45 season with the Bears. Returning from the '45 team were Bob Flowers, Clyde Goodnight, Tiny Croft, Baby Ray, Charley Tollefson, Bill

Kuusisto, Charley Brock, Bubo Barnett, Paul Lipscomb, Ed Neal, Nolan Luhn, Carl Mulleneaux, Ken Keuper, Larry Craig, Bruce Smith, Irv Comp, Russ Mosely, Roy McKay, and Ted Fritsch.

Lambeau split the squad into two teams to play an exhibition game for the benefit of the American Legion. A good house of 14,000 turned out to watch Hutson's "Army" beat Kiesling's "Navy" by a narrow 14-10 score.

In the front office, the stockholders re-elected the entire board of directors, and the board re-elected all the officers and executive committee to serve another year. Lee Joannes was beginning his 17th year as president of the corporation, and Frank Jonet was starting his 14th as treasurer.

With the first exhibition game in Milwaukee against the Eagles, Lambeau quickly read the handwriting on the wall. The Packers didn't have much of a passing attack without Hutson. None of the receivers came close to approaching the level of ability Hutson had displayed on his worst day. To make matters worse, not one of Lambeau's passers could come anywhere near to being as good as a blindfolded Cecil Isbell or a one-armed Arnie Herber. Recognizing this shortcoming in his team, Lambeau kept the ball on the ground and hoped his defense could hold the opposition. The defenders did their job and stopped Philadelphia, but the Packers lost anyway, 7-6.

The ground game had a good first half against the Redskins when the Packers played them in Denver the next week, but Washington pulled out a narrow victory, 35-31, in the late going. Green Bay led, 24-7, at the half, but failed to muster more than one scoring threat during the second 30 minutes as the Redskins figured out the Pack had to stay on the ground to move the ball.

In their third exhibition game, the Packers faced the Giants in New York. Lambeau's infantry didn't move the ball very well against a rugged Giant defense, forcing the Packers to take to the air. Irv Comp teamed up with Nolan Luhn for a pair of scores, and Green Bay amassed 275 yards through the sky. Even so, the defense fell apart, and the Giants ran roughshod over the Pack, 35-21.

With injuries to some of his best running backs piling up,

The Lambeau Years — Part Three

Lambeau was beside himself about what to do with his '46 Packers in the regular season opener at home against the Bears. Fritsch, Schlinkman, Smith, McKay, Nussbaumer, Keuper, Goodnight, and Brock were all out of the lineup. The Bears were in the pink for the contest, and it showed on the scoreboard at game's end: Chicago 30, Green Bay 7.

Besides being a Green Bay loss, the game was the first Packer contest since the club joined the NFL in which George Whitney Calhoun saw the opening kickoff. In all previous years, Cal was prevented from seeing the opening minutes of Packer home games by his duties as publicity agent. Cal personally handed out or mailed out all press passes to Packer games, then made certain that they were used only by the men to whom he had given them by sitting at the press gate and collecting them on game day. On this Sunday, all the passes came in a little early.*

To describe the game in a word, the Packers were pathetic against the Bears, and just about everybody knew it but didn't want to admit it. Art Daley tried to camouflage the situation by pulling a little history out of his typewriter at the *Press-Gazette*. He reminded his readers that the Packers lost to the Bears, 30-3, in the second game of the '36 season, then went unbeaten the rest of the way and won the NFL title. The story picked up the spirits of the fans and the players, and the Packers improved the next week, losing to the LA Rams, 21-17, in a disputed game. Lambeau claimed – and rightfully so – that the Rams were given an unnecessary officials' timeout in the final seconds that allowed LA to run the winning play. Since pro football has no protest system like pro baseball and pro basketball have, Lambeau's complaints of being cheated went for nought.

---

* A year later Lee Remmel wrote in the *Press-Gazette* that Calhoun would see his first Packer kickoff against the Giants in the first exhibition of the '47 season. Remmel was told this by Calhoun himself whose desk at the newspaper was next to Remmel's. This was a prime example of the faulty memory syndrome mentioned in the beginning of this history. See the Introduction, *The History of the Green Bay Packers: The Lambeau Years – Part One.* Also see Appendix D.

The two losses to the Packers' chief rivals for the division crown put Green Bay in a deep hole to start the season. Few teams in the history of the NFL had lost their first two games of a campaign and then gone on to win a division or league title.

Next up for the Packers was Philadelphia. The Eagles were undefeated in two outings. Green Bay's defense put up a stone wall, and Ted Fritsch had a big day, scoring 17 points on two TDs, two PATs, and a field goal to lead the Pack to a 19-7 win before an estimated crowd of 40,000 in Philly.

While the Packers were preparing to meet the Steelers at home the following Sunday, the NFL front office began bragging about how it was besting the upstart AAC in attendance. So far that year, the NFL had drawn 506,358 fans for an average of 31,647 per game. The AAC's figures were 648,861 total and 28,211 average. Bert Bell would have been wiser to keep this bit of information out of the newspapers because the numbers actually made the AAC look good.

When the Steelers visited Green Bay, the Packers donned white jerseys with gold numbers for the game because it was felt the black and gold of Pittsburgh was too close in contrast to the blue and gold of Green Bay and the white jerseys would prevent any confusion for the players and fans. The last time the Packers wore the white tops was in '45, and they lost to Cleveland. Art Daley disspelled any rumors about the shirts being a jinx by reporting in the *Press-Gazette* that when the Packers wore them prior to the Ram game they beat Detroit. The Packers didn't suffer from any jinx against Pittsburgh as they dumped the Steelers for the ninth straight time since Pittsburgh entered the league as the Pirates in '33.

With seven games still left to be played, the Packers (2-2-0) still had a good mathematical chance of catching the Bears (3-0-1) and the Rams (2-1-1) as they entered the fifth week of competition against the Lions at Milwaukee. A disappointing crowd of only 24,000 turned out to watch the two rivals put on what Lee Remmel of the *Press-Gazette* kindly called "the National Football league's finest defensive performance thus far this season." In reality, the Lions were a lousy football team, and the Packers played just well enough to win, 10-7.

The Western Division race received a boost that Sunday

when the Giants slipped past the Bears (3-1-1) and the Cardinals (3-3-0) whipped the Rams (2-2-1), allowing the Packers (3-2-0) to move into second place. All the Pack had to do now to take control of their own fate was beat the Bears the next time the two elevens met, and just by a quirk in the schedule that occasion was the following Sunday.

Lambeau spent the week before the Bear game psyching up his charges, telling them that they owed the Bears a little something for the thrashing that they had taken earlier in the year at Green Bay. The team responded with near perfection – on defense. The Packers held the Bears in their own territory throughout the first half, never letting the Monsters beyond their own 45; but the Green Bay offense was as dismal as the defense was awesome. Three times the Packers got inside the Chicago 25, and three times they came away with zilch. Ted Fritsch had been the hero a few weeks before; he was the goat in the Windy City. After missing a pair of field goal attempts in the first half, he got the ball on the first play of the second half and fumbled it on the Green Bay 30 where Bear end Ed Sprinkle scooped it up and ran it back for a TD. Later in the third period, the Bears mounted their only scoring drive of the game as they marched down to the Green Bay 21 where they had to settle for a 28-yard field goal by Frank Maznicki to put Chicago up, 10-0. The Green Bay offense remained impotent until late in the game when the defense gave the Packers their best scoring opportunity. Tiny Croft stole the ball from Dante Magnani and was tackled at the Bears' 13. Two plays later Fritsch broke over the goal to give the Packers their only score of the day.

The loss, coupled with wins by the Rams (3-2-1) and the Cards (4-3-0), dropped the Packers (3-3-0) into fourth place, a game and a half behind the Bears (4-1-1). With only five games left, it didn't seem likely that the Packers would catch Chicago.

The Packers traveled to Chicago again the next week, but this time to face Jimmy Conzelman's Cardinals. Conzelman was back for his second coaching stint with the Redbirds, having spent the last three war years as vice-president of the St. Louis Browns baseball team. His previous teams in Chicago (1940-42) hadn't done all that well, but most of his squads back in the

'20s – Rock Island Independents '22, Milwaukee Badgers '23-'24, Detroit Panthers '25-'26, and Providence Steamrollers '27-'30 had been much better than .500 clubs. His '28 Providence team won the NFL title, and five other years he finished in the first division. He had the Cards playing some good football in '46, and the Packers prepared for the Redbirds as if they were the Bears. When Green Bay dumped Chicago, 19-7, Conzelman confessed that the Packers were a better team than he had thought.

The Cardinal affray marked the end of George Whitney Calhoun's consecutive game attendance streak. Since the beginning of his involvement with pro football in Green Bay in 1918, Cal hadn't missed a single Green Bay contest, whether it was an intrasquad affair, exhibition, league battle, or title tilt – at home or on the road. He complained that his alarm clock had failed to ring, causing him to miss the train to Chicago.

Losing just about put the Cards (4-4-0) out of the divisional race as the Bears (5-1-1) had a commanding lead over the Packers (4-3-0) and the Rams (3-3-1) with only four weeks left on the schedule.

The pathetic Lions were next on the slate for Green Bay as the Packers traveled to Detroit for the November 17 contest. The results were almost the same as they had been in Milwaukee three weeks earlier. Detroit played lousy football, and the Packers played just well enough to win, 9-0, on a TD and a field goal by the league's leading scorer Ted Fritsch.

By winning, the Packers (5-3-0) merely kept pace with the Bears (6-1-1) and stayed ahead of the Rams (4-3-1). Although they still had a mathematical chance of taking the division title, the Packers knew it wasn't likely to happen because two of the Bears' last three games were against the Lions.

The only real excitement left for Green Bay was the "homecoming game" with the Cardinals. A full house packed City Stadium for the contest. At halftime, the fans were introduced to the "All-Time Packer Team" that had been chosen by them in a *Press-Gazette* poll.* As for the game itself, the crowd went away disappointed because the Cardinals knocked the Packers

---

*See Appendix A.

out of the race for the division crown by scoring three TDs in the fourth quarter to dump Green Bay, 24-6.

With nothing left to play for except pride, the Packers finished the season by whipping Washington, 20-7, but losing to the Rams in LA, 38-17. The loss to the Rams left Green Bay in third place for the second year in a row, and the 6-5-0 record was Green Bay's worst since '34 when the Packers finished with a 7-6-0 mark.

Art Daley summed up the Packers' season the week before the last game with the headline of his editor's column:

It's Hard to Imagine Packers Without Passing; But It's True

For the first time since he took control in 1919, Curly Lambeau didn't have a passing attack because he didn't have a true passer on the team. Irv Comp was a bust in '45, but Hutson's performance overshadowed Comp's deficiency. Without Hutson in '46, Comp's lack of ability stood out like the proverbial sore thumb.

In order to get the Packers back on top of the division in '47, Lambeau knew he needed a passer. Now if he could only find one . . .

§ § §

3
The AAC Challenge

In war, one does not give aid and comfort to the enemy. Someone forgot to tell that to former Packer Clarke Hinkle.

All Packerdom was rocked by a speech made by former Packer great Clarke Hinkle at the second annual Elks East–West–Central high school football banquet in late November 1946. Hinkle, who was living and working in De Pere, warned, "The Green Bay Packers are not going to be in Green Bay very long unless the city's civic organizations wake up and create more interest in the team. I don't know why, but there is absolutely no interest in the Packers any longer."

Hinkle's blast ricocheted all the way to New York where the national media picked up on it and began printing stories about the Packers moving to a big city such as San Francisco or Dallas or Baltimore. Some writers who didn't quite understand who owned the corporation that operated the franchise in Green Bay wrote how Curly Lambeau was planning to take the team elsewhere. Where they got the idea that Lambeau could do anything of the kind would be mere speculation at this point in time, but later events (described in subsequent chapters) did give rise to the possibility that Lambeau or someone very close to him had started the rumors.

Finally, it took a Midwesterner to put to rest all the rumors concerning the shift of the Green Bay franchise that were floating around the country. Edward Prell of *The Chicago Tribune* interviewed NFL Commissioner Bert Bell, then wrote, "Green Bay's Packers, rumors to the contrary, which have popped up more persistently than ever in the last two years, aren't going to pack up and find a new home." Prell quoted Bell:

"The National league wouldn't be the same without a Green Bay," declared Bell. "Any talk that the Packers, operating in Green Bay and Milwaukee, can't hold their own financially, just isn't so. I believe every team which played in Green Bay or Milwaukee took away more than the league guarantee of $10,000, and they (the Packers) more than hold up their end away from home where they have a terrific appeal. I would say that the Green Bay Packers, after 26 years in the league, are here to stay."

Prell explained that attendance for Packer home games in Green Bay and Milwaukee drew 113,500 fans for five home dates in '46 and 214,000 for six road games. The league total for 55 games was 1,800,000 for an average of 32,727. Bell said the Packers more than held up their end.

A closer examination of the numbers revealed that the NFL without the Packers five home games drew approximately 1,687,000 for an average of 33,740. The Packers averaged 22,600 at home, which was more than 10,000 less than the league average with them and more than 11,000 less than the league average without them. Bell was incorrect to say that the Packers were holding up their end in the league's attendance figures, and Prell was wrong to support Bell's statement with his statistics. The truth was the Packers weren't holding up their end of the bargain with the other clubs in the NFL. Each visiting team was taking home about $15,000 from playing in Green Bay or Milwaukee, while the Packers were raking in almost twice that amount when they played on the road. The Packers weren't holding up the league; the league was holding up the Packers.

Adding to the rumors about the Packers moving was the fact that the Miami Seahawks were booted out of the AAC because they were such a drag on the new league. The franchise reverted to the league at the end of the '46 season, which allowed the AAC a free hand to give it over to another owner in another city. AAC Commissioner Jim Crowley said interests in Baltimore and Philadelphia had the best chances of gaining the franchise. Talk had it that the AAC wanted to put a team in Baltimore *before the Packers moved there.* The AAC moguls considered the Maryland city to be prime football country and placing a team there would be a boon to their fledgling organization and it would further embarrass the NFL by beating the established league to the punch.

A bigger embarrassment to the NFL popped up in New York

when the Bears met the Giants for the NFL title in mid-December. New York players Merle Hapes and Frank Filchock were offered bribes to throw the title tilt. Alvin J. Paris, a minor official of a New York novelty concern, was charged with attempting to bribe the two players. Hapes admitted before the game that he had been approached by Paris, but Filchock flatly denied ever having discussed a bribe with Paris. Police reports, based on evidence gathered through wire-taps on Paris's telephone, supported both statements. Even so, Hapes was barred from playing in the game by Bert Bell because he didn't report the bribe attempt to anyone. Filchock played in the game, and he played harder than any teammate, but the Bears still won, 24-14.

Oddly, Paris had told his cohorts before the plot was discovered to bet on Chicago to win by 10 points, which turned out to be the Bears' margin of victory. But when the other criminals learned that Paris had lied to them about Filchock and Hapes being bought, the gamblers began hedging their bets which cut deeply into their winnings.

Finally, the NFL got around to holding its annual draft. Of course, it was done in secret because the owners didn't want to tip off the AAC to whom they were drafting, but this wasn't the reason some league magnates gave the press. Lambeau told the *Press-Gazette* that he was withholding the name of his top pick "because he is in a bowl game and publication of his name among football's draftees before January 1 might embarrass him and his coach." This was pure manure. Before the inception of the AAC, making known the names of top draft choices was headline news, and Lambeau was all for it. Now all of a sudden he was worried about embarrassing a player and a coach by announcing that he had made the kid a number one pick? The *Press-Gazette* compounded Lambeau's lie and insulted the intelligence of its readership by giving the statement credence.

Several other teams in the NFL announced at least a partial list of their draftees, including the Bears who had the first ever "Bonus Pick". In their infinite wisdom, the NFL owners devised a plan to give the top pick in the draft each year to the winner of an annual drawing instead of automatically awarding it to the team that finished the previous campaign with the worst record. Each team would have its name dropped into a hat, then one name would be drawn. That club would be allowed to pick first in the draft that year but wouldn't be allowed to participate in the Bonus Pick sweepstakes again until the every team in the league had received the Bonus Pick. As a further penalty for winning the Bonus Pick drawing, the winner was limited to 29 picks in the regular phase of the draft. George Halas used the pick to take Bob Fennimore, a halfback from Oklahoma A&M (State), who turned out to be a bust as a pro.

The AAC held its draft later the same week amid boasts by Jim Crowley that three of his loop's teams turned a profit in their first year. AAC champion Cleveland, Eastern Division winner New York, and San Francisco, runnerup in the West, finished in the black. At the draft meeting, Miami was permitted to make picks, which was odd because it was a foregone conclusion that the Seahawks were defunct. Even so, Hampton Pool, the Miami coach, chose Charley Trippi, the All–American halfback from Georgia that the Chicago Cardinals chose as their first pick.

On the last day of a year that a lot of Packer fans wanted to forget, a very large threat to the Packers was announced in Chicago. Jimmy Crowley resigned as commissioner of the AAC and became a partner in the new ownership of the Chicago Rockets. Joining Crowley in the venture were two other men who had very solid connections to Green Bay and Wisconsin. William S. Toohey and John J. Brogan were long–time friends of Crowley. The three men bought the franchise from John L. Keeshin, and Crowley immediately was named as general manager, vice–president, and head coach.

Crowley and Toohey were born in Chicago and Muscatine, Iowa, respectively, but they grew up in Green Bay, Brogan's native city. Brogan played high school football for West High at the same time that Curly Lambeau was playing at East. Crowley and Toohey played for East during the years immediately after World War I. It was during this time that they became friends with Brogan. Although each one went a different way after their school years, they continued to maintain their friendship. While Crowley was making a career of coaching college football, Brogan entered politics, then business in Green Bay; and Toohey moved to Chicago and went into business. At the time that they bought the Rockets, Brogan owned and operated the Fox River Boat Company and Toohey was known as "the syrup magnate" because he owned the Syrup and Fruit Products Company of Chicago and the Central State Produce Corporation of Lawton, Michigan, while he was also the vice-president of the D.B. Scully Syrup Company of Chicago.

All three men, especially Brogan, had close connections with Green Bay in particular and Wisconsin in general. Because of this, the rumor mill started grinding out plenty of grist to the effect that the Rockets would be moving to Milwaukee.

In his *Sports Cocktails* column in the *Press-Gazette*, Art Daley wrote that according to "officials at State Fair park, it was learned that the Rocket management sought to obtain the State Fair park gridiron for its home games . . . This effort, however, was blocked because the Packers and the Fair organization have signed a five-year lease which has four years to run."

John Brogan replied to the story in Daley's column:

"The Rockets never at any time sought to get into State Fair park. When a report to that effect was published several weeks ago in a Milwaukee paper we (the Rockets) went to Ammon (Ralph E. who manages State Fair park) and asked him why that report was given to the newspaper? (sic) We told him that that report hurt us in Chicago. The people there might be led to believe that we are trying to get out of Chicago. We are not trying to go anywhere, and we never made any attempt to get into Packer territory."

Being fair to all concerned, Daley published remarks by all the parties involved in the rumor:

From Ammon – "About a month ago, I bumped into Hugh Brogan (brother of John) in Madison. He inquired as to the type of tieup (sic) the Green Bay Packers had in State Fair park. I told him that the Packers had a five-year lease on State Fair park which has four years yet to run. Brogan also added that the Rockets would be interested in playing exhibition or league games if the Packers ever pulled out.

"These facts were made public in a Milwaukee newspaper

several days later. And about that time I received a telephone call from an official of the Rockets in Chicago. I don't recall his name, asking whether or not somebody from the Rockets had made an overture toward use of Milwaukee as a home grounds. A day or two later a story came from Chicago on the press wires that Crowley (Jim, president and general manager of the Rockets) denied that the Rockets were interested in Milwaukee."

From Hugh Brogan – "I chatted with Ammon on a street in Madison and Ralph asked me if the Rockets might be interested in playing some games in State Fair park. I told him that I was not connected with the Rockets and knew nothing of their plans."

From Ollie Kuechle, Milwaukee sports writer – "We published a story, which I wrote, about a month ago on information given me by Ammon. The information is exactly the same as Ammon told you (the Press–Gazette). We were never asked to print a retraction by the Rockets, although a couple of days later Crowley came out with his Associated Press statement that the Rockets definitely were not interested in Milwaukee."

Reading between the lines, Hugh Brogan admitted meeting Ammon in Madison and discussing the possibility of the Rockets playing in Milwaukee. However, he denied having initiated the conversation, actually placing the blame on Ammon. For his part, Ammon didn't say Brogan had initiated the conversation, only that he inquired about the tie–up the Packers had with State Fair park. Brogan didn't deny Ammon's statement, and Ammon didn't deny Brogan's. After putting the two sets of remarks together, it came out that:

Ammon and Brogan bumped into each other in Madison, and Ammon, knowing that Hugh Brogan was John Brogan's brother, asked Brogan if the Rockets might be interested in playing in Milwaukee. Brogan said he didn't know if they would or not since he wasn't associated with the club, but just in case they were, what kind of tie–up did the Packers have with State Fair park? Ammon then told him about the five–year lease, and that was that. By the time he got back to Milwaukee, Ammon was certain in his mind that Brogan was speaking on behalf of the Rockets and reported the conversation to Ollie Kuechle.

Kuechle didn't say that he had checked the story with either Hugh Brogan or an official of the Rockets. Neither Crowley nor John Brogan denied the story by Kuechle; they only said that the Rockets weren't interested in Milwaukee.

The bottomline was the Rockets were interested in moving to Milwaukee because the Bears and Cardinals had Chicago sewed up tight, but when Rocket officials learned that the Packers had a five-year lease on the stadium — a lease that prevented State Fair Park management from renting to any other professional football team without the Packers' approval —interest in Milwaukee didn't just wane, it vanished completely.

Although this set of rumors and stories about the Rockets moving to Milwaukee were put to rest, the saga of the Packers moving there was still an ongoing soap opera with many episodes left to hit the sports pages before they would finally be laid to rest.

At the NFL meetings in Chicago in January of '47, the league barons grappled with the idea of expanding their own organization and also expanding the minor league system. George Halas wanted to add a new western division to the all-eastern American Association. The new group would play in the parks of the American Association of baseball. It was a thought whose time hadn't come yet. At the same time, the moguls took under advisement an application by the owner of the Pacific Coast League's San Francisco Clippers, Frank Ciraolo, for admittance into the league.

Other matters before the league magnates were the addition of a fifth official for games, a proposal that was turned down the year before when Halas opposed it. His vote in '47 made the measure a unanimous ballot. Also, Bert Bell was given full authority to deal with any owner who should ever be involved in gambling activities.

On the league front, Charlie Bidwill, the owner of the Chicago Cardinals, died of pneumonia on April 19 after a long illness. He was only 51 at the time, and none of his heirs was old enough or capable enough to assume ownership responsibilities for the franchise, so command of the Cardinals passed into the hands of caretakers for a few seasons.

The war between the two big-time pro loops had an unofficial cease-fire until the first week of summer.

At a meeting of owners and coaches at the Baltimore Touchdown Club, new AAC commissioner, Admiral Jonas W. Ingram, said that there was "plenty of room for two professional football leagues in this country." Ingram played *unfairly* by saying nice things about the NFL. "Men of the National Football League have done a grand job of pioneering professional football over the past 20 years." Then he announced that the AAC "is here to stay. We have eight grand teams, and we have four outfits today better than the Washington Redskins." Then he declared that the AAC would "be honest right down the line . . . " This was a direct reference to the Hapes-Filchock episode in the NFL title game.

As the summer wore on, Commissioner Bert Bell and the other powers of the NFL continued to ignore the AAC. In an effort to endear the league to the colleges, Bell proposed a three point deal in which any player who still had college eligibility remaining would not be signed to an NFL contract without the consent of the player's college, conference, and coach. In return, the colleges had to allow their people to become officials for the NFL and they had to remove any and all rules, restrictions or discrimination against former NFL players becoming coaches in the college ranks.

At the same time, Ingram was touring the country, predicting that some day the NFL and AAC would merge into one league. This was the same man who had told the Navy that it was too large and needed to trim its sails. It was Ingram's idea that the two loops form a new organizaton that would more or less resemble Major League Baseball with two leagues of eight teams each. Ingram talked, but few people listened, especially NFL people.

In the meantime, the Chicago Rockets went into training camp right in the Packers back yard. Coach Jimmy Crowley had his charges report to the team's facilities at Two Rivers, Wisconsin, where they prepared for their forthcoming season.

Admiral Ingram issued the ultimate challenge to Bell in late August. He telegraphed the NFL leader with an offer to play a title game between the NFL champ and the AAC champ at the end of the season. Ingram told newsmen that it could be winner-take-all in a game that was sure to net the victor $250,000, or the proceeds could go to charity. The admiral spiced up his verbal thrust by stating: "We feel we have four teams better than anything they've got." He went on to name the teams: Cleveland Browns, New York Yankees, Los Angeles Dons, and San Francisco 49ers.

Bell replied: "Not interested." He elaborated by stating that the NFL forbade its teams from playing post-season games.

Ingram countered by calling Bell's excuse weak. The admiral was too much of a gentleman to say that Bell and the other NFL moguls were simply cowards, that they were afraid that Ingram might be right and the AAC champ might actually whip the NFL champ in a title match, and that would be too embarrassing for the NFL to bear.

As the '47 season rolled around, the war between the two loops moved to the box office. Teams from both organizations went head-to-head in New York, Chicago, and Los Angeles. The AAC had San Francisco, Baltimore, Cleveland, and Buffalo all to themselves, while the NFL had Boston, Washington, Philadelphia, Pittsburgh, Detroit, and Green Bay.

Of all the franchises in the two circuits, the magnates of both the AAC and NFL were most concerned over little Green Bay. Why the Packers? Simply because every single professional team owner outside Wisconsin believed that Green Bay could not survive the war between the leagues. Therefore, according to the thinking of the other owners, the Packers were the pivotal pawn in the conflict.

The AAC men worried that the NFL would move the Packers into one of their bailiwicks, such as San Francisco, and eventually drive their team out of existence or to another city. Either way would be catastrophic for the AAC.

The NFL bosses were considering exactly that sort of move,

and they were nearly unanimous in their desire to remove the Packers from Wisconsin to the West Coast. They even had an inside man in Green Bay who was doing what he could behind the scenes to make such a move possible. But that's getting ahead of the time-table.

For now, the AAC and NFL engaged themselves with playing football in 1947. The war would continue but at a later date.

§ § §

4
Turning Back Time

It's said you can't teach an old dog new tricks. Curly Lambeau picked 1947 to see if that was true or not.

Lambeau had the best running game in the National Football League in 1946. As a team, the Packers were tops in the league on the ground. Tony Canadeo, Ted Fritsch, and Walt Schlinkman ranked fifth, sixth, and eighth, respectively, among the league's top rushers; but no Packer passer finished in the top 12. To further show how inept the aerial game was in Green Bay, Nolan Luhn and Clyde Goodnight led the receivers with 16 catches each. Fritsch was the top scorer in the loop with an even 100 points, and he was the best TD man with 10, and the best in field goals with nine. The sad part of this was Fritsch accounted for all but 48 of the points the Packers scored in '46.

All the numbers added up to one thing: the Packers could go to the air about as well as a flock of ostriches. With that fact so glaringly in mind, Lambeau set his sights on drafting a topnotch passer to lead the new offense he was already designing for his '47 Packers.

As previously stated, the NFL held its draft in secret because the owners feared the AAC would beat them to signing their top choices, but this wasn't the reason some league magnates gave the press.

Lambeau told the *Press-Gazette* that he was withholding the name of his top pick "because he is in a bowl game and publication of his name among football's draftees before January 1 might embarrass him and his coach." Bunkum! Before the AAC came into existence, divulging the names of top draft choices was headline news, and Lambeau was all for that. To

The Lambeau Years — Part Three

believe that he was suddenly worried about embarrassing a player and his coach by announcing that he had made the kid a number one pick was really stretching his credibility. The *Press-Gazette* compounded Lambeau's lie and insulted the intelligence of its readership by giving the statement credence.

By the end of December 1946, Art Daley finally wheedled the Packer draft list out of Lambeau and published it in the newspaper. Topping the coach's wish list were Ernie Case and Burr Baldwin, the quarterback-end passing combination from undefeated UCLA. The remainder of his top 10 included Alex Agase, guard, Illinois; Ed Cody, fullback, Purdue; Bob Skoglund, end, Notre Dame; Mickey McArdle, halfback, USC; John Ferraro, tackle, USC; Jim Callahan, end, USC; Monte Moncrief, tackle, Texas A&M; and Eugene Wilson, end, SMU. It wasn't a bad list of players as far as talent went, but Lambeau was dreaming if he thought he could sign all those California boys to play in itty-bitty frosty Green Bay, Wisconsin when they had already seen the bright lights of big, sunny, warm Hollywood. As it turned out, only three of these men — Cody, Skoglund, and Wilson — ever saw any duty in a Packer uniform. Of the others, Case, Baldwin, and Agase signed with AAC teams, while the remaining four chose other careers.

As he did every year, Lambeau trekked off to California for the sunshine and bowl games and starlets (but not necessarily in that order as will be explained in a later chapter) in late December, but this time he didn't realize that his football bastion back in Wisconsin would soon be under fire again.

Because he needed a real passer, Lambeau used the annual owners meeting to trade for one. He sent halfback Bob Nussbaumer to the Washington Redskins for Jack Jacobs. The *Press-Gazette* described Jacobs as a "full-blooded Indian from Oklahoma" who played every backfield position for the Skins. Dan Reeves, the owner of the Los Angeles Rams, predicted Jacobs was exactly what the Packers needed and that Jacobs would make Green Bay very hard to beat in '47.

When the official statistics for the '46 season were announced, the Packers became the first non-T-formation team to win the league rushing title since '38 when the Lions won the rushing crown with their single-wing formation. Along with being first on the ground, the Packers were last through the air. Of course, Lambeau and the *Press-Gazette* played down this fact.

The '47 playing slate was announced in late February, and Lambeau was quoted in the *Press-Gazette* as saying "the six-game home schedule (was) most ideal. He pointed out that it was the first time *'we've ever had six contests in our territory'*." (Author's italics) The coach must have taken too many hits on the gridiron during his playing days because the Packers had not only played six games in their "territory" previously but they had done it almost every year before World War II, sometimes playing seven games in Green Bay and Milwaukee in a single season.

A month later on March 24 Green Bay was once again shaken by unexpected news. The most surprised man in the city was George Whitney Calhoun.

Calhoun reported to work that morning at the *Press-Gazette* like he always did, and he went about his routine as wire editor for the daily newspaper. It was his job to check the news service wires and determine which stories would be appropriate for the paper that day. As usual, he went right to the sports reports and discovered the following article:

"George Strickler, who resigned last week as director of public relations for the National football league, has signed a three-year contract as assistant general manager and director of public relations for the Green Bay Packers, it was announced today by Packer Coach Curly Lambeau.

"Lambeau stated that the addition of Strickler to the Packer staff *does not effect the status of George W. Calhoun* (Author's italics), veteran Packer publicist and director of press ticket arrangements. Calhoun has been with the Packer organization since its start and was the man who 'passed the hat' in the early days.

"Strickler, 43, started his newspaper career at the age of 14 with the South Bend Tribune. After two years at the University of Indiana, he returned to the South Bend Tribune as a police reporter and then enrolled at Notre Dame to become Knute Rockne's publicity man in 1924, the highlight of which was placing the Four Horsemen on horseback for a picture.

"He later played baseball with South Bend and Milton, Wis., where he worked for the Burdick Cabinet company. In 1926, Strickler became bureau manager of the International News Service and a year later joined the Chicago Herald-Examiner where his first assignment was Gene Tunney's camp for the first Dempsey fight. After serving as sports editor of the Daily Georgian and Sunday American in Atlanta, Strickler became publicity director for Chicago stadium.

"Strickler joined the sports staff of the Chicago Tribune in 1931 and remained there until 1941 when he became director of public relations of the National league under former commissioner Elmer Layden."

John Torinus, Sr., stated in *The Packer Legend* that this event occurred in 1945. He quoted an Associated Press release that read:

"General Manager Curly Lambeau of the Green Bay Packers announced today that George Strickler, formerly sports editor of the Chicago *Tribune*, has been named publicity director for the Packers in Green Bay. *He will replace George W. Calhoun, who has retired.*" (Author's italics)

Torinus either had a faulty memory in reporting the year or the book had a typo. The year is unimportant. The statements in the two articles concerning Calhoun are very important, however. Both were wrong about Calhoun's status. *His place with the Packers had changed, and he hadn't retired.* Lambeau had fired him, but he didn't have the guts to tell Calhoun to his face that he was fired.

Torinus, who was probably one of Calhoun's closest friends at that time and for the remainder of Cal's life, wrote that Calhoun "was a bitter enemy of Lambeau from that day forward," and that Calhoun "was somewhat surprised and deeply hurt" by his dismissal. Who could blame him?

Calhoun, more than any other individual, had made Lambeau what he was: a magnate in the NFL; and he had made the Packers what they were: a success in the NFL. Calhoun was the man who had suggested to Lambeau that he stay in Green

Bay and play for the town team in 1919 instead of returning to college at Notre Dame like his young wife and his father and mother wanted him to do. Calhoun was the man who had supported Lambeau and the Packers in the newspaper right from the first meeting Curly had attended with the other young men who had played for Nate Abrams's town team, the Green Bay Whales, in 1918. Calhoun was the man who put his own money into Lambeau's corporation when Lambeau picked up the NFL franchise *that Curly had caused the Clair brothers to lose in 1921*. And when Lambeau's venture in the business of pro football failed at the end of the 1922 season, wasn't Calhoun one of the men who rallied the community behind Lambeau's team and kept it in the NFL? Calhoun was Lambeau's friend and supporter all those years, and this was how Curly treated him.

Lambeau didn't know it at the time, but his popularity in Green Bay had peaked and was now headed downhill with increasing speed every day.

From the time of Strickler's hiring until mid–summer, little more than the usual occurred in Packerdom. Player contracts trickled into Lambeau's office, and Strickler made the appropriate press announcements. Art Daley wrote minor tidbits about various players in his column in the *Press-Gazette*, but other than that there was little news because Lambeau was in California most of the time.

Lambeau returned to Green Bay on July 16, which would turn out to be a very important date in the future. He hired a new assistant coach, and he acquired some new ballplayers.

Notable among Lambeau's acquisitions during the off–season were Bob McDougal, Ward Cuff, and Damon Tassos.

McDougal was a Wisconsin lad from Oconto, a small town just 30 or so miles up U.S. Highway 41 from Green Bay. He played freshman football at the University of Wisconsin in Madison, then transferred to a warmer climate to play for the University of Miami (Fla) before joining the Marines in '42. Like a lot of boys growing up in Wisconsin since the advent of the Packers, McDougal dreamed of playing for his favorite team.

The Lambeau Years — Part Three

Whereas McDougal was a rookie in the NFL, Ward Cuff had 10 full seasons under his belt. Lambeau purchased Cuff's contract from the Cardinals in April, hoping the aging veteran would do for the Packers what he had done for the Cards in '46, that is, act "as a wonderful stabilizer and really put fire and brains into our backfield," as Chicago's Jimmy Conzelman put it. Because he had business interests in Milwaukee, Cuff wanted to be traded to the Packers the year before when he was still with the Giants. The Giants traded him to Chicago instead. Lambeau had wanted to draft Cuff back in 1937 when he saw him running wild at Marquette University, but New York's Steve Owen beat him to the punch. The Packers were looking at Cuff primarily as a defensive back and as a ball-carrier secondly.

Tassos came to the Packers in a trade with the Lions. Lambeau sent guard Marv Pregulman to Detroit for Tassos and a fifth round draft choice. Pregulman hailed from East Lansing, Michigan and the University of Michigan, and it was his desire to play closer to home because he and his father were in the furniture business in the Michigan city. Nice guy that he was, Lambeau accommodated Pregulman who was coveted by Lions owner Fred Mandel. Like most owners, Mandel was a little short on football savvy. His coach, Gus Dorais, called Tassos the one player "I don't want to lose." Tassos, known as "the Greek", was a two-year veteran out of Texas A&M.

Former Green Bay player Bo Molenda was signed to teach Lambeau's V-formation to the backfield. Molenda played for the Packers during the triple-champ years of 1929-31, then he was sold to the New York Giants because Lambeau didn't like the way the big fullback was treating the coach's pet, young Arnie Herber. He played for the Giants for four years, then became an assistant to Steve Owen. In '41, Molenda became the ends coach at Lafayette College. He joined the Navy when the war broke out and became the coach of the San Diego Naval Base eleven in late '43. He was still there when Lambeau hired him. Molenda joined Don Hutson and Walt Kiesling on the Packer staff.

When Lambeau returned from California and found 22 signed contracts on his desk, he immediately began crowing about the forthcoming season. "Right now," he said, "we're almost three deep with a lot of contracts coming in soon." The coach planned to build his new offense around recent acquisition Jack Jacobs, saying, "I've heard nothing but good reports about the boy's playing ability." Art Daley quoted Lambeau's remarks about Jacobs's versatility, then wrote a piece of copy that his editor should have corrected before letting it reach print: "For instance, in one game with Washington last year Jacobs was forced to play every backfield position, including three in one game." Lambeau didn't care about the Oklahoma product's versatility as much as he did about his ability as a passer. To accommodate Jacobs, Lambeau planned to move Larry Craig and Ken Keuper, quarterbacks in the offense he was shelving, to new positions.

Another passer that Lambeau was counting on for the '47 campaign was Cliff Aberson, the minor league baseball player in the Chicago Cubs farm system. Aberson went through a hot streak at the plate in late June and early July which made the Chicago brass sit up and take notice. The Cubs' general manager, James T. Gallagher, said that the Cubs planned to bring Aberson up to the big club in September as long as he hadn't signed a contract with the Packers to play football. If he were to sign a deal with Green Bay before fall, the Cubs would step aside and let him play football. Or so they said. Aberson continued to hit well, so the Cubs decided not to wait until September to call him up. Gallagher gave him his chance in mid-July, and Lambeau publicly wished the lad well, while he privately expressed his hope that Aberson would be a failure in the Majors.

The biggest news of the summer for all of Packerdom was the retirement of Lee Joannes as president of the corporation. Joannes had been president since 1930 and had guided the club through *The Great Depression* and the second bankruptcy in Packer history. Just before the annual stockholders meeting, he told the executive committee that if the stockholders so desired he would remain a director but he absolutely had to be relieved of his duties as president and member of the executive committee. He cited his involvement in a new business as his reason for retiring. That was for public consumption. The real story was much deeper than that, but the truth wouldn't be known for two and a half years.

To replace Joannes, the board of directors elected Emil R. Fischer, president of the Atlas Warehouse and Cold Storage Company in Green Bay. Fischer had been on the board of directors since 1936.

At the same meeting held July 25, 1947, Gerald F. Clifford, the legal genius who had created the non-profit corporation, made a motion to increase the board of directors from 22 to 25 and the executive committee from nine to 12. The stockholders filled two of three new directorships with William J. Servotte and Russell W. Bogda. Replacing Joannes and filling the three new spots on the executive committee were Milan J. Boex, Harvey Lhost, Bogda, and Servotte.

Lambeau gave his annual "state of the team address" at this meeting. "We should be as good, and better, than previous years. One thing, the morale will be sky-higher than last year when most professional and college teams had trouble along those lines." He said his backfield of Jacobs, Bruce Smith, Bob Forte, and Ted Fritsch would match up with any in the league, and he couldn't wait to see Jacobs and end Gene Wilson in action. "Excluding Don Hutson, Wilson should prove to be one of our all-time best receivers. Don is in a class by himself." On the rest of the division, the coach stated that the Rams had the best material, that the Bears were always tough, that Detroit was building a powerhouse, and that the Cardinals would be good enough to beat anyone in the NFL. The Packers would go into training camp with only 42 players as opposed to the 60 of a year ago. It was Lambeau's plan "to work longer with each boy this season, and (we) haven't sacrificed a thing in starting with a smaller squad." Famous last words!

The first meeting of new executive committee, now consisting of 12 members, was held the following Monday night, July 28, 1947. The committee determined that running a professional football team was too much for one to handle, meaning Lambeau had too much to do and needed some help; therefore, a new system for running the corporation was proposed and put into effect. The decision was made to divide the executive committee into sub-committees. President Fischer and Lambeau would be members of every group because it was felt that their input was necessary to the success of the operation. The sub-committees were: Contracts and publicity — Andy Turnbull, chairman, Gerry Clifford, and Milan Boex; finance — H.G. Wintgens, chairman, William J. Servotte, and Russ Bogda; grounds — Fred Leicht, chairman, H.J. Bero, and Harvey Lhost; legal and league affairs — Gerry Clifford and Lambeau.

No longer would all matters concerning the team be left in the hands of Curly Lambeau. The executive committee would be assisting him in almost everything except coaching the players. No one knew it at the time, but a time bomb began ticking at that meeting; and there was no telling when it would explode.

That year the NFL moguls decided that 33 players were not enough to stock a team, so they increased the roster limit to 35. Lambeau hoped this would make his job easier when he began welcoming his charges to Rockwood Lodge at the end of July. Included in the early arrivals was Andy Uram, the hard-running halfback who had spent six seasons with the Packers from 1938 through 1943 who was trying to make a comeback after spending two years in the Navy and one year on the retired list. He failed to impress the Packer staff and was cut.

Fred Vant Hull had played guard for the Packers in '42, but then went off to war. Lambeau signed him for '47, but NFL Commissioner Bert Bell suspended Vant Hull from playing in the league for five years because he had played the '46 campaign in the AAC.

Finally, the pre-season rolled around, and Lambeau unleashed his new air attack against the Giants in an exhibition game in Green Bay. It netted a lot of yards but only 17 points. The coach was dissatisfied with Green Bay's performance and promised that corrections would be made. His promise failed to materialize in two subsequent practice games as the Packers could only score 17 against Pittsburgh and 14 against Boston, losing the former contest and winning the latter.

The real problem behind the Packers' lack of scoring was a rash of injuries to some key people. Typical among them was Urban Odson's back injury which was suffered when he was bounced off the incredibly hard ground at Rockwood Lodge's practice field. When Odson went down, the Packers were left with only one healthy right tackle, and in a day when players went both ways, this was disastrous to the Packers.

To bolster his depleted roster, Lambeau picked up end Johnny Kovatch in a trade with Washington, and he signed guard Al Forte who had been released by the Bears. Kovatch graduated from Notre Dame and joined the Redskins in '42. After one season, he entered the armed forces and returned to the NFL in '46. The Packers gave up a future draft choice to get Kovatch. Forte was a five-year NFL veteran who played his college ball at Montana.

The Packers prepared to open their 27th season in the NFL during the last week of September. Lambeau cloaked the final practices in secrecy because Green Bay's home opener was against the heavily favored NFL champion Bears and George Halas wasn't beneath sending spies to Packertown for a preview of things to come on Sunday.

Lambeau opened the campaign with a mostly veteran roster. Returning from the '46 squad were ends Clyde Goodnight, Nolan Luhn, Don Wells, and Larry Craig; tackles Baby Ray, Paul Lipscomb, Urban Odson, and Tiny Croft; guards Dick Wildung and Ed Neal; centers Lester Gatewood, Charley Brock, and Bob Flowers; and backs Bruce Smith, Bob Forte, Ted Fritsch, Tony Canadeo, Walt Schlinkman, Roy McKay, Ken Keuper, Irv Comp, and Herman Rohrig. Joining them were rookies Gene Wilson (end, SMU), Ed Bell (tackle, Indiana), Ralph Davis (guard, Wisconsin), Bob Skoglund (end, Notre Dame), and Ed Cody (back, Purdue). Other newcomers were backs Jack Jacobs, Ward Cuff, Bob McDougal, and Jim Gillette; tackle Damon Tassos; and guards Al Forte and Ray Clemens.

Because of numerous incidents of sucker-punching when the officials weren't looking, the NFL moguls decided to add a fifth official, a back judge, for the '47 season. Lambeau initiated the move and with good reason. In the first Bears-Packers game of '46, Irv Comp and Nolan Luhn suffered broken noses and Carl Mulleneaux took one on the chin that was so hard that he was given a brain concussion and was forced to retire from football. It was Lambeau's hope that the fifth man on the field might put a crimp in Chicago's style of play.

Lambeau got his wish.

The Bears came to town on the last Sunday of September and went home that night as losers, 29-20. A packed house of 25,461 fans watched the Packers steal the game by intercepting five Chicago passes. Ted Fritsch rushed for 99 yards to lead a strong ground game, and Jack Jacobs kept the Bears off balance with some timely passing, including TD tosses to Nolan Luhn and Bruce Smith. Jacobs also ran for a touchdown.

The Rams were the next opponent for the Packers. The game was set for Milwaukee, and it marked the 20th meeting between the two teams. Green Bay held a 13-6 edge over the Rams, but the last four games had gone to the Sheep. Los Angeles held the Packers to a scoreless tie in the first half, but the Packers came out of the lockerroom to score two third-quarter touchdowns; one on a run by Bruce Smith and the other on a blocked punt by Ed Neal. Fritsch kicked a field goal in the early going of the final stanza, then the Packers held off a furious LA comeback to win, 17-14. Tony Canadeo and Walt Schlinkman had big days rushing, gaining 87 and 83 yards respectively.

The Packers entered Week 3 of the campaign in a first-place tie with the Chicago Cardinals, which was ideal because the two teams were set to play in Green Bay that Sunday.

For the first time in two decades, the Cardinals had a very strong team. Jimmy Conzelman was once again at the Chicago helm, and he had a premier running back in Charley Trippi and a more than adequate passer in Paul Christman. Trippi and Christman led a steady offense, and Conzelman had a powerful defensive line to hold off the opposition. The Cards had few stars, but the players they did have knew the meaning of the word *team*.

Another record crowd, this one totaling 25,502, crammed into City Stadium to watch the Packers get ground down by the Cards, 14-10. Green Bay took a 3-0 lead on a Ted Fritsch field goal early in the second quarter, but Chicago came right back with a touchdown in the same frame and another in the third period. The Packers got a TD from Tony Canadeo in the third, but that was it for Green Bay. Three scoring opportunities presented themselves to the Packers in the fourth quarter, but they failed to convert on any of them.

Lambeau could have easily pointed his finger at Jack Jacobs for this loss because the kid from Oklahoma managed to complete only three of 17 passes. There were extenuating circumstances, though. Jacobs's father was critically ill, and the Packer quarterback's heart was back home and not in the game. Lambeau was sensitive to the situation and said nothing in public or private. Immediately after the game, Jacobs left to be with his family in Oklahoma.

The loss wasn't disastrous for the Packers (2-1-0), leaving them in second place with Los Angeles behind the undefeated Cardinals (3-0-0). Washington (2-1-0), Green Bay's next opponent, was tied for first with Philadelphia in the East.

The Packers had handled the Redskins rather easily in an exhibition game, but Washington's general, Sammy Baugh, played only the second half in which the Skins scored all 21 points they put on the board that day. He would be in the game from the start when the two teams squared off in Milwaukee. Lambeau wasn't too worried, though, because he had the top pass defense in the league, having held Sid Luckman (Bears), Bob Waterfield (Rams), and Paul Christman (Cards) to a total of 380 yards.

Green Bay scored 10 first quarter points on a TD by Fritsch and a field goal by Ward Cuff. Washington stiffened through the next two periods, holding the Packers scoreless while tying up the game. Then Canadeo hurled a pass to Nolan Luhn for six points to break the deadlock in the fourth quarter, and Fritsch booted a field goal to put some added pressure on Washington, forcing the Redskins to go to the air on every play in the closing minutes. Bob Forte picked off a Baugh pass and outraced the Washington pursuers for a 68-yard TD return.

Winning 27-10, the Packers (3-1-0) added to the confusion of both divisional races through Week 4. The Rams (3-1-0) downed the Cards (3-1-0) to create a three-way tie for first in the West, and the Bears (2-2-0) moved back into the race with a win over hapless Detroit. In the East, Pittsburgh (3-2-0) jumped past Washington (2-2-0) by dumping Philadelphia (2-2-0). Both division titles were still up for grabs.

Next up for the Packers was Detroit in City Stadium. Lambeau warned his team all week long that the Lions were a thoroughly dangerous crew, especially with flashy halfback Bill Dudley running wild. Detroit had faced the other three division opponents already, the same as Green Bay, and the Lions had actually scored two more points on these teams than the Packers had. The difference was the Packers had won two of three from them, while Detroit had lost all three. The moral: the Lions had plenty of offense but no defense. This fact became evident when the Packers dumped Detroit, 34-17. Green Bay rolled up 368 yards on the ground and 119 through the air, while holding Detroit to a total of 230 for the game. Ed Cody had his biggest day as a Packer, gaining 113 yards on just nine carries. Five other Green Bay ballcarriers gained a minimum of 34 yards each, and Ted Fritsch wasn't among them. Cody also scored a pair of TDs, and Fritsch and Clyde Goodnight each had one.

The division standings barely changed as the Cardinals (4-1-0) remained tied for first with the Packers but the Rams (3-2-0) slipped into a tie with the Bears. In the East, Pittsburgh (4-2-0) remained on top with Philadelphia (3-2-0) a half-game back.

Art Daley warned his readers in the *Press–Gazette* that the "Packers could get their ears pinned back Sunday" when they faced the Steelers in Milwaukee. Scout Wally Cruice said the same thing but in different words when he remarked that Pittsburgh was "one of the best teams I've seen this fall. It's the very best, in fact, in fundamentals. They really rock 'em. It has much better than average speed in the line, and it's rough defensively. There isn't great individual brilliance, but there is great team play."

Daley and Cruice proved to be prophets. The Steelers had never beaten the Packers in a regular season game in nine tries under their own identity and three tries as a combined team during World War II.* Pittsburgh had come close to defeating Green Bay on only one occasion, and that was in '42 when the Pack downed the Steelers, 24-21, in Milwaukee in the season finale. In the '47 game, which was Green Bay's final appearance in Wisconsin for the year, Lambeau made one of his classic blunders. As he had done so often before during his career at the helm of the Packers, he chose to forego attempting an easy field goal on fourth down early in the third quarter when the Packers held a 10-9 lead, and Green Bay lost the ball on downs at the Pittsburgh 11. The Steelers scored a touchdown later in the period, then tackled Jacobs in the end zone for a safety early in the final frame to take an 18-10 lead. The Packers bounced back with a TD pass from Jacobs to Luhn, but when Green Bay came up short on the final possession of the game, the Steelers had their first ever victory over the Packers, 18-17.

By winning, Pittsburgh (5-2-0) remained atop the East, still a half game ahead of Philadelphia (4-2-0). The Packers (4-2-0) slipped into a second–place tie with the oncoming Bears behind the Cardinals (5-1-0), winners over the fading Rams (3-3-0).

In the *Press–Gazette* the next day, Lee Remmel also proved to be a prophet of doom when he wrote in his column:

"In a black mood was E.L. (Curly) Lambeau, the Packer hed (sic) coach, who was unable to conceal his deep disappointment at a defeat which may well have wreaked considerable havoc with Green Bay's 1947 championship hopes — which burned so brightly a week ago."

Besides the loss, the Steeler game proved costly in another way. Tackles Baby Ray and Urban Odson were both injured. Odson missed the next game, and Ray, a 10-year veteran, wasn't as effective the rest of the campaign as he had been in past years. Their absence late in the game contributed heavily to the defeat by Pittsburgh, and their subsequent diminshed play compounded Lambeau's problems with his team for the remainder of '47.

The Bears in Chicago were Lambeau's next exercise in coaching. Since losing their first two games, the Monsters of the Midway had won four straight, thrashing Philadelphia, 40-7;

* See Chapters 16 and 17 of *The History of the Green Bay Packers: The Lambeau Years — Part Two* for details about the Steelers and Eagles combining in 1943 and the Steelers and Cardinals combining in 1944.

Detroit, 33-24; Washington, 56-20; and Boston, 28-24. Halas certainly had his team on a roll, and Lambeau was more aware of this than anyone. He had seen in the past how a streaking team seemed to get all the breaks and right bounces of the ball, no matter what the opposition did to prevent them. Some of his own squads had benefited like this, and now he feared the same would be true for the Bears.

Lambeau's fears were unfounded. His Packers got all the breaks and bounces. They recovered five Chicago fumbles and intercepted four Luckman passes. The Bears could only recover four Green Bay miscues and intercept no passes from Jacobs. Had the Bears not turned the ball over so many times, they might have beaten the Packers worse than they did, 20-17. As it was, Art Daley called it correctly when he wrote that the "Packers lost another one of those 'we shoulda won' games."

Once again, the culprit of defeat was not the players but the head strategist, Curly Lambeau. In the second quarter with the Bears leading, 14-10, the Packers had the ball on Chicago's two with fourth and goal–to–go. Lambeau called for a sweep instead of taking the almost sure three points from Ward Cuff's toe. Jim Gillette fumbled, and the Bears recovered it at the seven. Another scoring opportunity went to waste early in the third quarter. The Bears led, 20-10. Bob Skoglund recovered a fumbled lateral on the Chicago three. Three tries into the line got them to the one, and on fourth and goal, Lambeau eschewed the field goal again and tried to sweep the end only to have Irv Comp fumble it away this time. When he did choose to try a field goal in order to tie the game with 20 seconds remaining, the Bears blocked it to preserve their victory.

Lambeau and the sportswriters lamented that the Packers had lost three games by a total of eight points. Not one of them pointed out the fact that Lambeau passed up kicking field goals that might have won two of those three contests. Art Daley was half right when he wrote: "But the Bear game provided the ultimate in touchdown futility." He should have added: "It also proved that a field goal on the scoreboard is better than a touchdown in the huddle."

The Bears did contribute to the loss, too. Halas said, "We were lucky. We are thankful we won." Besides the two brilliant goal line stands that the Monsters put up, Halas made a considerable contribution when the telephone lines between the Green Bay bench and the coaches in the press box went dead at the most inopportune times. No one pointed any accusing fingers at the Chicago owner–coach, but Lambeau did say that "Bear officials failed to provide communications between the press booth and the bench. That is the phones were installed, but 'dead'." The smell of Halas was all over the incident.

The loss dropped the Packers (4-3-0) two games behind the Cardinals (6-1-0) and one behind the Bears (5-2-0) with five weeks to go. Pittsburgh (6-2-0) and Philadelphia (5-2-0) were in charge in the East and looking forward to their November 30 showdown that everyone figured would decide the division title.

However, all was not yet lost for the Packers. Following the Bears, they faced the Cardinals at Comiskey Park. Realizing that their season hung in the balance, the Packers — and the Cards —came out roaring. Chicago took the ball into the end zone on their initial possession, and the Pack came right back on a 35-yard field goal by Ted Fritsch. A Fritsch TD plunge and another Fritsch field goal in the second frame let the Packers trot into the lockerroom leading, 13-7. A Jack Jacobs–to–Bob Forte TD pass made the score 20-7 in the third period. The score could have been worse for Chicago, but Fritsch missed on two other field goal tries. The Cardinals started their comeback early in the fourth quarter. In two straight possessions, Chicago scored to take the lead, 21-20. In their final attempt at the Chicago goal, the Packers found themselves on the Cardinals' 16 with time running out. Lambeau sent Ward Cuff into the fray to kick a game–winning three. But Cuff missed wide, and the Packers' season was in the septic tank.

Art Daley made some interesting observations in his column a few days later when he pointed out that Lambeau routinely used Cuff in short situations and Fritsch in long attempts for field goals. Daley's own words and figures deny this assumption. According to Daley, Fritsch had made field goals of 21, 23, 35, 44, 49, and 50 yards, while Cuff's field goals were 13, 14, 15, 28, 28, and 39 yards long. He made no mention of the distances from which both kickers missed field goals. The fact that they made field goals from those distances did not mean that Lambeau used them exclusively for short or long attempts. Also, the fact that Cuff had a field goal of 39 yards contradicted Daley's conclusion.

Two questions: Why did Lambeau tell Daley that he always used Cuff on short attempts and Fritsch in long ones? And why did Daley go to all the trouble to prove it?

The facts state that Lambeau didn't always use Cuff and Fritsch the way he said, and Daley proved this to be true by trying to support Lambeau's statement with statistics. According to Daley, Lambeau put Cuff in the game because he felt that Cuff would be the more accurate kicker — not because of *the distance* but because of *the angle* of the try. The truth was Lambeau was angry with Fritsch for missing the two previous attempts, and he put Cuff in out of spite.

Daley's column proved that Lambeau was still a powerful force in Green Bay in 1947 because Daley failed to do his duty as a journalist by pointing up the fact that Lambeau had made some poor decisions that cost the Packers three games. Of course, Daley could be excused because one negative word in print about Lambeau could have cost him his job whether he was consciously cognizant of this possibility or not. Daley could also be excused because he was only doing what his predecessors had been doing since 1919, that is, making excuses in print for Earl L. (Curly) Lambeau.

With four weeks left in the season, the Packers (4-4-0) were practically out of the race. The Cardinals (7-1-0) were in the driver's seat, and the Bears (6-2-0) were riding shotgun up front. In the East, Pittsburgh (7-2-0) had already eliminated the Giants (0-7-1), the Packers next opponent, and Boston (2-5-1) and Washington (2-6-0). Only Philadelphia (6-2-0) stood any chance of overtaking the Steelers.

The Giants were suffering through their worst season ever when the Packers met them in New York the Sunday before Thanksgiving. Green Bay scored first, and it looked like it would be an easy victory for Lambeau's crew that would keep them in the hunt for the title for at least one more week. The Giants had different thoughts. They rallied to take a first quarter lead of

14-7 and were still on top at the half, 17-10. New York increased the margin to 14 with a TD in the third period, but the Packers fought back to eke out a tie, 24-24. Each team had an opportunity to win it in the final moments, but neither could capitalize on their possession.

Green Bay (4-4-1) still retained a mathematical chance in the West because the Cardinals (7-2-0) were upset by Washington (3-6-0). Even so, the odds were worse now because the Bears (7-2-0) moved into first with their Southside rival. Although they both lost, Pittsburgh (7-3-0) and Philadelphia (6-3-0) remained atop the East.

In order for the Packers to have any chance at the division crown, they would have to win all three of their remaining games, while the Bears and Cards lost two each and played each other to a tie on the final day of the season. This remote possibility would result in a three-way tie for first in the West, which would have caused all sorts of problems had it happened because the NFL had no tie-breaking system as it would have two decades later. Fortunately, the Bears took care of everything by downing the Lions in Detroit on Thanksgiving Day, ending Green Bay's hopes of taking the title.

With nothing but pride left to play for, the Packers walloped the Rams, 30-10, in LA, then crushed the Lions, 35-14, in Detroit the week after. While that was happening, the Cardinals were upset by the Giants before beating Philadelphia, and the Bears were surprised by the Rams, setting the stage for a last week showdown between the two Chicago elevens.

Out East, Philadelphia won its showdown game with the Steelers to move a half-game up on Pittsburgh, then the Steelers won the following week while the Eagles were losing to the Cards. This put the Steelers back on top by a half-game, and it gave the Packers' last game of the season some meaning because they were scheduled to play the Eagles in Philadelphia. A Packer win makes the Steelers the eastern winners; a Packer loss forces a playoff game between the two Pennsylvania squads.

The Packers went into their final contest as six and a half-point favorites, but the underdog Eagles were not to be denied their chance at the division crown. The Philadelphia defense blocked a Jack Jacobs punt that set up one score, and it intercepted six Green Bay passes to thwart the Packers at every turn. Philadelphia wound up on top, 28-14, forcing a playoff game with the Steelers the following week.

The Packers went home that winter as also-rans, finishing third with a 6-5-1 mark. They read in the newspapers how the Eagles beat the Steelers but were then defeated by the Cardinals in the championship game in Chicago as the Cardinals won their first undisputed NFL title. Many Green Bay players wondered how things might have turned out if Lambeau had only chosen to go for those field goals against the Steelers and Bears and if he'd let Fritsch kick, instead of Cuff, against the Cards. Just maybe it would have been them in the championship game against the Eagles instead. Just maybe . . .

§ § §

5
The First Winter of Lambeau's Discontent

The off-season was a time for reflection on the past and the future by the players and the coaches. Several of them would re-evaluate their football careers and make momentous decisions that would affect others besides themselves. Chief among those trying to make up his mind about what he should do was Curly Lambeau, but unlike everyone else, his choice would affect an entire franchise, a city, and a state. Heavy was his burden that winter of 1947-48.

For the first 25 years of his NFL experience, Curly Lambeau possessed the ability to change with the times. He recognized trends on the field and adapted to them instantly. As the strategy of the game of football evolved from field position and dropkicking to passing and running, he designed his offenses and defenses to meet the challenges of NFL foes. His teams passed more than most others during the '20s and '30s, and when everyone else was throwing the bomb during the war years, he was grinding out yardage with a ball-control attack that ate up the clock and kept the opposition from scoring.

Off the field, Lambeau was also able to foresee the future of football as a business.

Commercial radio began making an impact on sports as early as 1921 and on the Packers in 1930 when Harold T.I. Shannon and Hal Lansing made the first live broadcast of a Packers' game for Green Bay station WHBY. Station WTMJ carried Green Bay games later that same year in the Milwaukee market with Russ Winnie doing the play-by-play.*   For the 1947 season, the

---

* See Chapter 15 of *The History of the Green Bay Packers: The Lambeau Years, Part One.*

Green Bay *Press-Gazette*'s radio station, WJPG–FM, broadcast the Packers' games and was followed on the air by WJPG–AM when that station began broadcasting later in the year. These broadcasts originated with anchor station WTMJ.

Television became practical in 1939, but World War II halted its development as an economic enterprise. With the conclusion of the war, production of television receivers started again, and the first TV sets went on sale September 17, 1946.

Any knowledgeable person with an ounce of foresight must have realized in 1948 that television stations would soon begin paying for telecast rights to professional sporting events, and as television would naturally proliferate, the competition for those rights would increase, which would result in higher fees being paid to professional sports organizations. Lloyd Larson wrote in his column in the Milwaukee *Sentinel*:

"With television moving out of the novelty stage, it won't be long before a battle of not too many years ago will be repeated.

"Remember when broadcasting of football, baseball and other sports event (sic) first became popular? How many of the directors and promoters feared radio competition on the grounds that it would kill off their crowds and sooner or later run 'em out of business?

"Radio people, of course, insisted that word pictures of the action would build up interest and, in the long run, increase business all around. And that's the way it turned out. The trend has been up, up ,up. Attendance figures prove it. Besides, pro sport operators — even some of the more dollar crazy colleges —have made extra hauls they never dreamed of, through the sale of broadcasting rights.

"Just to give you an idea of the dough invovled in such behind–the–scenes deals, the New York Giants are reported to be working on a tie–up with a cigaret company which will give that company the privilege of broadcasting next year's baseball games at a total cost of a million bucks. The Giants, naturally, will take a big enough slice to make up for many thousands of admissions.

"Television faces the same struggle as radio. The new venture will be accepted with open arms for a while. Then will come the 'they'll ruin us' moans as t.v. becomes commonplace, to be followed by deals, bigger and better, which will make everybody happy."

Larson was so right, and no one knew this better than Earl L. "Curly" Lambeau.

Lambeau knew enough about advertising to understand that the larger the market, the higher the cost of air time. That was on radio. He also knew that television would employ the same system for its advertising rates. Just as radio had added to pro football's revenues, so would television; and sooner or later, pro football, like baseball, had to become big business, especially in the larger markets such as New York, Chicago, and Los Angeles. Smaller markets, meaning Green Bay and rural Wisconsin, would have to be replaced by bigger ones, such as St. Louis, San Francisco, Cincinnati, and Dallas. Since the NFL moguls wished to keep the league a closed club of only 10 franchises, Lambeau felt that the days of pro football in Green Bay were numbered, that sometime in the near future the Packers would have to move to a larger city, possibly Milwaukee, preferably San Francisco. However, he knew that the people of his hometown would never allow this to happen — as long as they owned the corporation that operated the franchise.

With this fact of life in Green Bay in mind, Lambeau began casting his line into other pro football waters. Rumors that he was headed to the West Coast to coach either the Rams or the Los Angeles Dons of the AAC began cropping up as early as November of '47 in the New York papers. Even Notre Dame's Frank Leahy was mentioned as going to LA to coach the Dons. Leahy vehemently denied the rumor, saying, "I can tell you that I will be back at Notre Dame next year." Lambeau also denied any such notion was in the works for him, saying, "No offers of any kind were made to me for next season." Emil Fischer, the Packers' corporation president, stated that "Lambeau's contract still had several years to run," and that Curly was going nowhere.

Lambeau's statement to the *Press-Gazette* said that no offers were made *TO* him. He didn't say that he hadn't discussed coaching elsewhere with the managements of the Rams and

Dons. Fischer, on the other hand, didn't deny that talks between Lambeau and other organizations hadn't taken place. He simply said that Lambeau had a contract with the Packers and that he, Fischer, intended to hold Curly to it.

There was more to this little episode than the general public was led to believe at the time, but to discuss it here would be taking it out of its proper context. Therefore, the complete story will be revealed later in this book.

Having set aside the rumors about his contacts with other organizations, Lambeau went about his usual winter business for the Packers, and the first item on the agenda was the annual draft of college seniors. Although he wouldn't admit it then, Curly had some serious holes to fill on his roster.

The 1947 Packers at 6-5-1 hadn't been a bad team. In fact, Green Bay led the NFL in fewest points allowed, 210, and the Packers scored 274 for a positive difference of 64 points. These were good numbers. Also, of the Packers' five losses, four were by a total of nine points; only in the last game of the year against Philadelphia were they truly beaten, 28-14. On offense, Green Bay was fairly potent with Jack Jacobs finishing as the second best passer and top punter in the Western Division; with Tony Canadeo and Walt Schlinkman third and fifth in the NFL with 464 and 429 yards gained, respectively; and with Nolan Luhn and Clyde Goodnight finishing fourth and sixth in the NFL with 42 and 38 receptions, respectively. Considering these facts, Lambeau felt that he didn't need much to improve his team for '48.

The biggest hole in Green Bay's lineup was at tackle. Age and injuries had taken a toll in '47. Baby Ray was in his 10th year; Urban Odson had suffered a serious injury that made him into a part-time player; and Tiny Croft and Paul Lipscomb also went down at one point or another.

The second biggest problem was at right halfback. In Lambeau's offensive scheme, halfbacks still carried the ball almost exclusively. Other teams around the NFL and AAC were following the Bears' example by using the T-formation and putting a man in motion who became a third downfield receiver on passing plays. Lambeau wanted a ball carrier and not another receiver.

The NFL draft was held in Pittsburgh and was supposed to be kept secret; that is, no one, meaning the AAC, was supposed to learn the results of the meeting until after the players were signed. This meant keeping the draft lists of all the teams unpublished. Knowing the nature of people to reveal secrets, especially to the prying press, the NFL moguls came up with a compromise whereby each team would release their draft lists in alphabetical order instead of draft order. That would keep the press and the public happy, but at the same time, it would deny the AAC the knowledge of whom the NFL considered to be the top prospects and thus would keep the AAC from signing those players first. It was a good idea in theory but nothing more than that.

Lambeau drafted 29 players. Topping his wish list were Earl "Jug" Girard (Wisconsin, back), George Walmsley (Rice, back, All–American), John Panelli (Notre Dame, back), Larry Olsonoski (Minnesota, guard), Clarence McGeary (Minnesota, tackle–end), Jay Rhodemyre (Kentucky, center), O. Ed Smith (Texas Mines, back), and Lou Agase (Illinois, end–tackle).

With the draft out of the way, Lambeau went about the task of signing players. He drafted Agase's older brother, Alex, the year before only to see him sign with the LA Dons. The coach's luck with the younger brother wasn't any better. Besides losing Agase, Lambeau also lost Walmsley, Panelli, and McGeary. He was able to sign several others, however; some after going to a lot trouble.

Jug Girard hailed from Marinette, a small city north of Green Bay on the Wisconsin side of the Menominee River. Lambeau took it for granted that Girard would sign with Green Bay because he was a local boy who had grown up with the Packers. After hearing that Girard had signed with the New York Yankees of the AAC, Lambeau called Girard in a panic, and the draftee told the coach that he hadn't signed anything yet and wasn't planning to do so until after talking to the Packers. Translation: Girard was considering the Yankees and if Lambeau wanted him he'd better make a good offer. Lambeau invited Girard to Green Bay, and Girard said that he'd come, that he'd be arriving on the *Northwestern 400* the next morning at 10:45. Lambeau and his top aide, George Strickler, waited half a morning at the

Green Bay train depot for Girard to show up as promised, but Girard never showed. Beginning to stress out, the coach jumped into his car and drove up to Marinette. He caught up with Girard just as he was getting ready to leave for California to play in an all-star contest. Lambeau bought a ticket for Green Bay and boarded the train with Girard. When the train reached Peshtigo, Girard signed. Lambeau got off in Green Bay, and Girard went on to California.

Ed Smith wasn't easy to sign either. Smith was in California for an all-star game when Lambeau caught up with him at practice. The coach followed Smith around during drills until he could finally get the Texas lad alone. After a good talk, Smith agreed to terms. Lambeau whipped out a contract and a pen and handed them to Smith. The pen was out of ink. No problem. Lambeau led Smith to his car where he put the big back inside with Mrs. Lambeau to keep him company while he went looking for a pen. Curly ran a block and a half until he came across someone he knew who had a pen that he could borrow. He returned to the car and signed Smith before he'd let him out again.

Of the 29 draftees, only seven of them ever played for the Packers. Girard, Smith, Larry Olsonoski, Jay Rhodemyre, Ralph Earhart, Perry Moss, and Fred Provo. Lambeau also drafted Stan Heath, a quarterback who was playing for the University of Nevada, but he didn't sign for the '48 season because he had college eligibility remaining.

Before Lambeau returned from California, he learned that the contract that Girard had signed was invalid because the young halfback was not yet 21 years old. The fact was Girard was less than three weeks away from being 21 when he signed on with Lambeau and the Packers. Hearing that his contract with Green Bay was invalid, the New York Yankees of the AAC renewed their efforts to sign the Wisconsin product. Ray Flaherty, the Yankees coach, was reported to be on his way to Marinette to meet with Girard and sign him to a contract that would pay him $10,000 and would allow him to play professional baseball, too. When word of Flaherty's move reached Lambeau, he called Girard from Los Angeles and said he would match any offer the Yankees made. In the meantime, Jerry

Clifford, the Packers' attorney, and Bob Conrad of the Packers' staff drove up to Marinette to get Girard's mother, Mrs. Ann Girard, to countersign the contract that her son had signed on the train in December. She told the *Associated Press*: "I didn't even know he'd signed with the Packers until some Packer officials came to the house last week and wanted me to sign the contract, too. It was very surprising because before he left for Los Angeles he told me he wasn't going to do anything until he came back. I thought probably he had signed in a hurry and I wanted to give him time to think about it, so I wouldn't sign. Saturday night he called me from Los Angeles and told me the Yankees had contacted him out there. He wanted to know if I had signed the Packer contract and was very pleased when I said I hadn't. He's going to make up his mind this weekend which team he'll sign up with and I hope he makes a good choice. It's up to him, though." Fortunately for Lambeau and the Packers, Girard chose to honor his contract with Green Bay, signing all over again on his birthday, January 25.

Adding to Lambeau's woes that winter were the rumors surrounding Bruce Smith, the big running back from Minnesota who had played for Green Bay in '45, '46 and '47. Bernie Bierman, the legendary head coach for the University of Minnesota, interviewed Smith for the job of assistant coach, and Smith told the *Press-Gazette* that he was considering the offer. "After last season I don't expect Curly Lambeau to send the contract I want. I want to hear from him before I decide." He heard from Lambeau, then met with Bierman again. After that meeting, he told the Green Bay paper that he would be inking his contract with the Packers when it arrived. "I'll be playing pro football with the Green Bay Packers again next season. I had no difference of opinion with Bernie (Bierman), but I couldn't afford to turn down the contract with the Packers. It was too good."

No sooner than the Smith affair was finished than Lambeau found himself in the rumor mill. A February 20 story released by the *Associated Press* had Green Bay buzzing again. "Coach Curly Lambeau of the Green Bay Packers was among the men considered for the job coaching the Los Angeles Dons, a Dons spokesman said late Thursday. Club spokesman Frank

Clement did not say, however, that Lambeau had applied for the post." And he didn't say that Lambeau didn't apply for the job. Lambeau did talk to the Dons about coaching their team, and he seriously considered jumping leagues but didn't because he had other plans that were centered around the Packers although not necessarily the *Green Bay* Packers.

Adding to Lambeau's press headaches was his top assistant, George Strickler. In early March, *The Milwaukee Journal* ran a story that the Packers would be playing an exhibition game in Green Bay late that summer against the Boston Yanks. Strickler reacted to the story like someone had called him a dirty name. "That's a lot of hooey," he said in the *Press-Gazette*. "The Green Bay Packers will not play the Boston Yanks in an exhibition football game this season." Famous last words. The Packers were set for a game with the Yanks to be played in Boston instead of Green Bay, and it was a regular season contest instead of pre-season. Strickler's gripe was more a matter of ego. He was upset that the *Journal* had stolen his thunder by making the announcement of the game before he could divulge the practice schedule on Earl Gillespie's radio show on WJPG. The *Journal* writer just got his facts a little wrong by writing that it was an exhibition game.

Lambeau's final Alka-Seltzer moment was brought on by Charley Brock. According to the news release, Brock quit willingly, claiming that he was getting too old for the game. He was 32 at the time. As he put it, "I'm getting old now, and if I stayed another year, I'd just be along for the ride." He was allegedly going to take a coaching job, but the college was unknown at this time. Rumors had it that he was taking the line coaching job at Omaha University. Brock denied the rumors, but he wound up taking the job. The truth was Brock wanted more money, but Lambeau, thinking Brock was bluffing with this retirement business, wouldn't give it to him because he had drafted a topnotch center in Jay Rhodemyre. Exit Brock.

Lambeau's year was off to a bad start. If he'd known in January that it was only going to get worse, he just might have jumped to the AAC Dons.

§ § §

6
Onward Football Soldiers

On the night of April 14, 1912, a distress signal went out from a ship sinking in the North Atlantic. The captain knew that a great loss of life was inevitable because the ship didn't have enough lifeboats to save the entire crew and all the passengers. The shortage of boats wasn't his fault, but the disaster was. He would do the honorable thing and go down with the ship.

As early as December 1947, Curly Lambeau began feeling like he was the captain of his own *Titanic*. His football ship was being ripped apart by the war between the National Football League and the All-America Conference, and sooner or later, his craft would be heading straight to the bottom of professional football. That was a disaster that he couldn't bear to endure. As much as he wanted to avoid the conflict, there was nothing he could do to stop it.

But there were others who thought they could end the fighting between the leagues.

Alexis Thompson, the wealthy young owner of the Philadelphia Eagles, recognized early on that the NFL and AAC couldn't continue to fight each other and survive. The continued warfare would only lead to their mutual destruction. Thompson realized that the first step in settling the differences between the two organizations was to agree to a common draft of college talent. He proposed such an idea as early as December 1, 1947, but his co-owners in the NFL and Commissioner Bert Bell opposed the notion. Admiral Jonas Ingram, Bell's counterpart in the AAC, and several other officials of the fledgling league were more than willing to accept Thompson's proposal, but their willingness to compromise was thought to be weakness by Bell and the NFL moguls. Bell gave the boys a wink that said, "It's just a matter of time before the AAC is history."

Bell's stance was given support just a week later when Jim Crowley, the former Green Bay lad who was the first commissioner of the AAC, resigned as head coach of the Chicago Rockets, and his partners, William S. Toohey and John S. Brogan, gave up their majority interest in the franchise. The Rockets had won only one of 14 contests in '47, and it was rumored that the club had lost $200,000. Bell crowed over Crowley's demise.

The fans in Green Bay got a kick in the shorts from an old friend a few weeks before Christmas when Cecil Isbell, the head coach of the AAC Baltimore Colts, declared that "Green Bay, where I used to play, is noted for being a sports town. I agreed it was tops until I came to Baltimore. The people here just push Green Bay right off the sports map as far as enthusiasm goes." Bob Rodenberg, the Colts' president, supported Isbell's claim with numbers, stating that the team had averaged 29,000 spectators in home attendance in spite of winning only two games and tying one during the '47 season. To add insult to injury, Rodenberg suggested that the NFL move the Green Bay franchise to either New Orleans or Dallas. (The *New Orleans Packers?* The *Dallas Packers?* Something gets lost in the translation.)

To counter Rodenberg's claims that Baltimore supported the Colts better than Green Bay supported the Packers, Art Daley made a feeble attempt in the *Press-Gazette* to compare attendance records on a per capita basis. Daley gave the population of Green Bay as 47,000 and the population of Baltimore as 1,046,692. The Packers' average attendance for games in Green Bay was 25,000, while Baltimore's was 29,000. On a per capita basis, Green Bay fans turned out at the rate of 53%, while Baltimoreans attended Colts' games at the rate of 2.7%. Daley conveniently forgot that the Packers didn't have two NFL franchises located within 100 miles of Green Bay; he forgot that the Packers draw from a state that had more population than Maryland had in those days; he forgot to include the games that the Packers played in Milwaukee and all that was entailed there; and he forgot to mention that the Packers had been around for more than a quarter of a century, while the Colts were a first-year team. Fortunately for the fans in Wisconsin, no one outside of Green Bay saw Daley's inane article. If Bert Bell, George Halas, and some of the other NFL magnates had read it, they might have come up with the idiotic notion that Green Bay didn't belong in the league and that their purposes would be better served by moving the franchise to San Francisco or Dallas or New Orleans.*

Up to the middle of December 1947, most of America's press treated the AAC like an interloper. Then George P. Marshall, the volatile owner of the Washington Redskins, tried to shoot Santa Claus.

The College All-Star game played at Soldier Field in Chicago each summer and pitting the NFL champion of the year before against an all-star squad of graduated college players was the brain-child of Arch Ward, the sports editor of *The Chicago Tribune*. It was a meaningless game played for a good cause. Proceeds from the contest were donated to charity.

A week before Christmas 1947, four months after the game had been played, Marshall demanded the discontinuance of the annual football game. He stated that the NFL had voted Bert Bell full authority to call off the game if he saw fit to do so. Marshall based his demand on the fact that the All-Stars had used Claude "Buddy" Young, the speedy running back from Illinois, and George Ratterman, the quarterback from Notre Dame, in the August game. According to Marshall, both players had college eligibility remaining and thus were ineligible under the rules set down by the NFL in its contract with the *Tribune*, the game's sponsor.

This was all bunkum. Marshall was furious with Ward for a number of reasons, and he was using the All-Star game as a way

---

* **The idea that Green Bay doesn't deserve to be in the National Football League was nothing new in 1947. It was begun in the '20s and was still alive as late as '80s when** *Sports Illustrated,* **published an article claiming that Green Bay wasn't sophisticated enough for the NFL. Like Art Daley's remarks of 30 years earlier,** *Sports Illustrated's* **story was just as inane and misleading.**

of getting a shot at him. Ward had the affrontery to suggest that the NFL and the AAC make peace and start playing world championship football with each other instead of against each other. Ward was also instrumental in getting the AAC going, and he was continually supporting the upstart league in his column in the *Tribune*. Worse than that, the aforementioned Buddy Young and George Ratterman had signed contracts with AAC teams. As Marshall put it, "Mr. Ward made personal efforts to lure players and even officials from the National Football league to the All–America conference, and we have documentary proof of it."

What a cry–baby! Marshall was upset because someone else had a ball and could play the game without him and the other NFL magnates.

After reading Marshall's remarks in the newspapers, Bert Bell said: "That's a Marshall story he gave out. I know nothing more than that."

Ray C. Bennigsen, president of the Chicago Cardinals, said: "Marshall had no right to speak for the National Football league in stating that the league should cancel its 10-year contract with the Chicago Tribune Charities, Inc., sponsor of the game."

Much to the commissioner's credit, Bell ignored Marshall's bluster and the NFL lived up to its end of the contract for the game. Bell realized, though, that Marshall had made a monumental mistake in attacking Ward who was well liked and respected by his colleagues in the newspaper medium. Columnists all across the country took up Ward's defense, and the AAC had the press that it couldn't buy before Marshall's tirade.

Early in the year of 1948 the AAC granted a franchise to Branch Rickey of the Brooklyn Dodgers of baseball. Rickey had no intention of operating a football team, but he was willing to let someone else do it under some sort of financial arrangement with him. He was never clear on what that would be, but he did say, "I understand that there are people of responsible caliber who are interested in operating the franchise. If they can guarantee continued football in Brooklyn and prove acceptable to the league, I will give them one year rent free."

The Lambeau Years — Part Three

To counter the AAC's news, Bell predicted that the NFL would have its greatest year ever in 1948. "It will take plenty of doing to top 1947," he said, "but watch us. Competition will be closer than ever. The real thing in spectator interest — the thing that means big crowds — is a close race. All 10 clubs have championship hopes for 1948." When asked about the AAC, Bell responded: "What's that? Never heard of it."

In one move, Bell had made himself look good by distancing himself from George Marshall's flap, and now he was making himself look assinine with his non–remarks about the AAC. Neutral writers of the time were beginnning to wonder how the NFL had lasted so long with such childish leaders at the helm.

At the NFL winter meetings, the owners rejected Alexis Thompson's proposal to enter into a common draft with the AAC. They did this without even bringing the matter to a vote. The owners did approve of the sale of the Detroit Lions by Fred Mandel to a syndicate headed by Lyle Fife, an electrical supply magnate. They also approved a few rule changes, all very minor; but they did do one thing that was very interesting and that would concern the Packers in the future.

The Pacific Coast Football League had teams from Seattle to San Diego. One of them was in San Francisco. PCFL President J. Rufus Klawans presented the Clippers' bid for a franchise in the NFL at the meeting in New York. Bert Bell tabled the application *for a year*, saying the league "did not care *to add an eleventh club at this time.*" (Author's italics.) He added that the Clippers, however, were given a prior claim to the next franchise.

Dissecting Bell's remarks meant nothing in early 1948, but they would be quite a revelation two years later.

After the winter meetings, the NFL began crowing about the college players it had signed. The Cardinals signed Charley Trippi and the Bears signed Bob Fennimore the year before, but the AAC got all the rest of the NFL's top choices. This year was different. The Bears signed Johnny Lujack and George Connor out of Notre Dame. The Giants inked Charley Connerly and Barney Poole out of Mississippi and Bill Swiacki from Columbia. The Redskins landed Harry Gilmer from Alabama, and the Packers got Jug Girard. The Bears also managed to get Bobby Layne under contract. Landing so many top collegiate names was a real feather in the NFL cap, but the AAC refused to fold up their tents and fade away into history.

Knowing that they needed Chicago in their loop, the AAC moguls made moves to bolster the Rockets, including finding new ownership for the club which consisted of some established owners. Also, the AAC magnates felt that the Baltimore Colts and the Brooklyn club needed help as well. All three teams received players from other AAC clubs to improve their rosters and hopefully their ability to compete in the circuit.

While this was going on, the NFL severed its relationship with the minor league American Association. The AAC immediately moved in and replaced the NFL as the AFA's partner.

One of the major factors that gave the NFL an advantage over the AAC was the strength of its so-called lesser franchises. The Chicago Cardinals, Philadelphia Eagles, and Pittsburgh Steelers had been also-rans for more than a decade before the 1947 season, but in that year, the Steelers and Eagles tied for the Eastern Division title and the Cards won the Western. Philadelphia won the playoff game with Pittsburgh, and the Redbirds took the NFL crown after that. Because of their newfound winning ways, all three teams stayed out of the Poor House in '47.

The Giants, Bears, and Rams were located in three of the country's largest cities, and although they faced head-to-head competition from the AAC, they were able to keep pace in the race to the bank.

Boston, Washington, Detroit, and Green Bay were another matter altogether. Boston and Detroit were bad teams that didn't draw because they were bad teams. Washington lost a lot of its attendance to the new Baltimore franchise in the AAC, and the Packers suffered because of the rising salaries of players.

Green Bay, Milwaukee, and rural Wisconsin did not have the affluence nor the numbers that Chicago, New York, and Los Angeles had. The Packers couldn't charge the same prices for tickets that the other NFL teams could. Although they drew well, their attendance figures didn't translate well into dollars and cents; at least, not as well as the same attendance totals did in the larger cities. Being unable to pay the same large salaries would eventually hurt Green Bay's ability to compete in the NFL.

Because of the sudden new financial strength of the Pittsburgh Steelers, the AAC moguls felt that Green Bay was the weak link in the NFL chain in early 1948. In their opinion, it would be only a matter of time before the franchise would go under, and once Green Bay folded, more than one AAC owner hoped to inherit the Packers' place in the NFL.

However, the AAC's thinking received a jolt in April when John "Jock" Sutherland, the head coach of the Steelers, died from a malignant brain tumor. Sutherland had guided the Steelers into contention in '47, and it was felt by many that Pittsburgh just might take the NFL crown in '48. With Sutherland gone, this seemed improbable now. More than likely, the Steelers would return to their losing ways, and that meant Pittsburgh would rival Green Bay as the weakest franchise in the NFL.

The sad occasion of Sutherland's untimely death was a horrible break for the Steelers, but it turned out to be a twist of fate whose effects couldn't be determined for years to come. Suffice it to say that Sutherland's demise was the beginning of Pittsburgh's slide in the standings, and because the Steelers started back down the ladder of success, the AAC found another chink in the NFL's armor, the first weak spot being the Packers. Or so the AAC magnates thought. Like so many big city types before them and so many since then, the AAC owners didn't understand the passion the people of Wisconsin have for their Packers, and those passionate fans would do whatever they had to do to keep their Green Bay Packers in the NFL forever.

§ § §

7
Once More into the Line

Like the swallows returning to Capistrano every year, Curly Lambeau returned to Green Bay from California in April and began preparing for the 1948 National Football League season.

As already mentioned, Lambeau had his troubles signing his draft choices. Of the 29 men he picked from the college ranks, only 11 of them signed to play with the Packers, and of these, seven made the team and played for Green Bay that year and one was traded before training camp opened. Charles Biggers (T, Catawba), Bob Cunz (T, Illinois), Ralph Earhart (B, Texas Tech), Jug Girard (B, Wisconsin), Perry Moss (QB, Tulsa & Illinois), Larry Olsonoski (G, Minnesota), Fred Provo (B, Washington), Bob Rennebohm (B, Wisconsin), Jay Rhodemyre (C, Kentucky), Don Richards (T, Arkansas), and O. Ed Smith (B, Texas Mines) were the draftees to sign with Green Bay.

Besides having his troubles with the rookies, Lambeau found himself in a real tight with some of his veterans. Bruce Smith played Lambeau for a raise with the rumors that he was planning to retire and take up coaching. Then Charley Brock hung up his cleats to go into coaching. But Lambeau's biggest headache came from an unexpected corner.

Nice-guy Tony Canadeo, "The Grey Ghost" from Gonzaga, was one of the steadiest performers in Green Bay in '47. He led the Western Division in rushing with 464 yards gained and finished third in the NFL. When he met with Lambeau to discuss his contract for '48, the boss made him an offer that he could refuse — and did. Canadeo walked out of the meeting.

"We would like to have Tony with us," said Lambeau, "but we'll be okay at left half back if he isn't. It has always been our policy to pay players as much as possible. Our aim is to give

The Lambeau Years — Part Three

Packer fans a good football team."

Lambeau's first sentence was true; he did want Canadeo in a Packer uniform that fall. The second one was iffy; beyond Canadeo, the left halfback slot was shallow. The third line was another scoop of Lambeau manure; since the earliest days of the league, Lambeau had tried his best to squeeze his players into performing for less than their worth; Packer salaries under Lambeau were never comparable to those of players on other teams. And the last remark he made that day in the *Press-Gazette* was very true; to his credit, Lambeau did do his best to put not just a winning team on the field but a championship team in the history books.

For his part, Canadeo revealed a more believeable picture of what happened in his meeting with Lambeau. "I don't want anything more than anybody else on the team. I just want as much as the fellows playing the same left halfback position. I like playing for the Packers and wish to create no hard feelings. I was told that I would be traded if I didn't sign in 24 hours."

There it was! The threat! A typical Lambeau tactic to get a player in line. Canadeo had already begun to set down roots in Green Bay, and knowing this, Lambeau threatened to send him elsewhere, thus disrupting Canadeo's life. It was a petty trick, but it was pure Curly Lambeau.

After being told what Canadeo said, Lambeau replied, "Last season we did a little better than break even, but it was accomplished by cutting operating expenses, not salaries. Moreover, our profit on the year's operation wasn't as much as the increase some of the players are asking. The only raises we are giving are to a couple of men who made less than $5,000 last year and whose play certainly warranted an increase."

He went on to say: "The honeymoon is over for professional football players. There is plenty of talent for all teams. Several years ago it was different. The players had the owners on a spot and they took advantage of it. But today it is no trick to sign 100 men."

After declaring that only four or five teams in the two leagues had broken even in '47 and fixing the losses of the other 13 teams in the millions, Lambeau said, "But the players got paid. The players make all the money in pro football today. And they are turning down contracts for four months work that call for more money than a competent executive — not to mention some of the top coaches in the country — can earn in the entire year."

Then he dredged up some history, recalling that Don Hutson and Bronko Nagurski were paid $175 a game when they started their illustrious careers in the NFL. He also recited some other statistics, such as the 100% increase in the cost of living since 1939 and the 400% increase in the salaries of football players. "Club executives took cuts or held the line to weather the financial storm in pro football, but the players' salaries continued to skyrocket. Clubs and club owners no longer can stand the strain. Men along in years, almost ready to retire, have put their savings into professional football and gone broke. But the players got theirs. The present situation is too cockeyed to be sound. Readjustment is imperative and inevitable."

Lambeau was right about plenty of talent being available, and a lot of it was willing to play pro football but not for the miniscule salaries that the owners were offering. He pointed out that the players were being paid good money for only four months of work. If they were auto workers on an assembly line, that would be true, but these men, the players, were in the entertainment business, much the same as all those Hollywood types that Lambeau called friends during the off-season. Would he have denied John Wayne the same money that he was refusing to pay Canadeo? Absolutely not! In the world of professional football, Tony Canadeo might not have been the equivalent of John Wayne in the world of motion pictures, but he was at least the equal of Van Johnson who was also making much more money than Canadeo was.

Just as most of the NFL magnates were doing, Lambeau was missing the point that professional football wasn't then (and isn't now) just entertainment like a motion picture. It's a form of passion, and people are willing to pay good money to release their passions. This theorem of life has been proven over and over again, but in 1948, Lambeau and the other moguls were unwilling to test it by raising ticket prices because they feared that fans would stay away in droves. Instead, they blamed the players for their problems and continued to fight the AAC for the best talent.

While Canadeo held out for more money, other veterans signed on to play again in Green Bay. Ken Keuper was the first, followed by Ed Cody, Ed Bell, Bob Flowers, Bruce Smith, Jim Gillette, Bob Forte, Ted Fritsch, Jack Jacobs, Paul Lipscomb, Bob Skoglund, Ed Neal, Dick Wildung, Larry Craig, Ralph Davis, Urban Odson, Gene Wilson, Walt "Big Inch" Schlinkman, Nolan "Big Mitts" Luhn, Baby Ray, Don Wells, Clyde Goodnight, Irv Comp, and Damon Tassos. Lambeau signed Fred Vant Hull again after he sat out the '47 season because of Bert Bell's ban on players who had been on AAC teams; Vant Hull played for San Francisco 49ers while he was in the Navy in '46.

Through trades and free agency, the Packers' mentor picked up several other players. Jack Mead (end, Wisconsin) played with NY Giants in 1946-47, got released, and signed with Packers. Lloyd Baxter (center, SMU) who was drafted by Green Bay in '44 but went into the Marines instead, signed on. Orman (Red) Horton, a T–formation QB out of Texas who also attended Southwestern U. and Texas A&I then played for Salt Lake City in the Pacific Coast Football League, came aboard. Lambeau acquired 6'-6" tackle Clyde Johnson, who played for Kentucky but went into the Army for two years before joining the pros in '46, from the Rams for a future draft choice. Roy McKay was traded to Washington for Don Deeks, a 6'4" tackle who went to the University of Washington. Deeks broke into the NFL with the Boston Yanks in '45 after a year with the Portland Rockets in the PCFL, then he was sold to the Redskins in middle of '46. Evan "Red" Vogds, a tackle who went to Wisconsin, jumped from the Chicago Rockets where he had played in '46-'47 to the Packers for '48. Frank Syzmanski (center, Notre Dame) and Ted Cook (end, Alabama) came over from Detroit in a trade for rookies Bob Rennebohm and Howard Brown. Free agents signing were Jim Reynolds (B, Oklahoma A&M), Bob West (B, Missouri), Mike Kalosh (E, LaCrosse State Teachers), Ken Roskie (B, South Carolina), and Ray Piotrowski (C, no college).

The final contract to come in before the opening of training camp that year belonged to Tony Canadeo.

Lambeau brought back his assistants from '47, Don Hutson and Walt Kiesling, and in March, he hired former Packer player Bo Molenda to work with his backs and offense.

Off the field, a few changes were made in the front office of the Green Bay Packers, Inc. Emil Fischer was re-elected president; Lambeau was renamed vice-president and general manager; and Frank Jonet remained as secretary-treasurer. Joining the board of directors was John Torinus, Sr., the news editor of the *Press-Gazette*.

Training camp didn't go well for Lambeau and the Packers in '48. Before camp opened, five players — Tiny Croft, Buddy Gatewood, Charley Brock, Ray Clemens, and Herman Rohrig — retired officially. Then on August 16, Ray Piotrowski, Bob West, and Don Richards quit the team, feeling they were overmatched by the talent on the squad.

The College All-Star game against the Cardinals was played on the 20th, and the Chicago eleven won handily, 28-0. In the game, Green Bay draftee Jay Rhodemyre was cited as Most Outstanding Player for College All-Stars. That was the good news. The bad news was really bad. Perry Moss, the quarterback that Lambeau had drafted out of Illinois, was injured on the last play of the game, suffering a shoulder separation; and Jug Girard injured his knee in practice, putting him out of effective action for some time to come.

Then Larry Olsonoski reported having a trick knee that was bothering him, and Don Deeks went down with a knee injury. This left the line a little weak, but Lambeau wasn't ready yet to panic.

The Packers played their first exhibition game against the Giants in Minneapolis on August 29, downing New York, 7-0. Radio station WJPG carried the contest in Green Bay via a hookup with originating station WTMJ in Milwaukee, and Bob Heiss did the play-by-play. The fans at home had a lot to yawn about as the defense played superbly, but the only twinkle on offense was a 43-yard TD run by Ralph Earhart. Lambeau's passing attack netted the Packers zilch, and now Lambeau was ready to panic.

The day after the Giants game Lambeau made a conditional trade with the Boston Yanks. Feeling he needed experienced passing help, he picked up Howie "Red" Maley, a quarterback out of SMU who was in his third year as a pro. The Yanks had their choice of either a fifth round draft choice the following year or first crack at any player that the Packers planned to release. Green Bay then released Bob Cunz, Clarles Biggers, and Mike Kalosh.

Lambeau then set about preparing to meet the Steelers in their second exhibition game. Because of the unexpected death of Jock Sutherland during the off-season, Pittsburgh had a new head coach, Johnny Michelosen. At 32, he was youngest coach in the NFL at that time. The Packers beat the Steelers, 9-7, in Green Bay. Once again, the defense was superb, but Lambeau's passing attack was still invisible. Making matters worse, Jack Jacobs suffered an attack of appendicitis and had to be hospitalized; and Walt Schlinkman injured a knee in the game, putting him on the sidelines for a while.

Panic Attack II hit Lambeau the following week. He traded center Frank Syzmanski to the Eagles for 275-pound tackle Jim Kekeris whom Philadelphia had drafted the year before out of Missouri. This left the Packers with Bob Flowers and two rookies, Jay Rhodemyre and Lloyd Baxter, at center, but the tackle corps was bolstered.

In August, a flap was started by Harry Gilmer, a rookie quarterback out of Alabama who was chosen to play in the College All-Star game. Gilmer was a draft choice of the Washington Redskins. George Marshall, the Skins' owner, had a beef with Arch Ward, the sports editor of *The Chicago Tribune*, originator of the All-Star game, and supporter of the AAC. Gilmer refused to play in the game against the Cardinals unless the sponsor of the game, Chicago Tribune Charities, Inc., insured him against a career-ending injury for the full amount of his contract with the Redskins, which was reportedly for five years and in the neighborhood of $80,000. Ward refused to insure Gilmer, and Gilmer sat out the contest. Ward then screamed that the contract between the NFL and the sponsor called for the suspension of Gilmer from playing in any exhibition games for the Redskins and if he did then the Skins and their opponent would both be subject to a fine of $25,000 each. Because of a leg injury, Gilmer had missed Washington's first two pre-season games, but he felt he should play in the third one because it was to be played in Birmingham, Alabama, his home town. Washington's opponent for the game was the Packers.

Green Bay's president, Emil Fischer, made the statement that the Packers had a contract with the promoters in Birmingham and therefore had no choice but to play the game. Lambeau said the same thing but added that he hoped Gilmer wouldn't play because of his injury and he didn't want to "him to participate even in a few plays" because he would be "jeopardizing his entire football career." Nice words but hollow. Lambeau could have cared less about Gilmer. His concern was the $25,000 fine that he feared the Packers would be forced to pay.

Well, Gilmer played a few downs for show, but he didn't help the Redskins as the Packers crushed them, 43-0. Neither team was fined for playing the game with Gilmer, and that was that.

The injury bug struck the Packers again in Alabama. Three ends suffered injuries. Bob Skoglund went down on one kickoff with a knee injury that Dr. H.S. Atkinson, the Packers' physician, said would lay him up for at least six weeks. Jack Mead suffered a similar injury on another kickoff and found himself in the hospital with Skoglund, but his prognosis was worse. "Mead will be out indefinitely," said Atkinson. Also hurt was Don Wells who had a foot injury that was aggravated when he was stepped on during the game.

Other Packers who were suffering were Jack Jacobs (knee and elbow), Walt Schlinkman (knee), Bruce Smith (shoulder), and Fred Provo (knee). Of this group, the loss of Jacobs was especially hard on the squad because he was the number one passer in Lambeau's offensive scheme.

The Packers then traveled to Boston to play the Yanks in the NFL opener for both teams. Green Bay walloped the Yanks, 31-0, behind a strong defense that intercepted four Boston passes, and the Packers looked like real contenders for the division and NFL crowns. The highlight of the contest was a 72-yard sprint for paydirt by Ralph Earhart in the third quarter. That was the good news. The bad news was Jacobs left the game with an aching elbow, Bruce Smith hurt his back, Irv Comp sprained an ankle, and the Bears were the Packers' next opponent.

On the Friday before the Chicago game, Lambeau was concerned with his troops attitude. "We'll be shellacked unless we snap out of it and get fired up," he said. Then he recalled the 1941 Bears, saying that the '48 version was the best since that team. He drew a comparison to the 1940 season when the Packers started their season with an easy win over Philadelphia, then faced the Bears at home. The result was Chicago 41, Green Bay 10.

When the two teams lined for the kickoff on Sunday, City Stadium was packed with 25,546 screaming fans. By halftime, they sat still in a catatonic silence as the Bears raced out to a 31-0 lead. When the final gun was fired, the Packers had been handed their worst defeat ever, 45-7. As if that wasn't bad enough, it had to come at the hands of the hated Bears. The Packers threw four interceptions and lost the ball on fumbles twice for a total of six turnovers. They only managed one interception of their own and recovered no Bear fumbles. "We are NOT as good as we showed today," said George Halas after the game. Such modesty! He was right, of course. The Packers were really that bad that day. Bruce Smith took a jarring hit on the second play from scrimmage after gaining 20 yards and fumbled, and the Bears turned it into a TD. Jacobs threw an interception to Johnny Lujack to stop the Packers on their next possession. Then his third down throw was picked off by Noah Mullins and returned for six points. After that, the Packers were never again in the game.

Besides the injury to Bruce Smith, Jay Rhodemyre suffered a concussion and spent the night in the hospital, and Larry Craig had his nose broken. This proved once again that Chicago–Green Bay games were never easy.

The *Press–Gazette* printed a letter written by L. F. Hansen, a fan from Oshkosh, the following week. It was adressed to the Green Bay Packers, Inc.:

Gentlemen:

Judging from the comments I heard at yesterday's game you are the recipients of plenty of beefs and gripes based on your performance in the

Bear game.

Admittedly, the team looked like anything but a football team, but then I doubt if those criticizing have met every test of their own lives without at least (once) falling flat on their faces.

Now that the Packers have that one bad game out of their system they should be ready to take the rest of their schedule in stride — and that includes the return game with the Bears.

I am sure Mr. Lambeau will drop the curtain on yesterday's performance, after due concentration on the various reasons for the letdown, and follow up with a record breaking run from here on in. This fan will do his part.

Lambeau could have cared less about Mr. Hansen's letter as he prepared the team for the Detroit Lions who were now led by Packer nemesis Bill Dudley. Lambeau's practices were light, however, as a total of 11 players were on the injured list that week. None of them were hurt too badly to play, but their injuries were sufficient enough to impair their play, especially Jacobs whose ailing elbow affected his passing considerably. Injuries or not, Lambeau put the squad through two hours and 20 minutes of drills in a steady downpour on the Thursday before the game, causing several players to come down with colds. Also, Rhodemyre suffered a broken thumb that day, and he was forced to miss the Lion game.

Ticket director, Carl Mraz, warned folks during the week that the game would be a sellout and that they shouldn't wait until the last minute to get their ducats for the contest with Detroit. This was so much hogwash and the fans knew it. A good crowd of 24,206 turned out to watch Tony Canadeo have one of his best afternoons ever as a Packer. He gained 118 yards on 17 carries as he led the Pack to a 33-21 win. The only bad news was the knee injury suffered by Larry Olsonoski.

The champion Cardinals were the next foe for Green Bay. Paul Christman, the Cards' quarterback, broke his wrist in a 28-17 defeat at the hands of the Bears on the previous Monday night and was forced to miss the Packer tilt in Milwaukee. Even with Christman out of the lineup, Lambeau was worried because his team had made so many mistakes against the Lions, amassing 141 yards on 12 penalties that made the game closer than he would have liked. A repeat of that kind of play against Chicago would certainly spell defeat. Lambeau proved prophetic once again as his charges had 12 penalties for 140 yards and threw four interceptions. A record crowd of 34,369 fans turned out at State Fair Park to see the Cards pound the Packers for 325 yards on the ground and gain a 17-7 victory.

After the game, Lambeau announced that he was "not feeling bad, I'm MAD" and that "salary adjustments will be made until we begin to play the brand of ball we're capable of. There was a decided lack of spirit today. This can't be applied, of course, to all 35 of them because we had a half a dozen boys out there who had it — but that isn't enough. We have always had a reputation for spirit. We haven't shown it once this year. But we're going to correct this situation this week — or else. There'll be salary adjustments and changes made until it is corrected — one of the big reasons it exists is that the boys are getting good salaries and they're content. For that reason, there's got to be a penalty for losing."

With four games played, the Packers were on a record pace for penalty yardage in a season, averaging 107 yards per game to date. The Bears set the record in '44 with 1,025 yards for one season, and if the Packers continued being penalized at their current rate, they would create a new mark of 1,284 yards. This was not a record Lambeau wanted his team to own.

On Tuesday that week, Lambeau announced a 50% pay cut on all players. The pay cut was meant for only one game. Having second thoughts on Wednesday, he announced that he was holding up the fines until after the game with the Rams. Also, on Tuesday, he put Bruce Smith on waivers, but he didn't change his mind about that decision on Wednesday. Smith was out of a job, and that was that.

The Rams arrived in Wisconsin early and took up residence at Sturgeon Bay. LA had played the Bears the week before but without star running back Kenny Washington. Even so, the Rams still scored 21 points on Chicago. Washington was scheduled to play against the Packers, and this had Lambeau worried. He really wanted to know what the Rams were up to, but LA's coach, Clark Shaughnessy who had taken over the team from Bob Snyder when Snyder was forced to cease coaching because of ulcers, barred the press from his team's practices. Art Daley complained in the *Press-Gazette* about Shaughnessy's proclamation, but Shaughnessy ignored him, even when Daley wrote that "Packer Coach Curly Lambeau has never barred the press and radio" from his practices. Such whining should have been beneath Daley's dignity as a journalist, and he should have known that Lambeau must have closed his practices to the press at one time or another during his 30 years as the Packers' leader.

Barring the newsmen from his practices didn't help the Rams on Sunday. Ralph Earhart hauled in a pass from Jack Jacobs late in the first quarter and made a 64-yard scoring play out of it. Walt Schlinkman found paydirt from four yards out in the second period, and Ted Fritsch booted a 43-yard field goal and a PAT to round the scoring for Green Bay. Meanwhile, the defense intercepted seven Bob Waterfield passes, and it held the Rams scoreless as the Packers won, 16-0. The major highlight for the Rams was Waterfield's 88-yard punt, which broke the record set by Ralph Kercheval of Brooklyn in 1935 against the Bears.

Shaughnessy warned the Packers that the return tilt in November in Los Angeles wouldn't have the same result. Of course, the local press pooh-poohed the Rams' mentor.

The win left the Packers (3-2-0) in third place in the division behind the Bears (4-0-0) and the Cardinals (3-1-0). The Rams were in fourth (1-2-1), and Detroit (0-4-0) brought up the rear. In the East, the Eagles (2-1-1) were perched on top, followed by the Redskins (2-2-0), Steelers (2-2-0), Yanks (2-3-0), and Giants (1-3-0). Only the Lions appeared to be out of the running for a division title at this point in the season.

While the Rams were in town, Bruce Smith met with Shaughnessy and signed on with LA. The Giants had tried to sign Smith, but the Rams offered more money. Evidently, Smith wasn't hurt as badly as Lambeau had led people to believe. The truth was he felt Smith was dogging it, so he dumped him. For his part, Smith was dogging it because he wanted out of Green Bay.

Although the Packers had defeated the Rams with the spirited play that Lambeau said had been missing in the game with the Cardinals, nothing was being said about the fines that Lambeau had imposed on several players. Why? No answer yet.

In a personnel move, Lambeau picked up Ted Cremer, an end who played college ball at Auburn, on waivers from Detroit.

Next up on the schedule was Washington in Milwaukee. Daley was fairly cocky in the *Press-Gazette* about the Packers' chances against the Redskins as he reminded the fans of the final score of their August exhibition game, 43-0. He forgot to mention that Sammy Baugh, Washington's Hall of Fame quarterback, only played the first quarter of that pre-season contest. When the Redskins defeated the Packers, 23-7, the *Press-Gazette* staff had a fistful of excuses for the loss, the best being:

(1) "With the count still 13-7, the Packers pulled a legal quick lineup on the Skins' 12 and Jacobs pitched to Ted Cook in the end zone but the official suddenly called his own time out, nullifying the play. He had noticed Dick Poillon, Washington back, putting on a sick act after the teams had lined up at the line of scrimmage. No touchdown."

(2) "After Bob Flowers' interception gave the Packers possession on the Washington 29, Jacobs threw to Nolan Luhn on the goal line and the end stepped over. However, just before catching the ball he pushed defender Howard Hartley (so said the official) out of his way and it was offensive interference. No touchdown."

(3) "Admittedly, there are always a few who growl, principally fans, about the officiating in defeat. But the wails were more evident and of greater duration than normal late Sunday afternoon. And, if the work of the striped-shirted fellows left something to be desired, it may be traceable to George Marshall's pre-game 'pep talk.' The laundryman wept copious tears on the collective shoulders of the arbiters, pleading, 'We've lost a couple of tough ones this year because of the officiating so let's not have any of that today.' Mr. Marshall apparently was unmindful of the NFL rule which prohibits a club owner or representative from attempting to 'influence' the officials."

In analyzing the game, the sportswriters should have pointed out that Lambeau took his team out of the game when he refused to go for field goals when he had the chance. The two drives that the officials allegedly stopped by calling back apparent TDs were golden scoring opportunities for the Packers. Green Bay turned the ball over on downs both times, once on the nine and the other on the three. The Packers were losing, 13-7, on both occasions. After the game, Lambeau claimed that the team "had another letdown." Of course, they did, and he caused it when he chose to go for broke twice and came away empty both times. Those two stalled drives came on successive possessions. Washington dodged the bullet twice and took advantage. The Packers misfired twice and threw in the towel. Who could blame them? Especially when their coach decided to go for six instead of a field goal on fourth-and-seven in the third quarter. Lambeau's decision took the spirit out of his team, and the Redskins pulled off the win.

To add insult to injury, only 13,449 fans attended the game in Milwaukee after the *Press-Gazette* bragged it would be a sellout.

The loss didn't hurt the Packers (3-3-0) in the standings because the Bears (4-1-0) lost to Philadelphia (3-1-1) to fall into a first place tie with the Cards.

That week Lambeau traded Ken Roskie to Detroit for fullback Pat West who played college ball at Southern California. West had just been traded by the Rams the day before to Detroit. He was in his third year in the league.

NFL statistics released in mid-week had the Packers still leading the NFL in penalties and penalty yardage with 63 and 599. Also, Tony Canadeo was leading the league in rushing with 381 yards in just 70 carries for an average of 5.43 yards a carry.

E.B. Bernard of Watertown wrote to the *Press-Gazette* to ask: "There are any number of season ticket fans who want to know why Perry Moss is kept on the bench. He was a standout in collegiate competition. These fans feel he can 'spark' and add glamour to the setup if used partially, at least. The Packers will need and have gotten our support. We feel we have a right to make this inquiry."

Daley replied that he felt Moss was slow to develop as a QB, but that wasn't what counted here. Bernard's letter was important because it showed that the fans were becoming a little discontented with the way things were going in Packerdom. As they had so often in the past, Packer fans were once again displaying their acute sense of football, and this would have a decided effect on Curly Lambeau before long.

Lambeau had complained after the Washington fiasco that his team was overconfident because of the way they had manhandled the Redskins in the exhibition season. That wouldn't happen again, he promised; the Packers would get back on the winning track in Detroit. Capital Airlines pilot, Capt. O.W. "Shutout" Fairchild backed Lambeau's statement when he told the Packers that "You can't lose when you travel Capital." Fairchild was the pilot for the Packers when they traveled to Birmingham to play the Redskins during the pre-season and to Boston for the season opener. Both games were shutouts for Green Bay, and he figured the Detroit game would be more of the same.

The Lions had other thoughts. Although they were winless in five games, Detroit had a young team that was improving every week. Much to Lambeau's chagrin, the Lions chose to enter the win column against his Packers. Green Bay had leads of 7-0, 14-7, and 14-10 before bowing, 24-20. Ted Fritsch missed two short field goal attempts from 17 and 27 yards out, and two fourth quarter fumbles finished off potential winning scoring drives. But the Packers didn't give the game away. Detroit also missed a few opportunities to score additional points. The bottom line was the Lions weren't as bad as the Packers were that day.

The loss just about put an end to the Packers' (3-4-0) hopes of winning the division. The Bears (5-1-0) and Cards remained tied for first, and Philadelphia (4-1-1) and Washington (4-2-0) were pulling away from the pack in the East.

Packers Face Worst Season in History

So read the headline in the *Press-Gazette*. For once, Art Daley was so right. Things weren't getting better for the Packers; they were simply getting worse. Dick Wildung hurt his back and would be out of the lineup against Pittsburgh. Tony Canadeo had a bad cold that he hadn't been able to shake for two weeks, and he would be playing in a weakened condition. So would Jack Jacobs who was stricken with appendicitis again and was hospitalized at St. Vincent's most of the week before the Steelers game. Damon Tassos was also hurt and unable to play.

The Steelers had defeated the Packers the year before for the first time in their history, and everyone said it was a fluke. They were out to prove differently in '48. Early in the game Larry Craig went down with an injury and was out for the rest of the game. His loss seemed to open the flood gates for Pittsburgh as the Steelers scored first, then second, then third, and so on until they led, 38-0. A token TD in the fourth quarter made the final, 38-7, and the Packers headed for home with their tails between their legs.

With the season virtually over, Green Bay (3-5-0) could only play the role of spoiler. They still had the Bears (6-1-0) and Cardinals (6-1-0) on their schedule. Beating one or both of them would be some consolation; not much but some.

The Packers had never lost more than three games in a row in the NFL, losing three in a row only three times before. Lambeau pounded this fact into the heads of his team all that week. They didn't want to be the first Green Bay eleven to lose four straight, did they? Of course not! With this factor and revenge for motivation, Lambeau and his beaten up team waved good-bye to a huge turnout at the railroad station and headed to Chicago to face the Bears the following Sunday.

Larry Craig, Bob Forte, Bob Flowers, Jay Rhodemyre, Dick Wildung, Tony Canadeo, Walt Schlinkman, Damon Tassos, Larry Olsonoski, and Don Deeks were banged up, but all of them played against the Bears. And they played valiantly. The Packers held the Bears scoreless into the third quarter before Bobby Layne connected with Ed Sprinkle for a 34-yard TD pass. Allen Lawler kicked the extra point, and the Bears were up, 7-0. That was all the points they would get that afternoon. Green Bay started a drive on their own 20 with five minutes left in the game, and eight plays later Jacobs connected with Nolan Luhn for a 13-yard scoring strike to make the score, 7-6. Much to the Packers' dismay, Ed Cody missed the extra point. The Bears took the ensuing kickoff down to the Green Bay 30, then kept the ball until the clock had only three seconds left on it. The

Packers got one last desperation play off, but there was no miracle in store for them that day. They went home that night battered and bruised and mathematically out of the division race.

Much to the surprise of the players and Lambeau, a throng of nearly 3,000 fans turned out at the railroad station to greet them when they returned from Chicago. The Packers might have lost four straight for the first time in their history, but their patrons still loved them. This outpouring of appreciation might have been caused by businessman Jerry Atkinson of Prange's, a Wisconsin department store chain. During the week before the Packers played the Bears, he addressed a luncheon of businesspeople and said: "Many of us in Green Bay have somehow dropped our close affection for the team; maybe we've taken them for granted too much." Atkinson blamed this on the fact that the Packers were "out of town", meaning they were practicing and living at Rockwood Lodge, and this put the townspeople out of touch with the players. He called for a display of support, and the people responded — as always.

The Chicago game finished Clyde Goodnight's season. He took a knee in the back that fractured "the transverse process of the third and fourth lumbar vertebrae."

The following week the Packers traveled to New York to face the Giants. Neither squad resembled the ones that had met in Minneapolis earlier in the year. The young Giants now had some experience, and the Packers were operating on crutches. New York hunliated the Pack, 49-3, erasing Green Bay's worst beating record that the Bears had set in September.

After the New York debacle, Daley fed his readers another crock by writing that the Packers' attitude was way off the mark. He ignored the obvious, meaning the plague of injuries to several key personnel. Besides Goodnight, now Baby Ray was down with an injury. So were Jacobs and Ed Smith.

Lambeau didn't bother replacing injured players on the roster because the Packers were trying to save money wherever they could at this time. Besides, the season was over as far as title hopes went. Why bother to fill out the roster for two meaningless games? Or so went the logic.

No sooner had Daley blamed the Packers' losing season on

their attitude than Lambeau told the squad to start playing for their '49 jobs in the last two games or face being released. He blamed their losing record on poor conditoning by 50% of team. To prove his point, he began holding two-a-day workouts in California to prepare the team for the Rams. At the same time, he announced a new formation. Although he didn't call it the "shotgun", it was. He called it "the short punt formation". The tailback stood seven yards back of center with the fullback and left halfback four yards back of each guard. The right halfback stood behind the right or left end, depending on the play. Lambeau designed it so he could use Girard's passing ability with his running talents. To keep defenses honest, he also planned to use Jacobs at the tailback position.

The Packers were given an omen of how their game with the Rams might turn out. A passing motorist threw a lit cigar or cigaret into the back of the truck carrying the Green Bay equipment from the practice field in Ojai to the Coliseum. A dozen uniforms and various padding sets were lost, forcing the Packers to borrow those items from the Rams. The new formation and the loaned duds didn't help all that much as the Rams drubbed the Packers, 24-10. Red Vogds added his name to the injured list by breaking his right hand in the game.

Lambeau continued to tinker with his team for the last game of the season against the Cardinals in Chicago. He moved Girard to left end with the hopes that he might turn into another Hutson or at least a Clyde Goodnight. It didn't help. The Cards were heading for a division title and a rematch with the Eagles in the NFL title game as they stomped the Packers, 42-7.

The coach summed up the season in the *Press-Gazette* in early December before he left for California:

"Although extremely disappointing and aggravating, the situation is not exactly a new one for the Packers. We faced it before — in 1933 and 1934 — and came back to win championships in 1936 and 1939 and a divisional title in 1938. We corrected it then and we can and will correct it now.

"It was not one or two or four big situations that kept us from winning more. It was fifteen or more little things. I made some mistakes, a lot of mistakes. My judgment proved wrong on numerous occasions. I wish I could make over a few decisions.

"We had some very good boys this year, players who measured up to every major league standard. We had other players whose performances would have been much more impressive had we been more successful as a team.

"But we also had some whose play and effort definitely were not up to championship requirements. And championship football is all we are going to tolerate in Green Bay in the future.

"Our passing, quite obviously, was far from being satisfactory and was a handicap all season. That and the fact that a number of veterans did not play the kind of football we expected from them and know they can play."

Lambeau was right as far as he went. He could have and should have mentioned the plague of injuries that his team suffered throughout the season. He remarked on the poor passing, but he said nothing about the fact that he continued to play Jacobs game after game when Jacobs was suffering from a sore elbow in his throwing arm. He said some veterans didn't play the kind of football that was expected of them, but he didn't say that most of them were hurt half of the time.

The one person that Lambeau didn't point a finger at long enough and hard enough was himself. He should have taken the blame for their lousy season. He was the man at the helm. He was the man who made his players go through two-a-day drills after every loss right up to the last game of the season. He was the one who put the team through heavy contact drills for more than two hours in a steady downpour from which several players, including his star running back, Tony Canadeo, contracted severe colds. Not even Vince Lombardi ever treated his players that harshly after a bad game.

Mr. Lambeau should have taken a long look in the mirror after the '48 season, and while he was staring back at himself, he should have asked himself if he still belonged in professional football as a coach. But he didn't because he had other things on his mind at the time.

§ § §

8
The War Drags On

At the tail end of the 1947 season, life in professional football wasn't looking good for the moguls of the All-America Conference. One of its cornerstone franchises, the Chicago Rockets, was broke, although not in bankruptcy. This was an embarrassment to the loop, and something had to be done about it and quick.

The first thing the AAC mentors did was take over the franchise from the triumvirate of owners from Green Bay, Jim Crowley, John J. Brogan, and Bill Toohey. Then new owners, preferably Chicago people, had to be found. This was accomplished by May when it was announced by R.E. Garn, the executive director of the club and a Chicago investment broker, that "the new owners that included more than 20 business, sports and professional leaders of the Chicago area." This group included Maj. Gen. Leo M. Boyle, adjutant general of Illinois; Walker Butler, Chicago attorney and Republican state senator; Hugh W. Cross, lieutenant-governor of Illinois; Joseph J. Lipp, president of Lipp Paper Company and Western conference football official; Daniel F. Rice, Chicago grain broker and a number of other Chicago area business and professional men.

After ownership, the Rockets needed coaches, and one of them was future Green Bay head coach Ray "Scooter" McLean, a former back with the Bears who had attended St. Anselm's College in New Hampshire. Hoping to bring more of a Chicago flavor to the team, the owners hired former Chicago Bear George Musso to coach tackles. Continuing their connection with Wisconsin, the Rockets announced that they would be setting up their training camp that summer in Ripon.

The other AAC owners decided that the Rockets and the

Baltimore Colts needed better personnel to make them more competitive in their circuit, so they *gave* several players to each club to bolster them. Satisfied that they had done all they could to keep Chicago in the AAC, the magnates proceeded with the 1948 season and hoped for the best.

Life for the Rockets didn't get any better in '48. They still finished at the bottom of the division, and attendance didn't improve at all.

The Colts were another story, however. Attendance in Baltimore was up to 206,000 for '48. This was an encouraging sign for the AAC.

Around the rest of pro football, attendance dropped nearly a half million, off 11%. The NFL was off 247,737, 12.96%; the AAC off 196,928; 10.85%. Only the Bears, Cards, 49ers, and Colts were up. Despite their undefeated season, the Cleveland Browns were down 74,141. The AAC's New York Yankees had the biggest loss: 96,567. The Brooklyn Dodgers in the AAC drew only 72,497 for seven games; the NFL's Boston Yanks only 73,010 for six games.

The Packers' attendance for 1948 was 147,645 for six games, three each in Green Bay and Milwaukee. Approximately 75,000 fans attended the games at Green Bay's City Stadium that had seating for less the 25,000 people, while less than that number saw the Packers play at Milwaukee's State Fair Park which could accommodate over 34,000 fans and was located in a metropolitan area that had 12 times the population as Green Bay. In spite of all the testimonials by NFL big-whigs, Packer officials, and some sportswriters, the numbers prove that Milwaukee was not holding up its end of the bargain. The question was posed: Why? Why didn't Milwaukee support the Packers in the same fashion that the people of northeastern Wisconsin did? The answer was quite simple and was proven out by history and the future.

The Milwaukee Badgers of the 1920s drew poorly and faded from the NFL. They were also losers. The Milwaukee Chiefs of the AFL drew well, but World War II put an end to them. Marquette University's football team drew fair crowds when the team was a winner. The Milwaukee Braves drew incredibly well in the 1950s when they were winning pennants and the 1957

World Series, but when the team skidded in the '60s, attendance dropped with them. The same was true of the Milwaukee Brewers in the '80s.

All of this proved that the fans of Milwaukee wouldn't support a loser, and the 1948 Packers were definitely losers.

With Green Bay's attendance figures staring him in the face at the end of the season, Bert Bell had to be anxious to forget his pronunciations of the summer of '48 when he predicted the NFL would have a great year and when he said on Earl "The Lip" Gillespie's sports show on WJPG radio, "Professional football can't exist without Green Bay; the Packers have done a grand job and their following around the country is tremendous." He also said, "The Packers in six games at home drew even with a team that plays in New York's Yankee Stadium." Of course, it was his duty to say things like this — publicly, that is. But what was he saying privately? And to whom was he saying them? Keep those questions in mind for now.

The article in the *Press-Gazette* that quoted Bell's recent radio remarks also repeated some comments that he'd made in the past when talk about Green Bay not being able to survive in the NFL was rampant. "Green Bay will always be in the National Football League," said Bell. "Green Bay is professional football; Green Bay is the greatest drawing card on the road in the professional game." This brought another question to mind: Why was the *Press-Gazette* bothering to rehash his remarks at this time? Keep that question in mind, too.

Adding to Bell's concerns during the '48 season was Alexis Thompson, the millionaire owner of the Philadelphia Eagles. In October, Thompson allegedly threw in the towel in his attempts to reconcile the NFL and the AAC. "It's hopeless," he was quoted as saying. "The leagues will never get together. I have been trying to do everything for the fans. I thought that the fans really wanted to see the champions of each league in a sort of world series of football." Thompson's frustration was caused by the warring New York clubs. He had arranged a meeting between two small groups of owners from each circuit; it would be a beginning toward formal peace talks. Then Dan Topping of the New York Yankees (AAC) told New York sportswriters that the Giants would lose $200,000 that year. This set off Tim

Mara who said, "Dan's auditing our books again." Topping's blurb and Mara's counterattack prevented Thompson's meeting from ever happening.

Unaware of Thompson's clandestine meeting before news of its cancellation hit the newspapers, Admiral Jonas Ingram, the AAC's commissioner, tried to rekindle the sparks of peace that Thompson had started by calling on the NFL to join the AAC in a common draft, co-ordinated scheules, and a title match between the champs of each loop. Once again, Bell snubbed him.

As if Thompson's private dealings weren't bad enough to upset Bell, he had to tell the world in an interview with *Sport* magazine that "visiting clubs take a financial licking at Green Bay because of the small population and small stadium." He went on to suggest that Green Bay should be "one of the clubs to be dumped in joining the National and All-America loops into one circuit with eastern and western sectors." Did this cause a furor? Lambeau was livid. He quoted some figures for the public to consume. The Bears were paid $76,158 for their game in Green Bay that year; the Lions $67,693.50; the Rams $72,319.50; and the Cardinals received a whopping $100,959.50 for their game with the Packers in Milwaukee. Of course, Lambeau failed to mention that the Redskins were paid diddly squat in their recent encounter in Milwaukee that drew just over 13,000 fans, and the Giants wouldn't get much more than Washington when they played in Milwaukee in November. He also didn't mention that the Bears paid the Packers twice as much for their game in Chicago.

To back up Lambeau, Bell made a mid-season "state of the league" address to the media in Philadelphia. He said receipts for the year were only down a meager 3%, "but any good Sunday could make up the difference." As for the Packers, he said that Green Bay had hit new highs in attendance for home games in Milwaukee and Green Bay and "contrary to some reports it's a mighty healthy franchise."

Bell's statement quieted matters for about a month, then *United Press International* released a story on a poll of players in both leagues that they had taken. The basic question concerned the ongoing football war: Should the leagues settle their differences and merge? Yes or no and why? Six teams — the Boston Yanks, New York Giants, Washington Redskins, Philadelphia Eagles, and Green Bay Packers in the NFL and the Buffalo Bills in the AAC — refused to permit their players to participate in the survey, and some of the players who did answer the question asked to have their names withheld. The results were surprising. A majority of the players wanted an end of the bickering between the two leagues so they could get on with playing football. Some players hoped the war would go on indefinitely because a settlement would probably mean their salaries would stop escalating and the owners would probably try to cut their wages back to what they had been before the pro football war began. Nearly all of them said, however, that a merger between the two leagues was inevitable, although not soon.

By mid-December, the merger began looking more like sooner than later.

Alexis Thompson, the Eagles' owner, took a look at Bell's attendance figures and immediately renewed his efforts for peace between two leagues. Lloyd Larson quoted Thompson in *The Milwaukee Sentinel* when the Philadelphia owner complained about "the fantastic situation that finds me with a championship football team that will lose close to $32,000 this year." Larson wrote that he was sure Thompson's "fellow National League owners feel the same way about the costly talent war that's making it almost impossible to make an honest buck in what was once a sound undertaking. But they're still clinging to the hope that the All-America will fold. Which would mean the end of outlandish bidding and fancy salaries." Thompson replied: "But darn it, they're in it. They haven't folded up. The competition has driven salaries up so high that nobody can make a franchise really pay. We must recognize this and act accordingly."

Most of the other NFL owners and Bert Bell remained adamant about settling with the AAC.

Then the rumors started. Cleveland and San Francisco were willing to join the NFL without the other AAC teams, said one. George Halas was feeling out the owners of the Los Angeles Dons and the New York Yankees about a settlement of the war, said another. New York writer Joe King predicted that San

The Lambeau Years — Part Three

Francisco and Cleveland would join the NFL and without them the AAC would fold up. Admiral Jonas Ingram was predicting a settlement with the NFL within 30 days. In the settlement, Ingram was to resign so Bell could be the commissioner over both leagues. Dons' owner, Ben Lindheimer, was rumored ready to sell his franchise in the AAC, then buy the Chicago Cards and take over the Chicago Rockets, and as soon as that was accomplished he would combine the two teams as the Chicago Hornets in the AAC, leaving the NFL with only the Bears in Chicago.

Most of the rumors had some basis of truth for them. Things were happening in the war. Secret meetings; announced meetings; all meetings were being held behind closed doors.

The owners of the Cleveland Browns, San Francisco 49ers, New York Yankees, Buffalo Bills, and Los Angeles Dons met in Philadelphia on December 19. The NFL owners were also in the City of Brotherly Love, ostensibly to watch the Eagles and Cardinals play for the NFL title, which the Ealges won in a heavy snowstorm that kept attendance down. It was announced that the AAC moguls were meeting with the hope of finding a way of joining the NFL as a group or in some combination. Actually, the magnates from both circuits held their first ever meeting together.

James Breuil of the Buffalo Bills had come to realize that pro football couldn't make it in Buffalo as long as the two leagues were at war, so he proposed to combine his team with another and become a part owner with the team still located in Buffalo. It was reported that LA's Ben Lindheimer wanted to merge his Dons with the Rams, but he was actually opposed to a merger with the Rams. Lindheimer reasoned that, if Chicago and New York could have two teams, then so could Los Angeles. He wanted his Dons admitted to the NFL, too.

When asked about their feelings on the AAC meeting and the proposal that the NFL take in the best franchises from the AAC, Curly Lambeau and George Halas agreed that the addition of the Browns and the 49ers would make an ideal NFL of 12 teams, putting Cleveland in the Eastern Division and matching San Francisco up with the Rams on the West Coast. The admission of the Baltimore Colts was vehemently opposed by George

Marshall, although he denied this a month later. "Actually," he said, "I'd prefer to have Baltimore instead of San Francisco in the league as far as traveling expenses are concerned, and think of the wonderful rivalry we could work up with Baltimore." Then he remarked on how Baltimore was a losing proposition in the AAC. "Why should the National league take on a loser when we already have some weak clubs of our own. I doubt if other NFL owners will want to take in more than two AAC clubs. Where does that leave Baltimore?"

An unidentified NFL spokesman told the *Associated Press* that the negotiations broke off because the AAC insisted on the Dons and Colts being admitted with Cleveland, San Francisco, Buffalo, and the New York Yankees. The Rockets or Hornets were a lost cause, and the AAC men admitted it. Three teams in New York might work, but it was felt that the NFL would be more agreeable to accepting the Yankees if the Brooklyn Dodgers were dropped. The AAC proposal would have 16 teams in one league of two divisions.

For their part, the NFL owners said they couldn't accept Baltimore because they felt two teams in a metropolitan area of less than two million people couldn't make it. Also, they felt Buffalo would never make it in the NFL, and Los Angeles wasn't big enough to support two teams. They wanted what Lambeau and Halas wanted: Cleveland and San Francisco.

The talks broke off for the holidays, then resumed in January when the two loops held their winter meetings.

The *Associated Press* reported that two big stumbling blocks to negotiations were the settlement of local rivalries and George Marshall. The three New York teams and the Boston Yanks were willing to meet and work out a solution for them, but Marshall was still totally opposed to allowing Baltimore to join the NFL. Ben Lindheimer, it was rumored, was willing to merge his Dons with the LA Rams if two conditions would be met by the NFL. (1) He would become a part owner in the Rams, and (2) the Colts were admitted with Cleveland and San Francisco. His proposal would give the NFL 13 teams. If the two AAC New York teams were to merge also, then the NFL would have 12 teams. This possibility seemed likely to happen in early 1949.

Then the NFL held its winter meetings in Chicago. The NFL

moguls tried to persuade the owners of the Browns and 49ers to jump leagues, but the other AAC owners, Ben Lindheimer in particular, threatened legal action if any such moves were made. That put the merger back on the table. The NFL was willing to accept Buffalo and Baltimore in the Eastern Division and Cleveland and San Francisco in the Western, but this plan was thwarted by Lindheimer again because he owned the LA Dons and was the primary backer of the Chicago and Brooklyn franchises in the AAC. Dan Topping was willing to go along with the merger plan because as owner of the New York Yankees baseball team he would become the landlord for the Boston Yanks when they moved to New York. While Lindheimer held up this compromise, someone figured out that a 14-team NFL wouldn't work because teams in one division would no longer be able to play each other twice a year in a home–and–home series. Thinking like this caused the AAC magnates to back off and announce that they would play the 1949 season with seven teams as they would merge the Brooklyn Dodgers with the New York Yankees and give the excess players to the new Chicago franchise. Negotiations broke off.

Bert Bell summed up the thinking of the NFL owners in a story that made the papers in early February. He argued that in his belief there weren't 16 cities, the number that he felt was necessary to make up two leagues, in the country that were capable of maintaining top–flight pro football teams.

This was antiquated thinking. With two teams each in New York, Chicago, and Los Angeles, pro football needed only 13 cities to support 16 teams. Also, it was quite evident that Mr. Bell hadn't heard about television yet, and he certainly didn't have any feel for what sort of impact television would have on football. Like most of the men he worked for, Bell was much better at looking behind than ahead, and it was this lack of vision that forced the pro football war into another long year.

§ § §

9

The Second Winter of Lambeau's Discontent

There is no fairer game for vulturous sportswriters who suffer from *frustratus jockitis* than a wounded coach, and after surviving his worst season as either a player or a coach, Curly Lambeau was about as fit as a one-wing quail with blisters on his feet. Fortunately for Lambeau, the Humane Society of Green Bay, better known as the editorial staff of *The Green Bay Press-Gazette*, was around to protect him. For one more campaign, at least.

As Lambeau was analyzing the failure of his '48 team, Green Bay fans were doing the same thing. The first rumblings of their discontent were polite, such as the letter that E.B. Bernard of Watertown wrote to the *Press-Gazette* asking why Perry Moss was being kept on the bench when it was obvious that the Packers needed a "spark" to get them going and at the very least Bernard felt Moss would "add glamour to the setup if used partially, at least." Even Green Bay businessman Jerry Atkinson of Prange's was reasonably friendly when he blamed the growing disaffection of the fans on the fact that the Packers were "out of town", meaning they were practicing and living at Rockwood Lodge, and that this put the townspeople out of touch with the players. Other complaints about the Packers and their season that didn't reach print were being vocalized around Wisconsin. Most pointed fingers at various players; some said the officials had it in for the Packers; and a very few looked straight at Lambeau.

Sportswriter Lloyd Larson of *The Milwaukee Sentinel* heard all these grass-roots stirrings and discarded every one of them. In his December 9, 1948 column, he calmly summed up the real problem with the Packers in '48, reprinted here with its headings, bold type, and italics as it appeared in the *Sentinel*:

What WAS the Matter With the Packers?
Rockwood Lodge Is No. 1 on the List

Here's a letter containing observations with which I agree and a perfectly logical question which has been asked many, many times during the season and in the days since it closed: "Things sure are out of balance in Wisconsin. A certain element has been putting on a smear campaign against the state university because of the losing football season. Twisting the truth and accepting rumors as truth, if not telling downright lies. Undermining and dividing by planting ideas. It goes far beyond shooting at individuals or expressing honest opinions. Yet this same element forgets all about another state institution, the Green Bay Packers. They were supposed to be championship bound and wound up with three victories and nine defeats and the worst record in history. Why the smear I don't know. But that's not my question. What I want to know is what WAS the matter with the Packers?"

Frankly, I feel the No. 1 trouble with the Packers was and is Rockwood Lodge, their living and training quarters outside the city of Green Bay.

There have been rumors galore and many opinions on the subject ever since the poor showing in the first game with the Bears.

Differences in pay, the blanket half-game pay fines, flops on the part of individuals, over-all strength (or lack of it) on the coaching staff and one thing or another are supposed to have contributed to the **"My Happiness"** theme in reverse.

It's quite obvious, too, that there was some over evaluation of material.

The Idea That Didn't Work Out

But I still feel that the spacious new Packer home, Rockwood Lodge, had more to do with the "situation" than anything else.

It seemed like a good idea when the Packer Corporation took over the ladge (sic) months before the 1947 season. There the Packers, noted for their college spirit, would have a campus of their own, with practice facilities outside their door. There they would live together, live football and become more closely knit than ever before. The aim was to stir up even more of the college spirit and, in the long run, gain added advantage over big city rivals.

Yes, it was a good idea. But it hasn't worked out that way at all. The players saw too much of each other. The football diet was too heavy.

"Morning, noon, afternoon and night we got nothing but football and it was too much," as some have explained. The players also resented being herded together like juveniles. Many of them are mature men with families. And the families, of course, were moved off the "campus" after a year's trial run.

Player–Fan Relationship Is Lost

Important as those considerations are, there's an even greater weakness in the Rockwood setup.

This has to do with the player–fan relationship — the very spirit responsible for the Packers' tremendous success through the years. Largely because of this spirit — the direct and loyal backing of Green Bay's young and old — the Packers became famous as the only professional team with the college touch.

The lost touch was best explained by a former Packer great who said:

"In the old days we lived in town and mingled with the people. Each one of us knew hundreds of fans by name and perhaps thousands by sight. They knew us and were our friends. With that mutual feeling of friendship came a deep sense of responsibility. We didn't care to face those people if we lost. And when we did lose, we wouldn't have dared face them if we hadn't put out to the limit. We had our gripes and naturally had our differences, even with the coach. But those people kept us together."

Larson had fired the first shot in the war over Rockwood Lodge, but this was not going to be a one–sided affair. Coming

The Lambeau Years — Part Three 119

to the defense was George Strickler, the Packers' publicity director. His article was printed in the *Press-Gazette* two days after Larson's column reached the public. The opening was intended to be flowery and literary, but it turned out to be rather stupid. Strickler wrote:

"It took an American, Mr. Hemingway, to explain the inner meaning of bullfighting, but no Spaniard has, as yet, returned the favor by explaining Rockwood."

Hemingway was trying to make Americans understand bullfighting; the Spanish already understood their barbaric form of entertainment. Strickler's analogy was pathetic.

In the next paragraph, Strickler implied that Packer fans were ignorant rubes:

"It would not be true to say that the people who flock to City stadium and State Fair park are not aware of Rockwood Lodge, home of the Green Bay Packers, but for the lack of a little practical and sensible analysis, some of them, at least, miss its ultimate worth."

To add insult to injury, Strickler called on Lambeau to be his accomplice in this crime against Packerdom. "I am sure," said Lambeau, "that if the fans were acquainted with the facts, they would agree that Rockwood is good for the Packers."

Strickler proceeded to list some so-called facts about Rockwood Lodge, citing that Lambeau and the corporation had become interested in the lodge during the height of the housing shortage in 1945. His next statement was a real beaut. "*Only* (Author's italics) the lodge enabled Lambeau to assemble a squad in 1946." Excuse us, Mr. Strickler, but how did Lambeau assemble all those squads from 1921 thru 1945 without the lodge?

"No Packer is obligated to live at Rockwood," wrote Strickler. "Several have resided in Green Bay every season. At the end of the present campaign, a survey of the squad revealed all but two men preferred Rockwood." If only "two men" didn't prefer Rockwood, why did several Packers reside in Green Bay? No room at the inn, Mr. Strickler? Hardly. Rockwood could house the whole team and then some. Strickler was simply blowing smoke at the fans. Most of the players hated the lodge, but it was all they could afford on the salaries that Lambeau was paying them.

Only one Packer player, past or present, was quoted in Strickler's article. Buckets Goldenberg said, "If we had had Rockwood in my years with the club, we would have won two more championships." He didn't qualify that statement, or if he did, Strickler didn't bother to quote him.

There followed glowing remarks about the lodge by Bernie Bierman, the coach at the University of Minnesota; George Halas; and Jimmy Conzelman. Bierman was envious, and why shouldn't he have been? Rockwood Lodge was a better setup than his athletes at Minnesota had. As for Conzelman and Halas, they were only seeing a building and a practice field; neither man was seeing what was happening to the players.

Strickler wrote about hotel food being unhealthy for athletes who needed more nutritious diets than ordinary folks. "At Rockwood their diets can be supervised carefully." He made the lodge sound like a fat farm instead of a football training facility.

"Contrary to popular impressions, Packer fans in Green Bay have as much opportunity to see and visit with the players now as they did before Rockwood." More manure! The lodge was 12 miles outside of town. Not every person living in Green Bay in the late '40s owned a car, and those who did own cars were a little more than reluctant to jump in the old jalopy and jaunt out to the lodge to visit with their favorite players.

Strickler's rebuttal to Larson's column was as effective as an eye-dropper on a sinking ship. For his part, Larson did the gentlemanly thing by reprinting Strickler's feeble attempt to defend Rockwood in the *Sentinel*. At the end of his column, Larson wrote: "There's the case FOR Rockwood. All right now, Mr. Strickler — take off the gloves and give us the pitch. What WAS wrong with the Packers?" Strickler didn't reply.

While the Rockwood Lodge controversy was raging, Lambeau was busy trying to land that much needed quarterback. In this case, the man in question was Stan Heath, the passer that Lambeau had drafted the year before but who wasn't allowed to be signed because he still had two years of college eligibility remaining. Commissioner Bell had made the first ruling the year before when Lambeau drafted Heath in '47, stating that Heath couldn't play in the NFL until the 1950 season. Lambeau made a solid argument with Bell that if they didn't let Heath into the league in '49 then he would sign with an AAC team. On November 17, Bell reversed his decision and declared Heath eligible for the '48 draft, but since the Packers already owned the rights to Heath, this point was moot. Bell was actually giving permission to Lambeau to sign Heath, hopefully before the AAC snatched him up.

Stan Heath's parents lived in Menomonee Falls, Wisconsin, a suburb of Milwaukee. Heath attended Shorewood High School in Milwaukee, then played his college ball at the University of Nevada in Reno. He led the nation in passing in '48. His services were coveted by the New York Yankees as well as the Packers. Lambeau felt that having Heath would help bolster sagging attendance for games in Milwaukee. Besides, he needed a pure passer, and Heath fit the description. A report out of New York had Dan Topping offering Heath $40,000 for a two-year contract. Those were some incredibly big dollars for an untried college quarterback in 1948. Although the Packers were hard-pressed to meet Topping's offer, Lambeau was able to sign Heath right after the college all-star games were concluded.

At the tail end of the '48 season, Ed Sainsbury wrote an *Associated Press* story that declared the college crop would be spotty at best for both pro circuits. He cited a shortage of stars. Beyond Doak Walker (back, SMU) and Chuck Bednarik (center, Pennsylvania), the draft would be short on talent. Quarterbacks Johnny Rausch (Georgia), Frank Tripucka (Notre Dame), Bob De Moss (Purdue), Bobby Thomason (VMI), and George Blanda (Kentucky) had potential but would need the right opportunity to make an impact in the pros. As far as fullbacks went, there weren't any. Shorty McWilliams (Mississippi State) and George Taliaferro (Indiana) were the only tailbacks available for teams like the Steelers, Lions, and Packers who used single-wing formations. Some topflight linemen were coming out of college that year, but their numbers were small.

With such limited talent available, the Packers were in trouble already for the '49 season. Walt Kiesling, Green Bay's line coach, was quoted by Hugh Fullerton of the *Associated Press* as saying, "The Packers need 11 or 12 good new players to form a winning team; they weren't available on the draft list, either." This remark cost him his job.

Of course, Lambeau didn't say this was the reason he didn't rehire Kiesling for the '49 season. Instead, he said, "Kies is one of the finest line coaches in the country, but he should, in the interest of his health, take a year's vacation from football and all other strenuous activities." Kiesling was ill twice during the previous season for a week at a time, but he refused to take the time off. Lambeau was just using Kiesling's health as an excuse to get rid of him. After being "nudged aside" by Lambeau, Kiesling landed an assistant coaching job with the Steelers for '49.

Lambeau's draft list was published in the *Press-Gazette* on January 15. Of the 23 players drafted, only eight ever played for the Packers. A big one that got away was Dan Dworsky, a center from Michigan. Lambeau said on Earl Gillespie's radio show: "For the kind of money he wanted, we're not sorry to lose Dworsky; he plays only defensive ball anyway." This was a typical Curlyism, and it was a sign that Lambeau wasn't keeping up with the times. Already, several coaches, pro and college, were thinking of platooning, and some of them actually used many players as defensive or offensive experts only. As proof of that fact, the NFL adopted the free substitution rule at the winter meetings. In another typical out-of-the-other-side-of-his-mouth remark, Lambeau said, "Now we can concentrate on two complete offensive and defensive units."

Another draftee who chose the AAC Colts over the Packers was Everett Faunce, a halfback out of Minnesota. Faunce asked for a signing bonus, a routine request during the pro football war, but Lambeau said flatly, "No signing bonus." Baltimore gave him the bonus for signing.

The Packers also lost Brad Ecklund, the center from Oregon that Lambeau had drafted the year before. Ecklund joined Dan Topping's Yankees.

Another man that Lambeau had drafted in '47 was Paul

Burris, the All-American guard from Oklahoma. Burris was the first consensus All-American to sign with the Packers since Dick Wildung.

In the midst of all this football business, the Packers received some tragic news. On January 1, 1949, Bob Skoglund, Green Bay's great end from Notre Dame, died from a kidney infection at St. Francis Hospital in Evanston, Illinois. Skoglund had missed the entire '48 campaign with a knee injury, but it was hoped that he would be able to play again in '49.

After the NFL winter meetings in Chicago, Lambeau went about the task of rebuilding his coaching staff. He started by signing Bob Snyder, the former head coach of the Rams, as the Packers' new backfield coach. Snyder replaced Bo Molenda whose contract wasn't renewed after the '48 season. Molenda moved south to Chicago to become the backfield coach of the Chicago Hornets, formerly the Rockets.

Joining Snyder on the new staff was Charley Brock, the former all-pro center for the Packers. Brock would be a scout and an assistant line coach.

The third new coach for the Packers was Tom Stidham who replaced Kiesling as the line coach. Stidham had lots of coaching experience, starting as an assistant at Haskell Institute in 1927. He moved with head coach Dick Hanley to Northwestern in 1928, then became an assistant under Biff Jones at Oklahoma in 1935. He took over as head coach and athletic director for the Sooners in 1937 and led Oklahoma to its first ever bowl game in 1938. In 1941, he moved to Wisconsin and coached Marquette University for five years, then was an assistant for the AAC Buffalo Bills in '46 and the Baltimore Colts in '47 and '48 under former Packer Cecil Isbell.

Of course, Lambeau rehired Don Hutson to coach his ends and defensive backs.

With the hiring of a new coaching staff, especially men the caliber of Stidham and Snyder, Lambeau seemed to be answering Lloyd Larson's question in the *Sentinel* earlier that winter. The trouble was he was wrong as time would prove.

§ § §

10
Who's On First?

For the first time in the history of the Packers, Coach Curly Lambeau reached outside of Green Bay for big-time assistant coaches who didn't have previous connections with the Packers when he hired Tom Stidham and Bob Snyder. With Charley Brock and Don Hutson also in the scheme of things, Lambeau was prepared to gather his troops and ready them to meet the demands of another National Football League season.

At the end of the '48 campaign, Lambeau lamented, "Our passing, quite obviously, was far from being satisfactory and was a handicap all season." He was so right. The Packers finished ninth in the NFL in passing, completing only 109 of 274 passes for 1,364 yards and eight touchdowns. This was pathetic. Clyde Goodnight was the team's only decent receiver, hauling in 28 passes for 448 yards but only one TD. Nolan Luhn and Ralph Earhart made 17 receptions each, gaining 285 and 194 yards, respectively, and both of them landed in paydirt twice. In contrast, rookie Tom Fears of the Los Angeles Rams caught 51 passes for 698 and four sixes, and Pete Pihos of the champion Philadelphia Eagles caught 46 passes for 766 yards and 11 touchdowns.

The numbers didn't lie. The Packers needed a healthy first-rate passer and one more quality receiver. Lambeau already had Jack Jacobs, but Jacobs's status was iffy. He'd had an appendectomy right after the season ended in December, then he had bone chips removed from his right elbow in March. The head coach and his staff felt that Jacobs's overall health was weakened by the appendectomy and that his arm was also questionable since undergoing the knife. Also, Jacobs was getting up in football years. He had played under Stidham at Oklahoma back in the late '30s and early '40s, then broke into the NFL with the Rams in '42. Thus, Lambeau felt the need for a younger offensive leader, preferably a T–formation quarterback.

Enter Stan Heath, the top collegiate passer in '48, and Bob Snyder, the man who taught the T–formation to the Fighting Irish of Notre Dame. Lambeau hoped that both of them could perform their magic in Green Bay in '49.

As for a topnotch receiver to compliment Clyde Goodnight, Lambeau had his sights set on a former Wisconsin Badger named Elroy "Crazy Legs" Hirsch. After a brilliant career in college and serving a short stint in the Marines, Hirsch was drafted by the then Cleveland Rams and the Chicago Rockets. Hirsch opted to play his pro ball in the Windy City because it was closer to home and his business interests. His three–year contract with the Rockets was up at the end of the '48 campaign, but the Rams held the NFL rights to him. Lambeau went through the proper channels and asked permission of Dan Reeves, the Rams' owner, to talk to Hirsch about playing in Green Bay in '49. Hirsch was willing, but a deal would have to be made with the Rams first. Lambeau couldn't make the deal because the Packers didn't have a whole lot that the Rams wanted and what they did have Lambeau was unwilling to relinquish.

In an attempt to help land Hirsch, Lambeau picked up Bill Schroeder who hailed from Sheboygan, Wisconsin, and who had played two years with Chicago Rockets after graduating from the University of Wisconsin. Lambeau hoped that Schroeder would help convince Hirsch to tell the Rams that he would stay in the AAC if they didn't let him go to the Packers. The ploy failed. Hirsch went to LA, and Schroeder was cut from the team.

Lambeau signed 14 rookies for the '49 season. Among them were Heath, Paul Burris (G, Oklahoma), Lou Ferry (T, Villanova) whom Lambeau called another Joe Stydahar, Bob Summerhays (B, Utah), William "Wild Bill" Kelley (E, Texas Tech), Glenn Lewis (HB, Texas Tech), Paul W. "Andy" Devine (B, Heidelberg), Dan Orlich (E, Nevada) who was Heath's top receiver in college, Joe Ethridge (G, SMU), Ralph Olsen (C, Utah), and Ken Kranz (B, Milwaukee Teachers). Lambeau traded fullback Pat West and the rights to draftee Jim Ford (B, Tulsa) to New York Giants for rights to Albert J. "Jack" Bush (T, Georgia) and Edward A. Kelley (T, Texas), but neither man ever played for the Packers, making the deal a waste. As a project, Lambeau brought in Howard Scalla from Compton (California) Junior College. Scalla was huge for those days, weighing in at 315 pounds and standing 6'6".

Veterans returning to the squad were ends Ted Cook, Larry Craig, Clyde Goodnight, Nolan Luhn, Don Wells, and Red Wilson; tackles Ed Bell, Jim Kekeris, Paul Lipscomb, Urban Odson, and Dick Wildung; guards Ralph Davis, Ed Neal, Larry Olsonoski, and Red Vogds; centers Bob Flowers and Jay Rhodemyre; quarterbacks Irv Comp, Jack Jacobs, and Perry Moss; halfbacks Tony Canadeo, Ralph Earhart, Bob Forte, Jug Girard, and Ed Smith; and fullbacks Ed Cody, Ted Fritsch, and Walt Schlinkman.

Baby Ray and Don Deeks retired, and Fred Provo quit pro football to get on with his life.

The first roster move of training camp was the release of Perry Moss who failed to show up for the first practice. The next day Jim Kekeris decided that his knee wouldn't be able to stand the pressure of another season of NFL football, so he announced his retirement from the game. On the plus side, Damon Tassos changed his mind about retiring and reported to camp.

Missing from the first practices were Jay Rhodemyre, Tony Candeo, and Red Wilson. Canadeo made it by the fourth day, having been delayed by the serious illness of his mother in Chicago. Wilson sent word that he'd gotten married and had purchased a tavern in Texas; in other words, he was retiring from football. Rhodemyre was still at home in Kentucky, trying to make up his mind whether he wanted to play or not. Causing his indecision was his father's health. The senior Rhodemyre had suffered a heart attack and a stroke within a six-weeks period, and Jay felt his place was with his father and not in Green Bay — yet. He finally joined the team the week of their first exhibition game.

The huge tackle from Compton JC, Howard Scalla, decided he wasn't ready for the pros yet, so he left camp after only a week of practice. The truth was the blubbery Scalla was way overmatched by nearly every other lineman in camp.

In some off-field news, the corporation re-elected Emil Fischer as president of the Packers, but Andy Turnbull, the man who started the move that turned the Packers into the first non-profit professional sports franchise in history, resigned from the executive committee and the board of directors. Replacing Turnbull on the executive committee was newspaperman John Torinus, Sr., and filling the void on the board of directors was Vic McCormick. Frank Jonet remained as secretary-treasurer, and Curly Lambeau stayed on as vice-president.*

As a publicity stunt, the Packers named twelve-years-old child actress Margaret O'Brien as the team's mascot for 1949. She declared that she had been a Packer fan for about three years — "ever since they told me the Packers were the biggest and best team and were playing in the littlest city." She remarked that actor Gary Cooper could play for the Packers "if he was good enough." Then she said, "Please let me promise you something. With O'Brien for mascot, we'll be champions this year!" As the saying goes, "Out of the mouths of babes . . . "

Bad news came during the second week of practice when Tony Canadeo broke his right wrist during scrimmage. Dr. H.S. Atkinson, the team physician, put Canadeo's arm in a cast and said "The Grey Ghost" would miss five to six weeks of action. Suffering minor ailments were Bob Forte, Ken Kranz, Ed Smith, and rookie Glenn Lewis; all halfbacks. Larry Craig left camp without notifying the coaching staff who were in Chicago to watch the Eagles play the College All-Stars. The first reports said he went home to take care of some unexpected business on his farm, but a later story said that he left Green Bay to consult an orthopedic specialist about his knee injury.

Packer fans were given a sign of things to come in the fall of '49 when their team met the NFL champion Philadelphia Eagles in the first exhibition contest of the pre-season. The Eagles mauled the Packers, 35-0, rolling up 335 yards on the ground to dominate Green Bay offensively and holding the

---

* A very interesting article appeared in the *Press-Gazette* the next day concerning Turnbull's role in the history of the Packers. See Appendix B.

Pack to a total of 167 yards to make the rout complete. The really bad news was an injury to Jug Girard that was administered by Philadelphia's center Alex Wojciehowicz, a man who reputedly knitted dainties for his four daughters. Also hurt was Red Vogds whose back was giving him trouble again.

After the debacle with the Eagles, Lambeau made a trade for running back Bob Cifers who had been recently released by the Steelers because he missed a bed check and was then recalled by the team for the trade with the Packers. Lambeau gave up a future draft choice for Cifers.

In other roster moves, Lambeau released two rookies to bring his squad down to 44 men.

The next pre-season contest for the Packers was against the Giants in Syracuse, New York. The Gothamites weren't the Eagles. In fact, they weren't even the Giants of old. They outplayed the Packers, but six turnovers allowed Green Bay to eke out a 14-7 win, putting joy in the city by the bay once again.

Winning was nice, but it cost the Packers the services of Jack Jacobs who suffered pulled ligaments in his ankle. Jacobs would be out indefinitely. Other minor injuries were incurred by Ed Neal (knee), Ed Cody (shoulder), Bob Summerhays (wrist), and Larry Olsonoski (stomach).

The Packers traveled to Pittsburgh to take on the Steelers for their third exhibition game. In another punchless game, the Packers went down, 9-3. Incredible as it was, Green Bay was penalized 190 yards in the game, and Lambeau went back to the drawing board shaking his head.

Lambeau signed Roger Eason, a guard out of Oklahoma who played three seasons with the Rams before being released that summer of '49. Other roster moves that didn't amount to much were the signings of another center and an end, neither of whom worked out.

The Packers played an intrasquad game at Marinette the following week, and rookie Stan Heath had an outstanding game, throwing three TD passes as his team won, 28-7, over Irv Comp's group. After the game, Lambeau and his staff were all smiles, saying that the Pack was up to about 50% efficiency, which was exactly where he wanted them to be at this stage of the pre-season.

After being absent from the team for more than three weeks, Larry Craig rejoined the squad on September 8, just in time for the Packers' fourth practice game, this one to be held at Rock Island, Illinois, against the New York Bulldogs, formerly the Boston Yanks. The name change didn't help because the Packers defeated the Bulldogs, 7-3, on a fourth quarter TD run by Ralph Earhart. Beyond that, the Green Bay offense was restricted to a ground attack that gained 213 yards. Jacobs did all of the passing, although Heath was supposed to get some air time. The veteran quarterback had an awful day, completing just three of 18 passes attempted and having four intercepted. It made no difference to the fans back home; it was a win, pre-season or not.

Going into the last exhibition of the summer, Lambeau's squad still had 46 players on it. The new roster limit was 32. He had to cut 14 men before the opening game. Instead of cutting, he added another back, Frank Seno, who had just been released by the Bulldogs. Seno was more of an insurance policy for the Packers than an addition; he was acquired because of injuries to Irv Comp who was a first-rate secondary man, Ed Smith, and Bill Schroeder in the New York game. Then just before the game Lambeau released four rookies: Jim Goodman, Floyd Lewis, Frank Williams, and Charley Tatom.

The Redskins were the final opponent for the Packers during the pre-season. Green Bay's offense matched its total of 24 points from the previous four contests but still came up short, 35-24, as Washington ran and passed at will in a wide-open game. Stan Heath blew his chance to become the starting quarterback when he managed to complete only five of 19 passes for a meager 57 yards.

With the last of the exhibition games completed, it was cut down time in Green Bay. Waivers were asked on John Mastrangeli, Damon Tassos, Ralph Davis, Bud Canada, Verne Gagne, Glenn Lewis, Bill Schroeder, and Ed Cody. Lambeau then sold Frank Seno to the Redskins. This brought the squad down to 34 men with four days left before the season opener against the Bears.

As usual, the fracas with the Monsters of the Midway was a sellout for the Packers. More than 25,000 fans jammed into City

Stadium hoping to see a classic Chicago–Green Bay struggle, which they did for three quarters of the game. The game was scoreless until the final minute of the third stanza when Johnny Lujack booted a 16-yard field goal for the Bears. Lujack then threw two TD passes and kicked the PATs in the final period, giving him a hand in all of the Bears' 17 points. In the meantime, the Packers were zero-for-13 passing, having four aerials intercepted by the Bears, and Green Bay managed to gain 187 yards on the ground. Unfortunately, none of them ended in the end zone. Tony Canadeo, whose wrist had healed, put on a good show, gaining 92 yards on 11 carries, and Walt Schlinkman tacked on 44 yards on just seven attempts. But no Packer could score. The Bears went back to Chicago as winners, 17-0.

After the game, Lambeau addressed his troops in the locker room. "This is only one game," he emphasized. "Only one game. And there are eleven more to go. Your effort out there today was all right and if you keep it up, you're going to win a lot of ball games." A prognosticator, Curly wasn't.

Lambeau released veterans Clyde Goodnight and Bob Flowers after the Chicago game. According to Lambeau, Goodnight's knee was never the same since injuring it the previous year, and Flowers was a victim of numbers in that the Packers had too many good centers, three of whom were younger than he was and came cheaper than he did at contract time. The truth about Goodnight was his contract; he was making too much money. A week later he was signed by the Washington Redskins and played out the season with them as a defensive back.

Before the next game, Lambeau dropped a bomb on everybody, including and especially the club's executive committee. The *Press-Gazette* reported:

"Curly Lambeau, founder of the Green Bay Packers and for 30 years the team's head coach as well as its vice-president and general manager, today placed his three assistants in charge of the club's field operations.

"For the time being, Lambeau announced, during workouts

The Lambeau Years — Part Three

and games the team will be handled by Line Coach Tom Stidham, Backfield Coach Bob Snyder and Defense Coach Charles Brock.

"Lambeau, meanwhile, will devote his time to rebuilding the club and to the manifold duties connected with his position as vice-president and general manager. He will confine his coaching, he said, to acting in an advisory capacity.

"Announcement of the change in Packer policy after 30 years, during which the club won six world championships under Lambeau and finished out of the first division only once, followed a special meeting of the Packer executive committee called at Lambeau's request last Monday night.

Wants Spirited Organization

" 'Under this arrangement,' Lambeau said today, 'I feel I can do the ball club more good. The duties of officers of a major league club, especially the head coach and the general manager, have increased so much in recent seasons that it is impossible for one man to do justice to three positions.

" 'I have three of the outstanding assistants in football, men in whom I have the utmost confidence, and I know that they can carry on the field operations successfully, leaving me to do what must be done to get Green Bay back in the championship class.

" 'My one aim is to have a solid, spirited organization from the waterboy on up and to build the Packers into a championship club again. And that is exactly what we intend to do under this new arrangement.'

Complete Surprise: Fischer

"Emil R. Fischer, president of the Packer corporation, said the executive committee had accepted Lambeau's proposal.

" 'It was a complete surprise to the executive committee,' said Fischer, 'but Curly feels he can be of greater service to the club under present circumstances, and we therefore were in no position to demur. After all, it must be remembered that Curly has been coaching for 30 years in the toughest football in America and I think all of us realized that some day, the way the business has grown, there must come a time when he would have to delegate some of his duties. We feel he could not have picked three better men than Snyder, Stidham and Brock to put his plan into effect.' "

The shock of Lambeau's announcement was enough to cause the stock of the Packers to drop to "Great Depression" depths all by itself, especially since it came just two days before the next game which was against the Los Angeles Rams, the possessors of the most potent air attack in the NFL. LA had Bob Waterfield and Norm Van Brocklin throwing, and Elroy Hirsch and Tom Fears receiving. All four of these stars could be found in the Professional Football Hall of Fame when their playing careers were over. The only future Hall-of-Famer on the Packers' roster was Canadeo. Four against one wasn't very good odds. Still reeling from Lambeau's announcement, the Packers were demolished, 48-7, for the worst home defeat in their history to that time. As Bob Snyder said it so aptly after the game, "We just got the hell kicked out of us pretty good."

The Packers flew to New York for a Friday night contest with the Bulldogs. Many of them limped off the plane when it landed at La Guardia Airport. Larry Craig, Dick Wildung, Ed Smith, Ken Kranz, Bob Cifers, Irv Comp, Lou Ferry, and Don Wells were all suffering wounds that would either keep them out of action or limit their play. Lambeau said that all those injuries worried him, and he didn't expect the Packers' chances of winning to be very good. At a meeting of the Quarterback Club the night before, Don Hutson said, "We're in for a rough season . . . We don't have a good football team . . . We're going to lose some more ball games this season, probably a lot more . . . " Despite all these negatives, the Packers completely dominated the hapless Bulldogs, 19-0, before a meager crowd of 5,099 fans at the Polo Grounds. The win ended their nine-game regular season losing streak, and it gave the fans hope for the future.

During the following week, Lambeau decided that Wells, Ed Smith, and Larry Olsonoski were too banged up to be of any further use to the Packers in '49, so he released them and signed men to replace them. Steve Pritko was a veteran defensive end who had played with the New York Giants, Los Angeles Rams,

The Lambeau Years — Part Three

and New York Bulldogs and who had gone to college at Villanova. Glen Johnson hailed from Arizona State and had played for the New York Yankees of the AAC in '48 and part of '49. Jack Kirby was a halfback who had been released by the Redskins earlier in the year.

With renewed hope, the Packers traveled to Milwaukee to take on the defending Western Division champion Chicago Cardinals. The Cards were just as strong in '49 as they had been during the past two seasons, and Green Bay hadn't found the win column against the Redbirds since their first meeting in '46. Chicago had the same record as the Packers (1-2-0), having lost to the powerful Bears and Eagles, but their defeats weren't nearly as bad those suffered by Green Bay at the hands of the Bears and Rams. A crowd of 18,464 turned out at State Fair Park to witness the game that saw the Cards snatch four Green Bay passes out of the air and recover two Packer fumbles. The first interception was run back for a TD, and another thwarted a Green Bay drive that had taken the Packers to the Chicago four. One fumble was turned into an easy field goal by the Cardinals, and another stopped another good Green Bay drive deep in Chicago turf. The Packers had better statistics for the game, but the Cardinals had the points, winning, 39-17.

Next up for the Packers was a trip to California and a second game against the division–leading Rams (4-0-0). If the men from Green Bay were to have any hopes of a title in '49, they had to defeat Los Angeles. To achieve that goal, Bob Snyder continued to rebuild the passing attack that had shown signs of promise the week before when Stan Heath completed eight passes against the Cards. The coaching staff hoped that the Rams could be had with a solid aerial game, and they might have gotten their wish if the young Packers hadn't self–destructed by throwing three interceptions and losing four fumbles. Once again, turnovers made big losers out of the Packers, 35-7.

Back in Wisconsin again with nothing more to play for than pride, the 1-4-0 Packers continued to work on their passing game as they prepared for a collision with the Lions in Milwaukee. R.G. Lynch, the sports editor for *The Milwaukee Journal*, called on Milwaukee fans to come in droves to support the struggling Packers, not so much because they needed the moral support as much as they were beginning to get desperate financially. The Packers needed the revenue from a sellout. They didn't get anything near a sellout as only 10,855 loyal fans turned out to see the Pack down Detroit, 16-14, for their last win of 1949.

Although it was only the halfway mark of the season, the Packers (2-4-0) weren't out of the race mathematically. Green Bay was only four games behind the Rams (6-0-0). Los Angeles could still be caught, but the big question was: By whom? The Bears (3-3-0)? The Cardinals (2-4-0) who weren't playing much better than the Packers. Certainly not Detroit (1-5-0). One more Lion loss or Ram win and the season was over for the Motor City eleven. The Packers needed a miracle, but Lambeau had used up his allotment of wonders. Green Bay had no wings left, and the prayers of the fans were going unanswered. The Packers were in for another crash similar to the one they'd suffered in '48.

In an effort to bolster the team for the invasion of Wrigley Field to play the Bears, Lambeau released rookie center Ralph Olsen and picked up center Roger Harding on waivers from the Rams. Harding had four pro seasons under his belt; one each with the Lions and Eagles and the last two with the Rams. The move hardly helped as the Bears kept the Packers out of the end zone again, dominating Green Bay, 24-3. The only bright spot in the game was Tony Canadeo's rushing. He gained 98 yards to give him a league–leading 644 for the season.

With Irv Comp and Jack Jacobs, Green Bay's two best pass defenders, on the sidelines, the Packers took on the aerial minded New York Giants at City Stadium in a rare November home game. Charley Connerly had a field day, completing 15 of 28 for 347 yards, and although the Packers managed to pick off four of his tosses, he also threw four TD passes to lead the Giants to a 30-10 victory. Tony Canadeo gained another 71 yards to up his season total to 715.

Canadeo gained 116 yards against the Pittsburgh Steelers in Milwaukee the next week, but only 5,483 fans turned out to see him do it. If the other Packers had played as well, the game might have been closer, maybe even a win, but the Steelers swamped the Pack, 30-7.

Canadeo had another big day against the Cardinals in Chicago, gaining 122 yards, but the Packers came away pikers again, losing 41-21. Green Bay surrendered 34 points to the Big Red in the first 20 minutes of the game, then roared back with all of their scoring before halftime. Unfortunately, the Packers were unable to do anything right in the second half.

During the week, Bob Cifers was dumped from the team.

The Packers hit rock bottom the following week when they fell into the cellar of the Western Division. The Redskins took Green Bay's measure to the tune of 30-0. The Packers were never in the game. Proof of that was the fact that Canadeo gained a mere 29 yards on 15 carries.

Right after the Washington game, Lambeau gave end Ted Cook his walking papers. This was strange because Cook was the team's leading receiver; some might have said Cook was Green Bay's only decent receiver. Everyone questioned this move by Lambeau, even Art Daley who usually defended Lambeau's decisions.

The Packers closed out the season with a trip to Detroit and a fight for fourth place. Green Bay's hollow, shallow secondary allowed the Lions to pass at will but not score much. The Lions won anyway, going away winners, 21-7, and taking fourth place in the division.

To date, 1949 was the worst season in the history of the Green Bay Packers. They finished dead last in the Western Division with a 2-10-0 record. Only the New York Bulldogs were worse at 1-10-1. The season lacked excitement on the field, but the action off the field was another story entirely.

§ § §

11

Peace At Last

On December 12, 1948, New York newspaper writer Joe King predicted the San Francisco 49ers and Cleveland Browns would join the National Football League and that the All-America Conference would fold up. That same day Admiral Jonas Ingram, the AAC's commissioner, predicted a settlement between the warring leagues within 30 days. Both men were wrong.

After negotiations between the two circuits broke off in January, the battles for players resumed, and both sides spewed the routine rhetoric at each other in the press which remained neutral for the most part until late in August when Bert Bell forgot that he was living in America where people have been guaranteed certain inalienable rights since our forefathers wrote the Constitution and gave us the Bill of Rights as a legacy. With imperial wisdom, Bell prevented sportscaster Tom Harmon from doing the play-by-play of the Rams-Redskins exhibition game because Harmon had done the broadcast of an LA Dons game earlier that summer. Bell's interference with the press aroused the indignation of the media and brought censorship from Southern California chapter of the Football Writers Association. (It's amazing how times changed. It's hard to imagine Bell's successor, Pete Rozelle, telling the American Broadcasting Company that they couldn't do Monday Night Football because that network telecast games of the United States Football League.)

The AAC elected a new commissioner in 1949, and like his predecessor, O.O. "Scrappy" Kessing was quite outspoken about the football war. He stated that the rivalry between the two leagues was "silly and stupid and should be stopped at once." And just like Admiral Ingram, he made good sense.

As autumn settled over the country and football was in full swing everywhere, new rumors about a settlement of the war began cropping up. Of course, Bell discounted them, saying they had "no foundation in fact." Columnist Irv Kupcinet expressed a different opinion when he wrote: "An arrangement has been worked out by interested members of both leagues which find only three members of the All-America conference surviving the merger — Cleveland's Browns, San Francisco's 49ers, and the New York Yankees."

Another rumor had it that owners from Chicago (Halas), Washington (Marshall), and New York (Tim Mara) had okayed the merger that Kupcinet outlined. The oddity there was these three men represented three-fourths of the old-time "Big Four" of the NFL. The fourth franchise and its man were Green Bay and Curly Lambeau. This raised a new question: Was Lambeau no longer the power that he had been in the '30s? Time would tell.

The next day George Halas issued a denial of his involvement in any merger talks, saying, "Nobody from the All-America conference has contacted me, nor do I intend to contact anybody in their organization."

In support of Halas, George Marshall vowed that he would block any attempt to merge the two leagues. "Under certain conditions," he said he might favor inclusion of the Cleveland Browns and San Francisco 49ers. Under NFL rules, any move to increase the size of the league required unanimous consent of all the owners. He said he would support the Browns and 49ers only if:

"(1) Their applications included sound financial plans for operation.

"(2) The NFL scheduling of the two clubs did not materially add to the cost of his operation."

Both teams would have to convince the NFL that they could gross $540,000 each for a season of their home games. Of the other AAC teams, he said that they either encroached on NFL teams or they were bad financial risks. Asked if he would okay more clubs if their location did not encroach on so-called NFL territory, he said Cincinnati and St. Louis "certainly offer tremendous possibilities."

All was quiet on the football war front until the middle of November when Ted Collins, owner of the New York Bulldogs, signed George Ratterman, quarterback, away from the Buffalo Bills of the AAC. Ratterman signed a four-year pact that would begin in 1950. To add insult to injury, Collins bragged that seven of the 10 NFL teams would make money. His club would lose money, but not much. He also said that all seven of the AAC clubs would lose money. This set off remarks by Mickey McBride, the owner of the Cleveland Browns, and Scrappy Kessing, the AAC commissioner. McBride said: "The National league is dominated by a couple of persons who would treat me as small fry. I've never been pushed around by anyone and I don't intend to let anyone push me around now." Anyone who knew anything about the inner workings of the NFL would have figured out that he meant Halas and Marshall and maybe Mara and Lambeau, too, besides Bert Bell.

After the Collins raid, everyone expected a counter-attack by someone in the AAC, but nothing happened. This was really strange.

Then it happened.

Peace!

The headline on front page of the Green Bay *Press-Gazette* for December 9, 1949 said it all:

Football Leagues Announce Merger

The sub-heads revealed more surprises:

13 Teams, Including Packers, In Set-Up

Fischer To Be President of National

Division; Three A-A Clubs Are Added

The Baltimore Colts, San Francisco 49ers, and Cleveland Browns would be merged into a new league that would be named the National-American Football League. The Buffalo Bills were to be merged with the Browns; the Dons and Rams were supposed to consolidate; and Ted Collins bought the New York Yankees and received a 10-year lease to play in Yankee Stadium. The only AAC team that was supposed to lose out completely was the Chicago Hornets. Six players on the Yankees were to go to the New York Giants as part of their compensation for the merger. Bert Bell would be the commissioner of the new organization, while Scrappy Kessing took a hike. Daniel Sherby of the Browns would be the president of the American Division.

Immediately, rumors began that Houston would be awarded a franchise so the NAFL would have an even number of teams at 14.

Larry Craig made a poignant remark when the Packers were informed of the merger: "Now you guys will have to go to work. There'll be a lot of ball players looking for your jobs nesxt season." Craig was retiring.

Of course, the best laid plans of mice and football moguls never quite work as planned. The people of Buffalo refused to let their team be shunted into limbo; they fought back. Because of this strong community movement in Buffalo to raise money for the Bills and keep the team afloat, Bert Bell included Buffalo in a tentative schedule for the new NAFL.

Just as rumors had said in December, wealthy Texas oil man, Glenn McCarthy, requested a franchise for Houston in early January, 1950. McCarthy was hoping that a franchise would be granted to either Dallas or New Orleans at the same time with Seymour Weiss, the New Orleans hotelman, owning the Louisiana team. Dallas businessman Edward T. Dicker also made an application for a franchise to be placed in his city. The possibility of a 16-team league was being seriously considered by the NAFL magnates as they headed toward their annual winter meetings in Philadelphia.

But before the NAFL magnates met on January 19, the Dallas franchise application was withdrawn. Dicker said he didn't think Texas could support two pro teams at this time.

The folks in Buffalo weren't about to give up. Their fund drive had raised $261,640 in cash and season ticket sales of $298,299.60 on 14,726 tickets. This put them over their goal of $500,000, which was the approximate amount George Marshall had said it would take to operate a team in the pros.

Prior ot the NAFL meetings, Lambeau proposed a dual draft: one for the college talent and one for the players of the AAC teams who weren't included in the merger. The New York teams would be kept out of the second draft because they were allowed to split up the players on the AAC New York Yankees. Lambeau also wanted all previous deals involving draft choices to be nullified, such as the one where the Bears traded Bobby Layne to the Bulldogs for their number one choice in 1950. His proposal was intended to strengthen the really weak teams, meaning the Packers, Lions, and Colts. The Bulldogs were already stronger because of the addition of the NY Yankee players. Lambeau suggested that the Packers, Lions, and Colts each be given two choices in the second, third, and fourth rounds.

Naturally, Lambeau's proposals were turned down.

To the surprise of many people, the NAFL owners turned down the Buffalo and Houston applications to join league. Houston was denied because no one cared to play in Texas, and Buffalo was turned down because two late season games would have to be played in Buffalo and no one wanted to run the risk of playing in winter weather, meaning they feared bad weather would mean small gate receipts which was why the Packers were never allowed to play in Green Bay late in the year.

The alignment of the new NAFL was finally set. The Packers, Chicago Bears, New York Bulldogs, Detroit Lions, Baltimore Colts, Los Angeles Rams, and San Francisco 49ers made up the National Division, while the New York Giants, Philadelphia Eagles, Pittsburgh Steelers, Washington Redskins, Cleveland Browns, and Chicago Cardinals made up the American Division. The Colts would the "swing" team that would play every other team in the league once, while the others played their division rivals twice each and would have one game against a team from the other division.

1946 Packers: Front row, left to right: Forte, Miller, Smith, Brock, Bennett, Nussbaumer, McKay, Canadeo, Rohrig, Schlinkman, Letlow, Craig, Luhn. Second row: Head Coach Lambeau, Riddick, Aberson, Lee, Wells, Adkins, Pregulman, Neal, Lipscomb, Flowers, Sparlis, Mitchell, Goodnight, Coach Kiesling, Coach Hutson. Back Row: Trainer Jorgenson, Asst. Trainer O'Brien, Fritsch, Gatewood, Comp, Odson, Croft, Ray, Zupek, Kuusisto, Keuper, Wildung.

1947 Packers: Front row, left to right: Asst. Trainer O'Brien, McKay, Wilson, Canadeo, Cody, Rohrig, Brock, Schlinkman, Wells, Goodnight, Craig, Trainer Jorgenson. Second row: McPartland, Davis, Fritsch, B. Forte, Keuper, Flowers, Luhn, Gatewood, A. Forte, Gillette, Jacobs, Tassos, Coach Hutson. Third row: Coach Kiesling, Smith, Skoglund, Croft, Neal, Lipscomb, Ray, Odson, Comp, Bell, Wildung, Head Coach Lambeau.

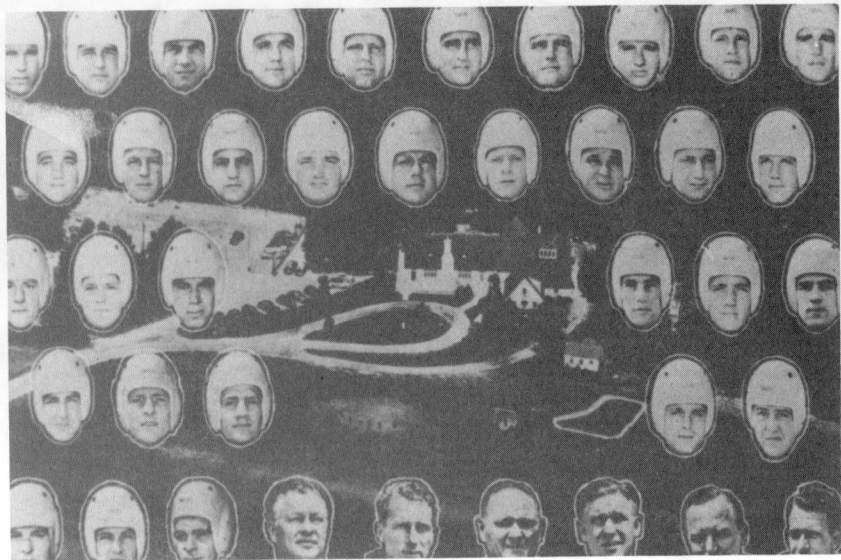

1948 Packers: Bottom row, left to right: Vogds, Earhart, Rhodemyre, Head Coach Lambeau, Coach Hutson, Coach Kiesling, Coach Molenda, Trainer Jorgenson, Asst. Trainer O'Brien. Second row: Baxter, Moss, Olsonoski, Smith, Deeks. Third row: Davis, Skoglund, Jacobs, Provo, Cook, Girard. Fourth row: Wildung, Wells, Forte, Odson, Schlinkman, Wilson, Tassos, Bell, Cody. Top row: Ray, Craig, Canadeo, Fritsch, Flowers, Comp, Neal, Goodnight, Lipscomb, Luhn.

1949 Packers: 82 Bell, 25 Canada, 16 Cifers, 51 Comp, 54 Craig, 41 Earhart, 35 Flowers, 64 Fritsch, 36 Girard, 39 Heath, 26 Kelley, 80 Lewis, 38 Luhn, 58 Neal, 19 Olsen, 49 Orlich, 7 Schlinkman, 21 Smith, 15 Tassos, 43 Wells, 44 Ray, 33 Burris, 3 Canadeo, 17 Cody, 48 Cook, 66 Davis, 40 Eason, 18 Ferry, 8 Forte, 57 Gagne, 23 Goodnight, 27 Jacobs, 42 Kranz, 47 Lipscomb, 31 Mastrangeli, 63 Odson, 46 Olsonoski, 22 Rhodemyre, 74 Schroeder, 77 Summerhays, 79 Vogds, 45 Wildung.

Jim Gillete (16) takes off on a long gainer around the left end against the Chicago Cardinals in 1947.

Ed Cody breaks away around the left end against the Bears in 1947. Clyde Goodnight is leading the blocking.

The Packers practice at Rockwood Lodge. At the end of World War II, Curly Lambeau bought Rockwood Lodge for the Packers with the plan to develop it into a training facility. It worked for a while, then the problems began to crop up, such as the hard practice ground that caused a myriad of injuries and the distance to Green Bay that kept fans away. The Lodge burned down in early 1950 just when the corporation needed some hard cash to stay in business.

George Whitney Calhoun, one of the men who made the Packers survive the hard times of the '20s, sits at his desk at the Green Bay Press-Gazette. Lambeau fired Calhoun in 1946 from his post as the Packers' publicity man, and this helped lead to Lambeau's downfall within the organization.

Curly Lambeau leaves Rockwood Lodge. Lambeau was always a natty dresser and a fine figure of a man as this photo shows. No one cared about his Hollywood ways until he began lording them over the people of Green Bay — and the Packers lost more games than they won.

Curly Lambeau's last coaching staff watches game films. From the left are Tom Stidham, Bob Snyder, Lambeau, Charley Brock, and Don Hutson.

The Packers received a visit from NFL Commissioner Bert Bell at Rockwood Lodge. From left to right are Andy Turnbull, the first president of the Packers' corporation; Lambeau; Emil Fischer, the president of the Packers in the late '40s; Bell; and Jerry Clifford, the attorney who did more than any other single individual to keep the Packers alive through 30 years of strife.

In 1949, Green Bay businessmen staged a benefit game on Thanksgiving Day to raise much needed cash for the Packers who were once again on the verge of bankruptcy. This group of old-time players pictured here were, standing left to right, Tiny Engebretsen, Herb Nichols, Lambeau, Jug Earpe, Lavvie Dilweg, Verne Lewellen, and Johnny Blood; kneeling are Charley Brock, Don Hutson, Arnie Herber, and Joe Laws.

This cartoon appeared in the Green Bay Press-Gazette on August 3, 1948. That's supposed to be George W. Calhoun with his chin on his hand, and he's saying, "Rainin' for twelve hours. We'll be lucky to have two or three hundred in the stands this afternoon. We'll lose over two thousand bucks if we play. Maybe we ought to just go home, lie on the couch, and listen to 'Three O'clock In The Morning' or somethin' on the phonograph." Joe Ordens is the man looking out the window and saying, "Yeah, Cal. Do you think we should call it quits, Mr. Turnbull?" With his hands on his hips is Andy Turnbull who is saying, "No, Joe. Listen, Curly. Go out there with your Packers and play that Duluth team . . . rain or shine. If you hope to put across professional football . . ." And, of course, standing in the right foreground is a very young Curly Lambeau. This was Erwin L. Hess's version of the scene in 1922 when the Packers' braintrust was trying to make up their minds about playing the Duluth Kellys on Thanksgiving Day in a rainstorm. Missing from the picture is Nate Abrams. If not totally accurate historically, the cartoon does capture the spirit of the moment.

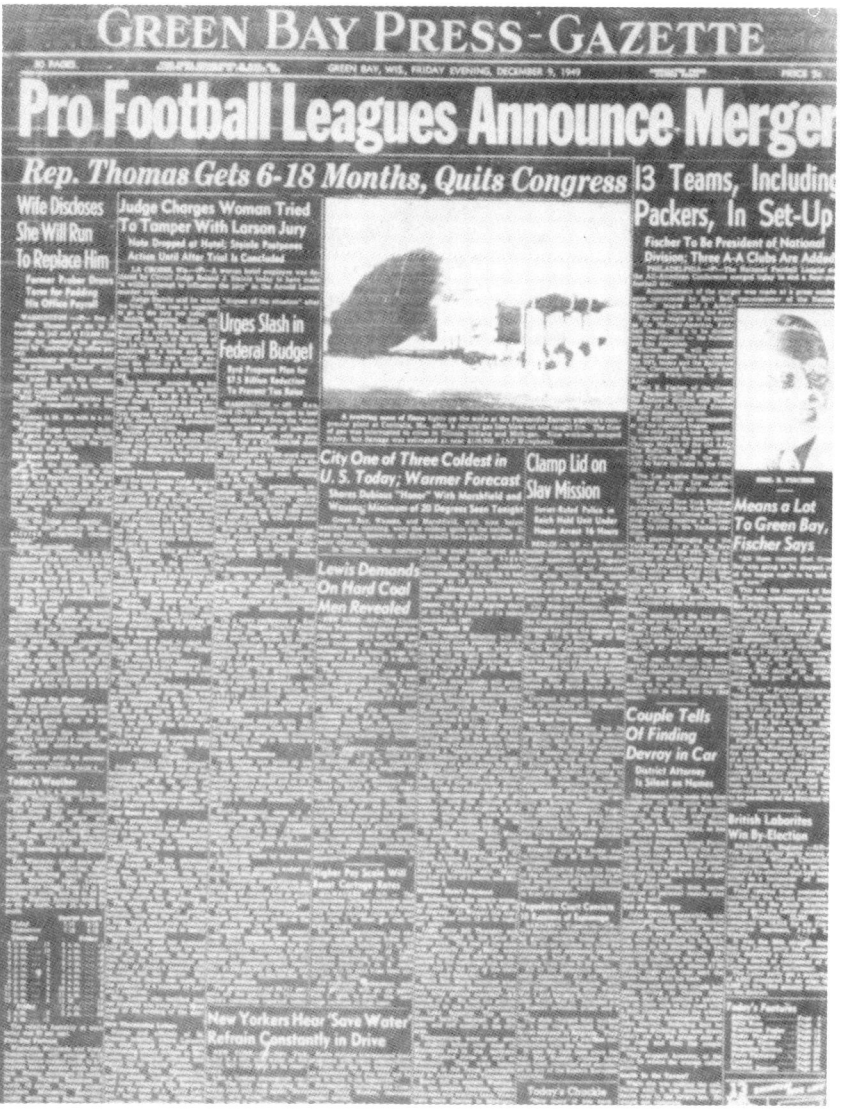

This was the front page of the Green Bay Press-Gazette on December 9, 1949. Like no other city in America, Green Bay loves its football team.

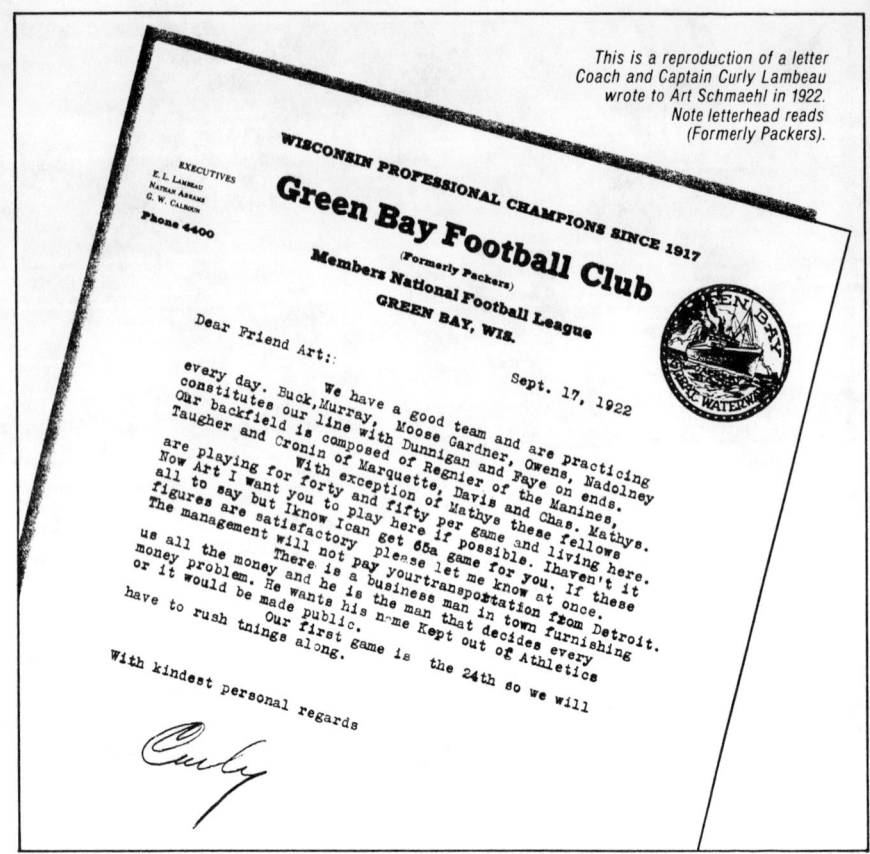

This is a reproduction of a letter Coach and Captain Curly Lambeau wrote to Art Schmaehl in 1922. Note letterhead reads (Formerly Packers).

This is photocopy of a page out of the 1983 Packer Yearbook. Note that the letterhead states plainly that the Green Bay Football Club has been "Wisconsin Professional Champions Since *1917*" and that the team was *formerly* known as Packers. The executives of the club are E.L. Lambeau, Nathan Abrams, and G.W. Calhoun. The letter is signed by Curly Lambeau. This is proof positive that the Packers weren't founded in 1919, but were only nicknamed the Packers that year.

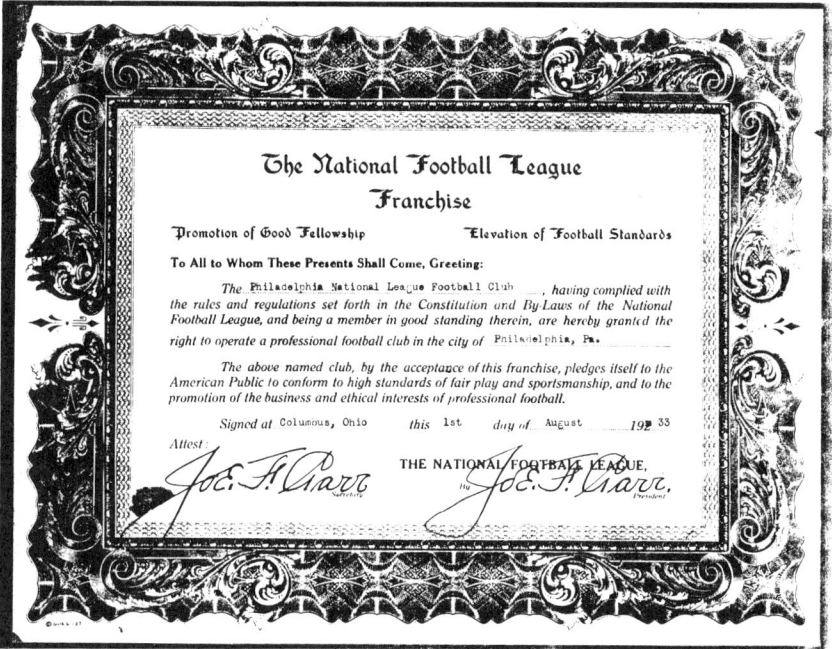

This is a photocopy of the Philadelphia Eagles franchise certificate that was issued on August 1, 1933. The original is on file at the Pro Football Hall of Fame in Canton, Ohio.

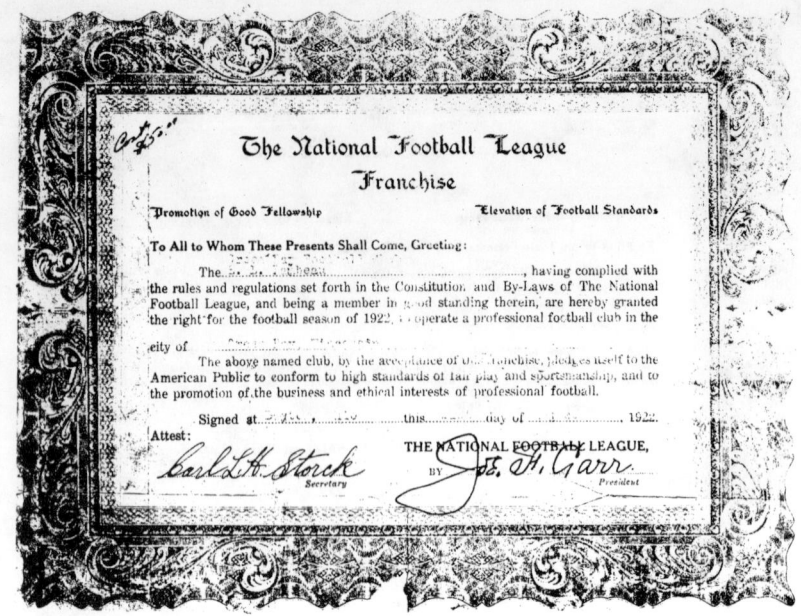

This is a bad photocopy of an already bad photocopy of Curly Lambeau's franchise certificate that was issued to him for the Green Bay Football Club on August 21, 1922. Compare the signatures on both and see how Joe Carr's autograph changed over the years.

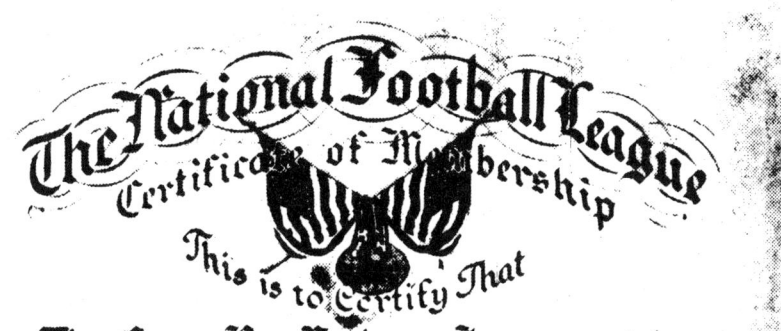

Did you ever see this before? It is the franchise of the Green Bay Packers in the National Football league. It was issued in July 1935 and represents the transfer from the Green Bay Football corporation to the Green Bay Packers, Inc. Its value has been estimated by sports writers around the country from $100,000 to $250,000. Lee Joannes, president of the Green Bay Packers, Inc., declines to estimate its value. He says: "What is the difference how much it's worth, it's not for sale and it is owned by a non-profit corporation. It cannot be transferred without a majority vote of the 461 shares of stock owned by 104 stockholders which would be practically impossible to obtain because a comparatively small number of the shareholders own more than one or two shares and these are mostly manufacturing and mercantile business concerns. It doesn't seem that any of these would vote to send the Packers away from Green Bay."

This alleged franchise certificate appeared in the Green Bay Press-Gazette on November 9, 1945. It bares absolutely no resemblance whatsoever to the two certificates on the previous page. Why? Was it a phony?

It's hard to believe that the Packers ever had to push to sell tickets. This is a Season Ticket Gift Certificate that was sold in 1947 as a Christmas present.

Business wasn't as good as the Packers wished it would be in 1948. So they ran stories like these in the Press-Gazette in order to spur season ticket sales. This article appeared on April 22, 1948.

All but one of the first All-Time Packers Team that was selected by a poll of fans. Left to right, kneeling, are Lavvie Dilweg, Jug Earpe, Buckets Goldenberg, Charley Brock, Mike Michalske, and Don Hutson. In the backfield, left to right, are Johnny Blood, Arnie Herber, Clarke Hinkle, and Verne Lewellyn. Missing is Cal Hubbard.

Walt Schlinkman was a hard-hitting fullback in the late '40s. He breaks through the Cardinals' line with the help of several teammates, including Clyde Goodnight, Nolan Luhn, and Larry Craig.

The man who saved the Packers for the people of Wisconsin and Upper Michigan, Gerald, Clifford.

As on final piece of the new puzzle, the players from the Bills, Hornets, and Dons went into a draft pool.

The two leagues were now one — at last.

But what did this near Armageddon really mean to the history of the Green Bay Packers?

Everything.

§ § §

12
Humpty Dumpty Sat on a Wall...

A lousy record on the field was only the tip of Green Bay's iceberg of problems. The real trouble was behind the scenes, behind closed doors, in the meetings of moguls from both the National Football League and the All–America Conference, in the meetings of the Packers' executive committee, and the cause of those troubles was the man who cried persecution because he spent the off–season basking in California sunshine instead of freezing his butt in sub–arctic Wisconsin.

Prior to Monday, July 28, 1947, Curly Lambeau had been allowed almost absolute power over the operations of the Green Bay Packers, Inc. He was the coach, the general manager, and vice–president of the corporation. He called all the plays — on and off the field. Whatever Curly wanted, Curly got. This was good; the Packers were winners, and money kept flowing into the corporation, allowing Frank Jonet to balance the books every year without using red ink. But on the evening of the aforementioned date, this was all changed.

Just a week before this meeting, Lee Joannes announced that he was retiring as president of the corporation and as a member of the executive committee. He would stay on as a director if the stockholders so desired, but he absolutely had to be relieved of his other duties as president. He cited his involvement in a new business as his reason for retiring. That was for public consumption. As previously stated,[*] the story was much deeper than that.

Joannes retired because he was tired of butting heads with

---

[*] See Chapter 4.

Curly Lambeau and because Lambeau coveted the corporation's presidency. Joannes had been at the helm of the corporate ship since 1930, and he had guided it through some pretty dark waters in the '30s and through World War II. Of course, he had lots of help in these matters, particularly from Frank Jonet and Jerry Clifford. This trio had led the charge that saved the Packers for Green Bay. During this same period, Lambeau had been allowed to run the football team as he saw fit, and the Packers were quite successful on the field, winning five NFL titles, six division crowns, and finishing below .500 only once. Joannes and Lambeau attended all the NFL meetings, winter and summer, together. Through the first five years, Lambeau went as head coach and general manager, while Joannes represented the corporate end of things. After Lambeau was elected a vice-president in 1940, he was allowed to take an active role in the inner workings of the NFL because he was a corporate officer of the Green Bay Packers, Inc. It was at this point that he and Joannes began to part ways openly, although the real schism had begun seven years earlier.

After the 1932 season, Johnny Blood arranged for the Packers to play a series of exhibition games in Hawaii and California.** On the boat going to the Islands, lineman Joe Zeller struck up a conversation with a lady. Zeller was doing fairly well with the woman until he introduced her to his boss, Curly Lambeau, who moved in and took charge. Lambeau found her to be more than attractive; she was downright friendly and free to make the passage more pleasant for both of them. This tryst might have carried over to Lambeau's stay in Hawaii and then California; gossip of the day was uncertain about that. It was, however, the first *affaire d'amour* that Lambeau would embark upon during his visits to California. One thing was certain about the 1932-33 trip: Lambeau was seen with actress Myrna Kennedy in Hollywood, and she did sit on the Packers' bench when they played in Los Angeles. She might have been the object of his attention or she might not have been. No matter. Lambeau sent word back to Green Bay

** See Chapter 1 of *The History of the Green Bay Packers, The Lambeau Years, Part Two.*

after the last exhibition in California that he was going on a scouting trip through Arizona and Texas before returning home. His players knew better. He was taking his Hollywood honey, whoever she might have been, for some fun in the desert sun.

By the time Lambeau did return to Green Bay, tongues were wagging about his extended stay in the Southwest. Of course, the gossip was started by some of his players who returned to Green Bay ahead of him. No one paid much attention to the talk at the time because Curly was Curly, Mr. Football, the man who put Green Bay on the map with his three-time champions; Curly would never do such things. And if he did, so what? He was Curly Lambeau, and he had done so much for Green Bay. No sense in making a big deal out of a few rumors started by some guys who were probably just jealous of Curly anyway. Besides, it all happened out West, which meant it had nothing to do with life in Green Bay.

So was the thinking in Green Bay for the most part. Not everybody agreed that looking the other way was the best thing to do, however. Lee Joannes was among the latter who privately cautioned Curly to restrain himself from such escapades because they reflected on the Packers and the city of Green Bay.

Marguerite Lambeau, Curly's wife, was also in the minority when it came to looking the other way. After Curly took another extended trip to California at the end of the '33 season that resulted in more embarrassing rumors for her, she divorced Curly.

Possibly another casualty of Lambeau's indiscretion was Joe Zeller. The big guard from Indiana didn't return to the Packers in '33.

Free from marital constraints, Lambeau began to spend more and more time in California after the season. Scouting trips, he called these excursions, as he charged many of his traveling expenses to the Packers.

When Lambeau returned to Green Bay in 1940, he brought a new bride with him. The following year, he came home alone, having gone through another divorce, but that didn't mean the lady was finished with Curly. She showed up in Green Bay during the week of the Packers second pre-season game. When Lambeau heard that she was in town, he put out the word to the local hostelries to turn on their *No Vacancy* signs to her, and they co-operated quite willingly because Curly was Curly, Mr. Football, the man who put Green Bay on the map; never mind that the lady was very much pregnant with child, Lambeau's child, or so she claimed. Curly said differently. The unborn infant was allegedly fathered by his ex-wife's paramour, who was rumored to be one of Lambeau's former players, one who had played for the Packers in 1940 but who wasn't on the roster in '41.

No matter. The point was the lady said Lambeau was the father, and she was in Green Bay to establish residency in order to use the courts to force Lambeau to pay child support as well as the hospital bills when her time came to deliver. When she was thrown out of the Northland Hotel and no other hotel would accept her, she turned to the only friend she had in town: Mrs. Arnie Herber.

The Herbers welcomed the former Mrs. Lambeau into their home because she had no other place to go and because she didn't have enough money to leave town. When Lambeau learned of this, he ordered Arnie to put his ex-wife out of Herber's house; Arnie had until Monday morning to do this simple chore or risk being fired from the team. Herber, much to his credit, refused to buckle under Lambeau's threats. The lady stayed, and on Monday, Lambeau fired Herber from the Packers, stating in the newspapers that it was because Herber couldn't control his weight. Arnie Herber became another casualty of Lambeau's California connections.

During World War II, many professional athletes were drafted into the armed forces, while others volunteered to serve their country in its time of need. Of course, not every man thought it was his patriotic duty to lug a rifle through the hedgerows of France or the jungles of the Pacific. Some wanted to stay home and play their professional sport. In order to do this, they had to have a physical defect, such as Ted Fritsch had with his bad ear, or they had to have a job that was vital to the national defense. Even if they did have a defense job, they faced travel restrictions by the government that had the potential to prevent them from playing.

Due to these government rules, Lambeau conceived the idea of stockpiling players for the Packers by giving them jobs in Green Bay, or the immediate area, that were defense-related. This wasn't exactly a positive display of patriotic spirit by Lambeau. In fact, his behavior throughout the war years showed a definite lack of patriotism unless the activity was connected with football, and this rankled Joannes who opposed Lambeau's plan to bring dozens of players to Green Bay on the dual grounds that should they not make the team they would be stranded in Green Bay working at a menial defense job or they would be forced to enlist in the armed forces; either way, their services wouldn't be available to other teams, which would work to the Packers' advantage in the short run, according to Lambeau, and would work their disadvantage in the long run, according to Joannes.

Other minor collisions occurred between Lambeau and Joannes in the succeeding years, but the two that stood out the most were the firings of Dr. W.W. Kelly as team physician and George Whitney Calhoun as publicity director. In neither case did Lambeau consult with the executive committee before acting nor did he even have the decency to go to either man and tell him to his face that he was being replaced. Both acts were considered to be as dastardly and as cowardly as the assassination of Abraham Lincoln by John Wilkes Booth.

Lambeau's complete disregard of such old friends as Kelly and Calhoun, men who had gone that extra mile for him when he needed them, aroused the suspicions of another old friend. Jerry Clifford, the legal genius who had saved the Packers for the fans on two occasions already, mounted his white charger and prepared to do battle for Packerdom once again.

Shortly after Calhoun's dismissal and replacement by George Strickler, a man who might have been popular in some circles but who was an outsider to Cal's friends, Clifford began investigating Curly Lambeau's activities on behalf of the Packers. Working with Frank Jonet, the attorney was able to determine that Lambeau was abusing his expense account. Whether intentionally or not was yet to be determined, but that was neither here nor there. The point was Lambeau needed to be put on a leash or he would personally bankrupt the corporation.

Clifford took his facts and figures to Joannes. The president of the corporation wanted to dump Lambeau right then and there, but Clifford cautioned him against making such a move. The private feud between Joannes and Lambeau was a well known fact in Green Bay. Any move to oust Curly would most likely be misconstrued as an act of vengeance by Joannes and the executive committee for Lambeau's treatment of Kelly and Calhoun. Clifford reminded Joannes that, to the average fan, Curly was Curly, Mr. Football, the man who put Green Bay on the map; the newspapers, with their help, had spent most of the last three decades immortalizing the Belgian; you don't fire a man like that; you control him.

But Leland Joannes was the wrong man to do the controlling of Curly Lambeau. The job needed someone with more patience, with less hostility. Lambeau would never accept restraints from Joannes, not without a fight, a real out-in-the-open battle, a struggle where one man had to win and the fans would be big losers. Joannes would have to step down from the top post in the corporation and let someone else put a bell on Curly the cat; but if he did resign, Lambeau, who was known to be coveting the presidency of the Packers, would surely make a try for the office, an attempt that Joannes and Clifford and others would be forced to oppose openly. Their opposition could have a disastrous effect on the organization. It could polarize the directors and the stockholders and the fans, and that would lead to total destruction of the corporation. Lambeau had to be stopped from running for president, and then he had to be controlled by someone who could make Lambeau take his medicine and like it. Clifford suggested Emil R. Fischer, president of the Atlas Warehouse and Cold Storage Company in Green Bay, as the man for the position.

Fischer had been on the board of directors since 1936. He knew Lambeau and Joannes well, and he knew about their feud. He was able to remain neutral and stay friends with both men. Even so, he felt his first duty was to the stockholders and fans of the Green Bay Packers. He accepted the challenge of putting a leash on the Belgian and let himself be elected president of the corporation at the stockholders meeting of July 25, 1947.

Clifford then made a motion to increase the board of directors from 22 to 25 and the executive committee from nine to 12. The stockholders filled two of three new directorships with William J. Servotte and Russell W. Bogda. Replacing Joannes and filling the three new spots on the executive committee were Milan J. Boex, Harvey Lhost, Bogda, and Servotte.

The first meeting of new executive committee, now consisting of 12 members, was held the following Monday night, July 28, 1947. (The date of this meeting is important as will be shown later.) The article in the *Press-Gazette* failed to mention who attended the meeting, but it has to be assumed that at least eight men were present, including Lambeau because he was in town and he was eager to show the new members of the committee that he was the real power in the organization.

The committee determined that running a professional football team was too much for one man to handle, meaning Lambeau had too much to do and needed some help; therefore, a new system for running the corporation was proposed and put into effect. The decision was made to divide the executive committee into sub-committees. President Fischer and Lambeau would be members of every group because it was felt that their input was necessary to the success of the operation. The sub-committees were:

Contracts and publicity — Andy Turnbull, chairman, Gerry Clifford, and Milan Boex; finance — H.G. Wintgens, chairman, William J. Servotte, and Russ Bogda; grounds — Fred Leicht, chairman, H.J. Bero, and Harvey Lhost; legal and league affairs — Gerry Clifford and Lambeau.

No longer would all matters concerning the team be left in the hands of Curly Lambeau. The executive committee would be assisting him in almost everything except coaching the players.

If Lambeau objected to the new plan initially, he failed to voice his discontent in the pages of the *Press-Gazette*. He went about his job as usual and put together a team that came within nine points of winning four games and copping the division title. It wasn't until the middle of the following year when he realized what a loser he had for a team that he began to show his true feelings for the reorganization of the corporation, but by then it was too late to do anything about the changes.

Or was it?

§ § §

13
Humpty Dumpty Started to Fall...

Exactly where Lambeau got the idea to buy Rockwood Lodge proved impossible to discover, but the fact that he initiated the purchase wasn't. Lambeau convinced the executive committee that the lodge was exactly what the Packers needed to make them the classiest organization in the National Football League When prospective players heard about it, he said, they would jump at the chance to come to Green Bay to play their pro ball. Lambeau was wrong. Many of the players resented being treated like they were in the armed forces or college again. They were adults and expected to be treated as such.

As previously stated, in the fall of '48, Jerry Atkinson of Prange's said at a luncheon of Green Bay businesspeople: "Many of us in Green Bay have somehow dropped our close affection for the team; maybe we've taken them for granted too much." Atkinson blamed this on the fact that the Packers were "out of town", meaning they were practicing and living at Rockwood Lodge, and this put the townspeople out of touch with the players.

This was exactly what Lambeau wanted. He wanted his players segregated from the fans so they could concentrate on playing football from the start of training camp until the last game was played in December. It was his feeling that living in town was distracting them from this purpose. Lambeau failed to understand that not everyone lived and breathed football like he did. Some people had other interests in life. From his earliest days in the game, he was nearly impossible to live with during the season, growing more tense with each day of the week until game day arrived, and in those days when the Packers won many more than they lost, he barely took more than an evening to celebrate a victory before he was thinking and talking and planning the next game. And when the Packers lost! He was worse.

Another sad fact about Lambeau was his reluctance to accept the blame for the Packers' misfirings and misfortunes on the field. Typical of Curly was how he blamed his assistants, Walt Kiesling and Bo Molenda, for the team's worst-ever showing in '48. Kiesling was quoted by the *Associated Press*'s Hugh Fullerton right after Christmas that year as saying, "The Packers need 11 or 12 good new players to form a winning team; they weren't available on the draft list, either." Lambeau reacted by not renewing Kiesling contract, stating that "Kies is one of the finest line coaches in the country, but he should, in the interest of his health, take a year's vacation from football and all other strenuous activities." Kiesling was ill twice during the previous season for a week at a time, but he refused to take the time off. As for Molenda, Curly just dumped him. Kiesling and Molenda landed on their feet, however. Kies found employment with the Steelers after being "nudged aside" by Lambeau, and Molenda signed on as the backfield coach with the Chicago Hornets, formerly the Rockets, of the AAC.

After the first game of the season in '49, Lambeau read the handwriting on the wall that stated simply: The Green Bay Packers are worse than mediocre. Not willing to take the blame for a repeat of the '48 campaign, he made his suspicious announcement that he would cease to be the field coach and would be an advisory coach in the press box for the remainder of the schedule, handing the coaching duties to his trio of assistants, Bob Snyder, Tom Stidham, and Charley Brock.*

Lambeau was really saying that the Packers were in deep financial trouble and when the crisis came, as it surely would, he didn't want to be blamed for it.

Although he wasn't the first to recognize the problem, R.G. Lynch, the sports editor for *The Milwaukee Journal*, was the first to try to do something to help the Packers. He wrote an open letter to the football fans of the Cream City which is quoted verbatim

---

* See Chapter 10.

here because to abridge it would detract from its importance in the history of the Green Bay Packers:

"Milwaukee sport fans have got to face the facts and decide whether or not they want major league sports. It is time they understood that big league sports — baseball, football, hockey, basketball — have become big business. A club can drown quickly in a flood of red ink. So the fans must realize that to have major league sports they must support teams, year in and year out, winning or losing. The Oshkosh All-Stars folded up after last season with some $70,000 in losses, and Milwaukee was partly responsible, for Oshkosh looked to Milwaukee for help and did not get it. Instead, the Stars lost about $10,000 on their games here.

"Now, it is the Green Bay Packers who need help. Really need it. If it was merely a matter of making money or losing it, this column would not be written. But it is a matter of survival. There is a chance that the Packers may go the way of the Oshkosh All-Stars. The chance is so real that it may depend on the attendance at the remaining home games, here and in Green Bay. The Packers have no millionaire owner to write off losses. The club is a community affair.

"The Packers drew about $44,000 at the recent Chicago Cardinal game. They need $60,000 at state fair park (sic) to break even. And it is not enough to break even on home games, for the $20,000 guarantee which they get for road games does not cover the overhead. Only at one or two games do the Packers have any chance to collect substantially more than the guarantee.

"If the support at the two remaining Milwaukee games is not better, the season could become a debacle for the Packers and create a financial crisis.

"Milwaukee is just at the stage of blossoming into a bigtime city. A fine sports area is nearing completion. An outdoor sports stadium is about to be started. The machinery is in motion to see about bringing the St. Louis Browns franchise here.

"It might be a calamity at this stage if the Packers flopped in Milwaukee simply because they had a losing team. The

American League owners might say, 'Why move to Milwaukee? It would be as bad as St. Louis.'

"Over the years, the Green Bay Packers have provided a good deal more entertainment for Milwaukee and Wisconsin fans than the price of admission paid for — yes, they provided something more, a big spiritual lift at times. The writer feels sure that thousands of others spent many a Sunday afternoon, as he did, at the radio, season after season, listening and thrilling to the Packer games.

"For the sake of those memories, for the sake of sports in Milwaukee, everybody who can afford the price should go out to state fair park (sic) next Sunday for the Detroit Lions game and again Nov. 20 for the Pittsburgh Steelers game.

"Let's save the Packers."

Milwaukee area fans chose not to heed Lynch's plea as they stayed away from State Fair Park in droves. A mere 10,855 turned out for the Lions game. Possibly, very few of them read Lynch's column; possibly, very few really cared to help the Packers; most likely, they went apathetically to the corner bar to watch the game on television because not every household had a TV in 1949, but many drinking establishments did. Those people who did have a television probably invited friends over to watch the game, and of course, refreshments were served, probably the alcohol variety. The probability that many fans watched the game on television makes the most sense for two reasons: (1) Why spend money to watch a loser; and (2) drinking made the game more palatable.

After the poor showing by Milwaukee area fans, Art Daley joined the crusade in the *Press-Gazette*:

"Much has been said pro and con anent the playing of Packer games in Milwaukee; the attendance there; and the professional football situation in general. Without taking sides, we'd like to present both views of the Milwaukee setup and touch on other points along the way.

"Attendance at last Sunday's Packer–Detroit game in Milwaukee, 10,855, has resulted in many Green Bay fans asking the question: 'Why can't all six league games be played in Green Bay?'

"Let's use John Jones, the salesman at any local store, as an example. Mr. and Mrs. Jones attended all three Packer games at City stadium at a cost of $28.80 which includes two $4.80 seats ($9.60) for each game. Now, the question is: Will Jones be willing to double that amount ($57.60) if six games are presented at City stadium each season. Think it over.

"The Packers, being a $500,000 business, must have some assurance — especially in these high-salaried days — that City stadium will be virtually sold out for all six games. Sellouts at the stadium assure the Packers of enough profit to absorb any road losses.

"Most of you Bay residents will recall that in 1933 the Packers played all six games at the stadium. It can be added that half of those games produced virtual sellouts. Attendance at the other three was considered poor. The split in games with Milwaukee started the next season. The season of 1933 indicated that this area could not absorb a full league schedule.

"However, possibly some inducement could be worked out that might guarantee the Packers sellouts for all six games at City stadium. As an example, maybe the price of a six-game season ticket ($57.60) could be reduced to $50 or $52. Start the ticket drive in January, for instance, and permit fans to purchase them on some sort of an installment plan. It would have to be a gigantic drive and would have to cover practically every city in the state — with emphasis on communities in the Fox river valley (sic), Milwaukee, Racine, and Kenosha.

"Playing of six games in Green Bay definitely deserves consideration.

"The other view or present setup — playing three games here and three in Milwaukee — has been taking a beating, so to speak, in the past two seasons (1948-49). The '48 season opened in Milwaukee with a record-breaking crowd for the Packer-Cardinal game but since then attendance has failed to reach 20,000. The attendance dipped with the fortunes of the team. Which seems to prove that Milwaukee will not support a losing team.

"Milwaukee fans apparently take a realistic, cold–blooded (in comparison to Green Bay fans) attitude toward the Packers — similar to that of fans in any large city toward their own pro teams. This is true in New York or Chicago where a losing team in the standings also loses at the gate. In Green Bay and surrounding communities, where the Packers are their pride and joy even in defeat, the fans are more sentimental; they might react, for instance, to a call from the Packers for help at the gate.

"At any rate, fans will get an opportunity to 'answer' that call a week from Sunday when the New York Giants play at City stadium. Roughly, 16,000 of the 25,000-plus seats have been sold.

"The split with Milwaukee was started back in 1934 on a winning–team principle, so to speak. Milwaukee has never seen a loser until the second game in 1948. If the split is continued new promotional ideas based on the 'Wisconsin Team' idea will have to be launched.

"It's no secret that the entire recent history of the Packers is built on the fact that the Packers are a state team. Naturally, it's more advantageous for the Packers to expand to statehood. The Packers certainly have a better 'talking point' in league circles if they represent an entire state — Wisconsin. It must be remembered that other clubs in the National Football league take a practical viewpoint toward football — more specifically, dollars and cents. If they can be assured a cut of a 25,000-plus crowd at every game in Green Bay but must settle for a cut of 18,000 or less at Milwaukee, then they will be happy to play at City stadium. On the other hand, Packer opponents assured of a 28,000 or 30,000 crowd in Milwaukee will naturally want to play there.

"The Packers have faced some pressure, it can be assured, from other clubs on playing games in Milwaukee. The Giants, for instance, never wanted to play in Green Bay — possibly because they (the big city) think they can do wonders in Milwaukee. The Packer–Giant game in Milwaukee last year drew poorly. If you'll pardon the plug, a sellout for the Giant–Packer game here Nov. 13 might change a lot of New York minds.

"Statements in this column are presented today merely as food for thought. In private circles, it is assumed the Packer corporation is discussing the Milwaukee situation but that's all far off yet. All of the returns for the 1949 season aren't in yet and these returns include results of the Packers' next six games. A victory for the Packers over the Bears Sunday or over the Giants in Green Bay the next Sunday would be a terrific boom to community spirit. The reported 'peace' between the National league and All–America conference no doubt will have a bearing on future decisions by the Packer corporation. For one thing, such a peace would sharply reduce operating expenses.

"As a parting word, let's be optimistic about the future — not down in the mouth or pessimistic. Never forget that there will always be a Green Bay Packer team. We have the word of NFL Commissioner Bert Bell for that!"

The question arises here: Was Daley speaking for himself or was he merely fronting for Lambeau as he had done so often in the past, whether wittingly or not?

Quite oddly, just a few days before Daley's column appeared in the newspaper, Lambeau was a guest speaker at the QB club. During the question–and–answer period, he "was asked if there was any truth to the rumor that a group of businessmen planned to buy the Packers and move them to Texas. The coach laughed and added that 'the Packers will always be in Green Bay.'"

Lambeau answered the question by not answering it. He would have made a brilliant politician. He didn't say that *a group of businessmen weren't planning to buy the Packers.* All he said was the Packers would always be in Green Bay. He denied the rumor with a non–denial, that is, he didn't deny the rumor with actual words but with a physical reaction and a reply that really did nothing to address the question.

After Daley's column appeared, Lambeau blamed the pro grid war as the start of Packer financial difficulties but added that "we think there will be peace by the start of 1950." He pointed out: "We've lost money but other clubs have lost much more." Concerning Milwaukee, Lambeau said that "we did well there until after the Cardinal game last year." He declared that "we'd like to play all of our games in Green Bay."

The people of Milwaukee didn't hear about this last remark. Or maybe they did and that was why attendance at the final game in Milwaukee that year was barely 5,000 fans.

On November 11, 1949, Art Daley wrote in his column:

"Attendance at the Packer–Giant game at City stadium Sunday afternoon might have a bearing on any Packer decision to play more than three games in Green Bay next season. During the past few weeks, there has been much discussion — some rumor — on the site of the Packers' home games, Green Bay or Milwaukee. The Packers shifted half their games to Milwaukee in 1933 because the community and area was unable to absorb six contests. After attendance skidded in Milwaukee last year, many fans urged the playing of the entire schedule in Green Bay. In a column at that time, we pointed out that a near sellout would be needed at each of six games here to satisfy visiting clubs and also to make it profitable for the Bays. Unless tomorrow's game is a sellout, the Packers may find it difficult to even consider moving any more games to Green Bay."

Attendance for the Giants game was 21,051. Not a sellout, but better than any one of the three games in Milwaukee that year; better than the last two combined.

As November and the 1949 season wound down, it was becoming quite evident in professional football circles that something had to be done about the Green Bay Packers — one way or the other. Rumors were a dime a dozen, and many of them were positively scary to Packer fans in Green Bay. The most frightening piece of verbal flotsam floating around town was the one that the Packers would no longer be in existence in 1950.

§ § §

14

All the King's Horses and All the King's Men...

On December 18, 1947, a rather curious story was released by the *Associated Press*. It concerned the gathering of the National Football League's annual draft meeting to be held in Pittsburgh the next day.

"Items reported to be disturbing the calm of some owners included:

"1. A suggestion by George Preston Marshall, owner of the Washington Redskins, that the annual game between the league champion and the College All–Stars in Chicago be canceled. Marshall charged the 'game's sponsor violated the contract.'

"2. *The future of Earl L. (Curly) Lambeau, vice president, general manager and coach of the Green Bay Packers.*

"3. The prospective sale of the Detroit Lions and its effect on Coach Charles E. (Gus) Dorais.

"4. Future policy toward the rival All–America Conference. Alexis Thompson, young and wealthy owner of the Philadelphia Eagles, has indicated he's one owner who favors some sort of rapproachment. The leagues have no relations."

The article went on to tell how Commissioner Bert Bell had arrived for the confab ahead of the owners but that he didn't know anything "except what I've read." As far as he was concerned, the purpose of their meeting was to hold the annual draft and nothing more, but a quote in the final paragraph contradicted his plea of ignorance.

"The National League's boss declared that Lambeau 'told me definitely that there's nothing to the story' that the Green Bay tutor may turn up as head coach of the Los Angeles Dons of the All-America Conference."

Bell denied knowing anything about the situation with Lambeau, but he took the trouble to talk to Lambeau about it. Which one of them brought up the subject was undiscernible, but they did talk about it. Why?

Imagine yourself as an NFL owner in 1947. You're in a war with a rival league, the AAC. Some of the owners in the AAC have so much money that losing a million bucks on football only offsets the profits of their other businesses. Meanwhile, you don't have that sort of luxury; if you lose $50,000 in a season, it really hurts. Even so, you have to compete in order to survive, and survive, you must. You hate the owners of the AAC because they threaten your survival by hiring your best players away from you or, at the very least, by offering them bigger contracts than you can afford but which you have to beat or risk losing your players. For two years, you and your fellow NFL owners have managed to survive the onslaught of the AAC. You're confident that it's only a matter of time before these good businessmen of the AAC tire of taking their financial lumps and throw in the towel, leaving the pro football field to you and the other NFL magnates.

But suddenly, your world is shaken by a story out of Los Angeles that states a traitor is in your camp. Curly Lambeau, a living legend in the world of pro football, an honest-to-goodness breathing and eating and never sleeping modern Horatio Alger, a hero of the game, a god of sports mythology whose prominence you helped to promote by inventing and embellishing tales of his wondrous feats — the man founded the Green Bay Packers in 1919, he saw the team through bankruptcy, his teams were the Davids who slew the football Goliaths of Chicago and New York, etc., etc., *ad nauseum* — Curly Lambeau, the football Paul Bunyan of Wisconsin, the story relates, is switching sides in the war. He's planning to do a "Benedict Arnold" and betray your precious NFL by jumping to the Los Angeles Dons as head coach, general manager, and a minority owner with full authority over all football operations.

Lambeau jumping leagues could be catastrophic. It would be worse than Benedict Arnold's act of treason; it would be more like George Washington going over to the British. Lambeau leaving might mean you and the NFL would lose the war, and you're humongous ego could never stand for that. What do you do? Get on the phone and call Green Bay.

"Hello, Curly? Tell us it ain't so, Curly! Tell us it ain't so!"

Curly Lambeau never was at a loss for self-confidence, but until his phone started ringing off the hook in December with calls from George Marshall, George Halas, Tim Mara, Art Rooney, and Bert Bell, not to mention Packer fans, stockholders, board members, and officers as well as dozens of sportswriters, all of them wanting the inside poop; not until this time did the Beligan realize exactly how much power he wielded in the world of professional football.

"Fellas, fellas, please! Me jump to the AAC? It is to laugh. I started the Packers, and I'll always be with the Packers. You can take that to the bank."

Just the same, you have enough knowledge about the ins and outs of sports reporting to know that most journalists don't invent stories like the one Braven Dyer exploded in Los Angeles. Despite Lambeau's denials, you worry that there might be something to it, and if there is, you'd better be prepared for the worst. You call your fellow owners, starting with Emil Fischer, the president of the Packers.

"Emil, what's this about Curly jumping to the AAC?"

"There's nothing to it," says a nervous Fischer. "Curly's not going anywhere. Especially not to the AAC."

"But what about the Rams? There's talk that Dan Reeves wants Curly to take over out there."

"You'd better ask Dan about that."

You call Los Angeles.

"What about it, Dan? Are you tinkering with Curly Lambeau and the Packers? You know that's against the rules, don't you?"

"The only time I saw Curly this year was when the Packers were here to play us. We hardly said more than hello to each other. But I'll tell you this much. If it meant keeping Curly away

The Lambeau Years — Part Three 161

from Ben Lindheimer and the AAC, I'd break the rules and make him an offer he couldn't refuse. I wouldn't let you boys down you know."

"Sure, Dan, we know. See you in Pittsburgh."

You and the other owners meet in the Smoky City to conduct the college draft, but it's Lambeau's status with the Packers that has you worried. You and the other owners corner Emil Fischer and demand to know the truth about the situation in Green Bay.

"It's like this, boys," said Fischer. "Curly's been dipping into his expense account a little too much, and we told him to stop it because the club can't afford it. To make sure he stopped, we changed our organization a little. Curly can't do anything any more, except coach, without someone else approving his move first. Don't worry about Curly. He's not going anywhere without us letting him go."

"That's good, Emil," says you, "because you know there ain't no Packers without Curly. As far as we're concerned, Curly is the Green Bay Packers."

"That's the way we feel up in Green Bay, too," says Fischer.

"That's good enough for me," says Bert Bell.

But is it good enough for you? An idea comes to mind. You get George Halas, George Marshall, and Tim Mara to meet you in private to talk about Curly's situation.

"I say this league needs Curly Lambeau. We need Curly whether he's in Green Bay or Timbuktu. If we let him get away to the AAC, we're dead in the water, boys, and we'll have to give in to the AAC and take them on their terms. What do you think we should do?"

"Maybe we should get Curly another job," suggests one mogul.

"But with who? You know he loves California, and Dan Reeves doesn't need him."

"Maybe we could put a team in San Francisco or San Diego."

"The last thing this league needs is a new team."

"I wasn't thinking about a new team. I was thinking about the Packers."

"The Packers? Fischer and those boys up there will never let their franchise go. You know that."

"They won't have any choice if the Packers go under, and if you ask me, that's where they're headed."

"They beat a bankruptcy rap before. Five will get you ten that they can do it again."

"No bet here."

The confab breaks up, but you're still not sure about Curly's loyalties. Maybe you need a little insurance. Better go on the Q.T. and ask George Halas. He's Curly's best buddy in the NFL. If anyone would know what's in Curly's mind, it would be Halas.

"Well, George, what's the deal with Curly? Is he going to jump to the AAC or what?"

"I've talked to Curly, and I'll tell you this much. He no more wants to jump to the AAC than I do, but he's unhappy up in Green Bay. Those local businessmen on their board of directors have put the kabosh on him. He tells me they're all butting into things, trying to tell him what players to keep and what plays to run and all. It's not like the old days when they let him do just about anything he wanted."

"That's yesterday's fish wrapper, George. What's Curly planning to do now? Is he staying in Green Bay or what?"

"He's staying, but I don't think he's going to put up with things the way they are for very long. Curly's not one to be pushed around, and I should know. I've been playing him for almost 30 years now." Halas pauses, then says, "But that's not what I'm worried about. It's the Packers I'm worried about. Sure, they were a tough go this year, but Curly can't keep up with the rest of us when it comes to rounding up talent. I can't see him signing a whole bunch of those boys he drafted, and without the horses, you might as well get out of the race. If the Packers turn out losers, I'm wondering if the folks up in Wisconsin will continue to support them."

Now that was food for thought.

All the owners go home or to Florida or wherever for the off–season. At the summer meeting, everything seems normal, and the '48 season comes off without a hitch, except for one minor problem, or maybe two, such as the Packers' last two games in Milwaukee that draw a few non–drinkers who don't own television sets. The Packers lose money on both contests, and the two visiting teams only receive their guarantee, which makes them financial losers, too.

At the winter meet in Chicago in January of '49, you feel its time something was done about the Green Bay situation and the AAC. You and the other owners have been talking with some of the boys from the other league, and there seems to be some hope that you guys can get together and put an end to the war.

Let's take the AAC deal first. The NFL has 10 teams, and the AAC has eight. Total 18. But there's three teams in New York, three in Chicago, and two in LA. That's one too many in both New York and Chicago. So you cut out the worst of those, meaning the Dodgers in Brooklyn and the Hornets in Chicago, and that leaves 16 clubs. Still too many. Not to worry. Boston doesn't support pro football; it never has and never will; ask George Marshall. We can merge the Boston Yanks with the New York Yankees, and we got 15 left. Still too many. There's no need for two teams in Los Angeles; the town can't support two. We can merge them, and that leaves us with 14 franchises. Baltimore is too close to Washington for George Marshall, so we can forget about the Colts. Now we're down to 13 teams. Just about everyone else is pretty solid, except for Buffalo and Green Bay. Buffalo didn't draw all that well, and the Packers have been around since the beginning, well, almost since the beginning. Besides, the Packers play half their home schedule in Milwaukee; that should count for something. No, wait. The last two games there this past year didn't do well. Why was that? Wrong opponents maybe? Sure, that's it. Wrong opponents. Maybe if the Packers played the Bears and Cardinals in Milwaukee they'd draw better. After all, the Packers do just fine in Green Bay no matter who they play there. We'll change the schedule for '49 and have the Bears and Cardinals play the Packers in Milwaukee instead of Green Bay. So we can forget about the Buffalo Bills and get on with a merger with the AAC by taking in the Cleveland Browns and the San Francisco 49ers. That's 12 teams. What a concept! Let's go for it.

The AAC says no. No merger without Baltimore. They say the NFL should dump the Packers. Didn't Cecil Isbell say that

Baltimore was a better sports town than Green Bay? He should know, shouldn't he? He played in Green Bay and coached in Baltimore. No merger without Baltimore.

So the merger is off. But what about playing those games in Milwaukee instead of Green Bay. Halas loves the idea; so does the Cardinals' management. The Lions want to play in Milwaukee, too. Emil Fischer shakes his head with an emphatic NO! "The fans of Green Bay will never give up the Bear game," says Fischer. "Fine," say the Lions and Cardinals. "Play the Bears in Green Bay. We want Milwaukee." Fischer compromised and played the Cardinals and Lions in Milwaukee, but the Bears still had to go to little Green Bay. The last laugh was on the Lions and Cardinals. The Bears drew better in Green Bay than either of them did in the Cream City.

Finally, you and the other NFL owners decide you have to merge with the AAC or die. Your weakest link is Green Bay. You go to Emil Fischer and say, "Emil, buddy, it's been nice, but if you boys up there in Green Bay don't show us that you can keep up with the rest of the league financially, then we'll have to take your franchise away."

To show the other NFL magnates that the people of Green Bay want their team and would support them no matter what, an intrasquad game was set for Thanksgiving Day in Green Bay.* The idea was to raise $50,000 to fill the empty Packer coffers and convince the world that the greatest fans in the world lived in Wisconsin and Michigan's Upper Peninsula. The scheme worked completely. Bert Bell and the remaining doubters were convinced. The Green Bay Packers weren't going anywhere.

With that resolved, the NFL owners met with the AAC owners, and a merger was finally hammered out. Everyone could relax at last. Everyone except Curly Lambeau.

§ § §

* See Appendix G for full details.

15

... Kept Humpty Around to Play Again

When reading the pages of America's sports sections, it's hard to tell which rumors are based in fact and which are the pure machinations of America's sportswriters. This observation is true today, will be true tomorrow, and was definitely true in 1947.

Late in that pivotal year of 1947 two rumors made the sports sections of newspapers from coast-to-coast. Both concerned the head coaching position of the Los Angeles Dons of the All-America Conference. One revolved around Notre Dame coach Frank Leahy, while the other had Curly Lambeau as its subject. Leahy denied the rumor about him vehemently, saying, "I can tell you that I will be back at Notre Dame next year." Packer officials scoffed at a report by Braven Dyer, a Los Angeles columnist, that Lambeau might resign and become the head coach and general manager of the Dons. Two years would pass before it would be determined which rumor was based in fact and which was simply creative journalism.

The rumors about Leahy and Lambeau going somewhere continued to persist, but only Lambeau's name came up again in connection with the Dons.

In response to a mid-November 1949 story in *The New York Daily News* that claimed the Packers would forfeit their franchise at the end of the season and Lambeau would become the general manager of the Los Angeles Dons, Bert Bell said: "We in the National league are very strong for Green Bay and we always will want a Green Bay team in our circuit. I am most happy to hear that there is no foundation to this story that Green Bay may surrender its franchise."

Of the same tale, Tim Mara said: "We want to see Green Bay remain in the league. You people up there (Green Bay) have nothing to be ashamed of on attendance. The Yankees (New York team in the All–America conference) are averaging only 16,653 and the Hornets (Chicago team in the AAC) are averaging only a little over 13,000. The Dons are averaging a little over 20,000."

Emil Fischer remarked: "Any idea that Lambeau is quitting the club is ridiculous." Famous last words!

The New York story stated that Lambeau and Ben Lindheimer had met in Chicago the week before to discuss Lambeau's move to Los Angeles if the war between the two leagues continued for another season. Naturally, both men denied the rumor.

An *Associated Press* story from this same time stated that the Packers were staging their Thanksgiving Day intrasquad game in order to avoid bankruptcy. Angered by the report, Fischer replied: "The Thanksgiving day game is a civic undertaking sponsored by Packer fans in Green Bay and came entirely unsolicited by the Packer organization. Green Bay will remain permanently in the National Football league."

It would seem from Fischer's statement that someone suspected the Packers might jump leagues much the same way as the Brooklyn franchise did in 1946, but that was hardly the case as far as Fischer was concerned. But was it a possibility that Lambeau was considering? Only he knew for certain the answer to that question.

Rumors about Lambeau and the Packers persisted to permeate the talk of just about everyone who gave a thought to the team. When the executive committee held its weekly meeting on November 21, Fischer announced that "cognizance was taken of press reports to the effect that Coach Curly Lambeau was being asked to resign." He added that "the matter of asking Curly to resign has never been discussed by the executive committee or any member of it." The story about the rift between the executive committee and Lambeau came out of Milwaukee earlier that day. Ollie Kuechle of *The Milwaukee Journal* said that "a determined effort" would be made to oust Lambeau as general manager of the Packers at the executive committee meeting. The story stated that a faction on the committee had questioned Lambeau's choice of George Strickler as director of publicity, Lambeau's move to play some games each year at Milwaukee and Lambeau's expansion moves, including the purchase of Rockwood Lodge as a club base.

Two days later at the ninth meeting of the Quarterback Club, Lambeau made this reply to the rumors that were circulating around Green Bay: "Many persons are under the impression that I own the franchise; this is incorrect. The franchise is owned by Green Bay Packers, Inc. I paid $50 for the original franchise at the league's first meeting in Canton (Ohio) but *when the club was later reorganized the franchise was taken over by the corporation.* (Author's italics.) I own one share of stock myself."*

In a pre-game pep talk with the team before the Cardinal game in Chicago the following Sunday, Lambeau said: "We have some unpleasant situations — I think you all have heard about them, and it makes for a bad situation on the ball club. It's unfortunate that it does exist — but it does. I think the stories going around Green Bay are highly exaggerated, but, nevertheless, it's still a bad situation."

Many Packer fans were blaming Lambeau for the Packers' poor showing in the league, citing the fact that he had stepped down as field coach back in September. Art Daley tried defending Lambeau's move in his column: "Curly had good reason (for stepping down as head coach and becoming advisory coach) – one of health – for making his move . . . The mistake, in our opinion, was made when Lambeau did not appoint one of the three assistants to take charge." According to Daley, all three assistants said the same thing to him as well as at least 10 players who complained that no one was really in charge of the team.

To say that the atmosphere of Green Bay was charged with dangerous electricity would be an understatement. Men were actually fighting over Lambeau. Should he go? Should he stay? If he stayed, should it be under the same system or should the system be returned to the way it was before the executive

---

* See Appendix H.

committee stripped Lambeau of his autonomy back in '47? Maybe the corporation should be reorganized. Should more games be played in Milwaukee? Fewer games in Milwaukee? All of these questions and more faced the board of directors when they held their meeting on Wednesday November 30 at the Brown County Courthouse.

Dozens of stories about the events that transpired just prior to that meeting have been told over the years. One that was told to this author by John B. Torinus, who was present at the meeting, went something like this:

"Jerry Clifford had heard a rumor that Lambeau and Vic McCormick and two other fellows whose names I can't recall right now were planning to take over the franchise from the corporation. Clifford stopped them on the courthouse steps and took Lambeau aside. He told Lambeau not to try taking the franchise back from the corporation. If he did, Clifford would make public Lambeau's abuse of his expense account and he would bring charges against Lambeau for malfeasance in office and misappropriating corporate assets. He promised Lambeau that he wouldn't use the evidence to get him fired as head coach and general manager of the Packers. That's how Jerry Clifford stopped Curly Lambeau from taking back the franchise."

The precise details of this tale or any other about that moment in time may never be known because as far as this author has been able to discern none of the principals left a written account of it. However, the results of the board of directors meeting are a matter of record.

A resolution to renew Lambeau's contract for two years was passed at the meeting of the board of directors. The vote wasn't announced, but 21 of the 24 directors were present. According to *The Milwaukee Journal*, Jerry Clifford, Dr. W.W. Kelly, and George Whitney Calhoun voted against retaining Lambeau. The newspaper also stated that it expected that those three would be ousted as directors when the election of directors came around the following spring. Clifford was called the leader of the anti-Lambeau faction. He tried to call a "rump" session in the afternoon but couldn't round up enough directors. At the meeting, he called for a secret ballot but was voted down.

The Lambeau Years — Part Three

The biggest news, however, was the announcement that the corporation would issue 20,000 new shares of stock for $10 each in order to raise $200,000 in working capital. Carl J. Hansen, James W. Lang, and Arthur H. Mongin, Jr., of Kaukauna, offered to buy the first shares, one each the next day.

Lambeau said: "I am satisfied we now will have complete harmony in the organization for the first time in four years. Wednesday's meeting cleared the air. All major points in connection with our operation and my contract were settled on the floor and only a few minor details need to be clarified. The executive committee is straightening out these points now.

"I will take a definite part in the coaching of the team next year. I still believe we have one of the best groups of assistants in football and they will be back with the club next fall."

Emil Fischer said: "The Packers have successfully passed another crisis and are back on a sound footing. As far as Green Bay is concerned, this can be the start of a new era. Such interruptions are embarrassing and apparently unavoidable, occasionally. But they are far from fatal. We're ready to move toward a championship again.

"We have a sizeable backlog in investments, including Rockwood, which could not be replaced for $100,000. We own our own stadium and there is a considerable amount in paid-up insurance policies. Along with the $50,000 the fans of Green Bay raised voluntarily on Thanksgiving as a gesture of good faith in the club, we are in good, sound shape.

But we are operating with an obsolete organization, geared to professional football 15 years ago, an organization that is too inflexible to meet the many new and complex problems that have grown out of the game's rapid and tremendous progress in recent seasons."

Fischer was right, but he was only saying half of what he was thinking. In his mind, he felt that a change was necessary and Curly Lambeau was it. George Halas was successful in Chicago because he knew how to delegate authority; his prime interest was money, not fame. Lambeau was deprived of having money as his major concern by the fact that the Green Bay Packers, Inc., was a non-profit corporation. Fame was all that was left to him, but he had plans to change that.

On December 14, 1949, two very important articles hit the newspapers. One concerned the Packers directly at the time, and the other concerned the Chicago Cardinals and the Packers indirectly for the moment.

The Packers announced that four regular season games would be played at City Stadium in 1950 and only two would be scheduled for Milwaukee. This brought a round of cheers from the folks in Green Bay and a resounding yawn from Milwaukee. The Packers had their nerve making this statement at this time because the merger between the NFL and AAC was barely a week old and the makeup of the new NAFL was yet to be determined.

Mrs. Violet M. Bidwill, chairman of the Chicago Cardinals' board of directors and widow of Charley Bidwill, said: "The Cardinals are prepared to pay the highest salary in pro football to get a top flight head coach for 1950, and furthermore, I will not be pushed around in any deal in (the) formation of the new league. The league must be lined up to give an equitable schedule to the Cardinals or I'd just as soon retire from football. We must have (a new coach) before the first meeting of the new league January 19. This is big business. We're going to sign the best coach money can buy — if we have to pay him the highest salary in the league."

Lambeau was in California at the time of Mrs. Bidwill's announcement, but a remark he made when that immortal comedian, Bob Hope, interviewed him during half-time of the Rams-Eagles NFL title game in Los Angeles raised a lot of eyebrows in pro football circles. Hope asked: "You're going to be back with the Packers again next season, aren't you, Curly? I see you have a new two-year contract."

Lambeau replied: "You never know, Bob, you never know."

This little tidbit came right on the heels of another shocker coming out of Green Bay on December 15, 1949. Dr. W. W. Kelly, former president of the Packers, resigned as a member of the board of directors. In his letter to Emil Fischer, he wrote:

"As everyone is aware, I was strenuously opposed to the renewal of E.L. Lambeau's contract as manager and coach of the Green Bay Packers. My motive for opposing this renewal of contract was not from any personal feeling toward Mr. Lambeau, in spite of propaganda to the contrary; but was based upon my belief that a complete reorganization of the club was indicated at this time. I was supported in my position by only two other directors, and the vote of the board was practically unanimous in rejecting my ideas."

Kelly was an original member of the "Hungry Five" with Andy Turnbull, Lee Joannes, Jerry Clifford, and Curly Lambeau. Clifford and Lambeau were the only two left now. Although they hadn't started out as a "last man's club", the "Hungry Five" was beginning to look like one, and bets were being taken in Green Bay on which of the two survivors would win the struggle that they seemed to have engulfed them.

Christmas came and went, and everyone was looking forward to the New Year. But the old year, 1949, wasn't over yet, and it still held one more little surprise.

On December 30, a story that shook the NFL came out of one of the most unlikely places in America: Iron Mountain, Michigan. *The Iron Mountain News* published an interview with Gene Ronzani, a hometown boy who had made good by playing three varsity sports at Marquette University in Milwaukee, one of them being football. After college, he moved into the pro ranks with the Bears. In recent years, he had become a head coach for a minor league team, then returned to Chicago as a player and assistant coach to George Halas. In the interview Ronzani supposedly said that he had met with Packers officials and that "I don't know what sort of a deal I'll be offered until I meet with the Packers."

Hold the phone, folks! Green Bay went nuts. Lambeau was the Packers' coach. What was this business about Ronzani? A Bear, no less. This had to be a hoax.

Reached in Chicago by Art Daley, Ronzani denied the story, saying that he had never been contacted by any Packer officials. Daley wrote a bunch of other words to support Ronzani's denial, and everyone was satisfied for the time being.

New Year's Day came and went. All was quiet on the football front until January 10, 1950.

Lambeau still hadn't received his new two-year contract from the executive committee. When he was asked about this, Curly said he would work under the assumption that he would be the coach and general manager for the next two years, but he also expressed a need for harmony within the organziation. He explained that "no group of 12 men can get together once a week during the football season, for an hour and a half, including lunch, and run a professional football team. That can't be done. There are no miracle men." He added that "I can't possibly bring the corporation up to date in such a short time. I am not a brilliant man, but I certainly feel qualified to run our organization." As a closer, he emphasized, "We also must sell stock."

Heading the committee working on the stock sale was Lambeau's good buddy and rumored benefactor, Vic McCormick.

In a telephone conversation with a reporter from *The Milwaukee Journal*, Emil Fischer, who was vacationing in Florida, said that the delay in Lambeau's contract was due to his and Lambeau's absence from Green Bay, indicating that as soon as the two of them were in Green Bay together that it would be done. As for reorganizing the corporation and issuing additional stock, that would wait until the annual stockholders meeting. When asked if Lambeau's contract would wait until the stockholders' meeting, too, Fischer replied, "Not necessarily." In response to questions about the dissatisfaction of certain board members and their effort to oust Lambeau, he said, "I don't think anything will come of it. The stockholders' meeting will take care of everything. That's why it is a good thing to wait."

Emil Fischer was a wise man.

Just for spice, a new rumor that Lambeau was being offered the general manager's job with the Rams popped up. Lambeau denied the story, of course, but the source said that Dan Reeves, the Rams owner, had pegged Lambeau as his choice to be the new GM in Los Angeles.

Talk of reorganizing the corporation was buzzing around Green Bay. The big question: Should Lambeau be given complete authority over the operations of the corporation? Curly had a lot to say on the subject. Lambeau proposed:

"Stock should be voting stock and profit sharing and should sell at $25 per share with a goal of $250,000. The reason the stock should not be sold at $10 a share is that we'd lose money in handling it — mailing it, etc.

"I feel that there are enough buyers (of stock) in Green Bay and vicinity to insure that the control of the Packers would remain in Green Bay. Everyone who puts money in the Packers should have a voice in operation.

"Professional football is a battle of managements. In the old days, the battles for success in the league were fought on the field. Today, there is an added battle — management. Therefore, we must operate efficiently.

"We must have men who are thoroughly qualified to do the work assigned to them. Furthermore, professional football demands that business be started in January. In fact, I believe that January is the most important month in a new season. We can't wait until the leaves start to fall.

"I would like a setup similar to the one we had previous to 1947 or before my authority was decentralized. I believe that the present situation is unworkable and we cannot exist under the present arrangement of operation through committees and subcommittees.

"Most important is that we have complete harmony from top to bottom.

"I am not in favor of abolishing the present executive committee. The majority of the members are very helpful and useful to the Packers. I would like to see at least one football man on the committee and my choice there would be Don Hutson. A football man on the committee would substantiate the things that I report on football (field) matters."

There it was! He said it himself. Lambeau's rift with the executive committee was a result of the changes that they had implemented to control him. He admitted it. Curly wanted to be top dog in everything, and he actually expected to become the king that everyone had been building him up to be since 1919.

According to *The Milwaukee Journal*, "Lambeau was shorn of his power at *a meeting of a quorum of eight of the 12 men on the executive committee that was held on June 13, 1947 when he was out of town.* A resolution introduced by Jerry Clifford, club lawyer, and adopted, designated subcommittees on finances, grounds, contracts, publicity, league representation, and the draft, and it left Lambeau no alternative but to work with them."

This little tale proved that *The Green Bay Press-Gazette* wasn't the only newspaper to have reporters, writers, and editors who failed to check their facts before putting a story into print for the whole world to see. It was true that Lambeau was out of town on June 13, 1947; he was still at his home in California. But that was all that was true. Not until the stockholders meeting held on July 25, 1947 was the executive committee changed from a nine-man group to 12, and it wasn't until the first meeting of the newly elected executive committee that the changes that Lambeau came to abhor were made. And he was present at the meeting!

Obviously, the *Journal*'s reporter got his so-called facts from Lambeau who appeared to be trying to gain sympathy for being persecuted by the executive committee, especially Jerry Clifford who was trying to get even with Lambeau for removing Clifford's buddies, George Whitney Calhoun and Dr. W.W. Kelly, from their posts with the Packers as publicity director and team physician. The gambit was working with the press and the average fan on the street, but it wasn't working where it counted. At least not the way the Belgian wanted it to work.

Clifford countered Lambeau's ploy by letting it be known around Green Bay that Lambeau's buddy, Vic McCormick, a wealthy Packer booster and board member, was all prepared to purchase a large block of the new stock that Lambeau was proposing to be sold in order to fund the club properly. Lambeau laughed at the idea, saying, "How would anybody put a lot of money into any setup like this since the stock is nonprofit? Sure, I'd support the club, but a lot of people would support it." Lambeau forgot that he had proposed that the non-profit status of the corporation should be changed to profit sharing in order to bring in the kind of money that was needed to make the Packers into a competitive NFL team.

As a booster shot, McCormick was being mentioned as the next president of the Packers.

Lambeau went to the league meetings in Philadelphia that January and carried out the same duties that he had carried out so many times in the past. Emil Fischer was there, too. Strange, but they didn't do much together, and when they did, it was as if they were two prizefighters just entering the ring, eyeing each other, trying to gain some psychological advantage before they came to the real blows.

After returning to Green Bay, Lambeau denied the rumor that he would turn over the head coaching duties to Tom Stidham, while he stayed in the front office. "There is no truth to the story at all," he said. "Such things must be started by people who want to embarrass me. I was granted a two-year extension of my contract by the board of directors two months ago, and the contract calls for both coaching and handling the front office affairs of the club. It is on that basis that I am going to continue." He also denied that Cecil Isbell would be engaged as his backfield coach. Isbell had been fired as head coach of the Baltimore Colts and was out of work.

Both denials bear examination. What contract? No mention was made anywhere of Lambeau signing a new contract with the Packers. Had he been offered a contract and was mulling it over? And what about Isbell? No mention was made anywhere that Bob Snyder was on his way out the door. Why would anyone think that Lambeau was thinking about hiring Isbell? Answers later.

A catastrophe seemed to be stalking Curly Lambeau, and possibly he knew it, especially when Rockwood Lodge burned to ground on January 25, 1950. Faulty wiring in the attic was blamed as the cause by caretaker Melvin Flagstead, and his version became the official verdict later on, although a joke or two about the fire circulated around Green Bay as to the real cause. One asked if anyone knew which board member of the

Packers set the blaze. Some might have thought this funny, but it was actually repeated in bad taste. A little thought about the facts of the fire would have told anyone that it was an accident. (1) Flagstead's children and a few of their friends were in the house at the time. (2) Flagstead's son discovered the fire in the attic. (3) The five cottages on the grounds were not damaged. (4) The Flagstead family lost all of their possessions. (5) Flagstead suffered a three-inch slash on his left hand when he had to break a second-story window in order to escape. He had tried to extinguish the fire and was trapped upstairs, forcing him to break the window and jump two stories into the snow. The family left the building as soon as the fire was discovered, then watched helplessly as the lodge burned.

There was that statement back in December by Emil Fischer. "We have a sizeable backlog in investments, *including Rockwood, which could not be replaced for $100,000*. We own our own stadium and *there is a considerable amount in paid-up insurance policies*. Along with the $50,000 the fans of Green Bay raised voluntarily on Thanksgiving as a gesture of good faith in the club, we are in good, sound shape."

Frank Jonet said that the lodge was insured for $50,000. Now the Packers had $100,000 for the coming year.

Before the disaster at Rockwood Lodge could sink in, a new rumor popped up. This one said Lambeau was in line for the Cardinal coaching job. An *Associated Press* story the next day said Lambeau was in the running with Clark Shaughnessy, the head coach of the Los Angeles Rams. Lambeau laughed off the rumor saying it was too ridiculous for comment.

Lambeau was still laughing two days later on the first day of February when he made the front page of the *Press-Gazette*:

Lambeau To Coach Chicago Cardinals

Leader of Packers

For 31 Years Quits

Will Also Become Vice-President

Of Club, Submits Resignation Here

"Earl L. (Curly) Lambeau, coach of the Green Bay Packers for 31 years, today was named coach of the Chicago Cardinals of the National American Football league.

"Lambeau signed a two-year contract. Ray C. Bennigsen, Cardinal president, said he would also serve as a vice president of the club and would be in complete charge of player personnel. His appointment is effective immediately.

"Lambeau mailed his resignation as Packer coach and general manager to President Emil R. Fischer of the Packer corporation yesterday. He and his wife left for Chicago Tuesday afternoon and he met with Bennigsen in Chicago this morning, from which meeting the announcement emerged.

"Lambeau, in leaving Green Bay, ended the longest tenure of any coach with one football team in the history of professional football. In recent years with his teams on the losing side of the ledger, he had withstood several battles with the board of directors for renewal of his contract, the latest coming last Nov. 30.

"In his resignation he said that these 'differences of opinion have brought about a dangerous disunity of purpose within the corporation, one which in my opinion threatens the existence of the club.' He said he hoped his action 'will restore the harmony so mecessary if the Packers are to keep their place in major league football.' He also said he felt his action 'is in the best interests of the Packers and the fans of Wisconsin.' "

Lambeau's resignation:

Dear Mr. Fischer:

It is apparent that there is a growing reluctance to alter the policies under which the corporation has operated the last several years.

Unfortunately, I have not and cannot now subscribe to those policies. This difference of opinion, honest tho it be, has brought about a dangerous disunity of purpose within the corporation, one which in my opinion threatens the existence of the club. No organization can survive divided against itself.

Therefore I am resigning as vice president of the corporation and relinquishing the positions of head coach and general manager, effective as of this date (Jan. 31). I hope this action will restore the harmony so necessary if the Packers are to keep their place in major league football.

I take it with the deepest regrets and only after long and careful deliberation. One does not easily break away from something which he has devoted 31 years. But I feel my decision is in the best interests of the Packers and the fans of Wisconsin, to whom the Packers really belong.

With every good wish for their future success.
(Signed) Curly Lambeau

Nobody seemed to notice at the time, February 1, 1950, but Jerry Clifford had won.

§ § §

16
Let The Truth Be Known

There's always been this thing about not speaking ill of the dead. Well, Curly Lambeau wasn't dead in 1950, and neither was anyone on the Packers' executive committee. Translation: It was open season for the sportswriters on ex–demigods.

On the same day that Lambeau shocked most of Packerdom, Emil Fischer said that Lambeau's resignation "was not entirely unexpected. The Packer corporation also wishes Curly all the success in the world in his new position, and feels, like Curly, that it is in the best interests of both Curly and the Packers."

The truth was the executive committee was hoping that Lambeau would resign. That austere group realized that firing Curly would be a bad move on their part because public sentiment was with the so–called founder of the Packers. Fischer and company realized that the powers behind the Packers, i.e., Andy Turnbull and each of his successors, the board of directors, the stockholders, and the sportswriter of *The Green Bay Press-Gazette*, had spent nearly three decades making a demigod out of Lambeau, and now that their hero had proven to be human they couldn't terminate him and maintain their own credibility and, more importantly, their own power.

Because the deal between Lambeau and the Cardinals was made in such secrecy, the question of tampering came up. Did Ray C. Benningsen, the Cardinals' president, have permission from the Packers to talk with Lambeau about the vacant Cardinal job? This was a very pertinent point because league rules forbade tampering with coaches and players of other teams without their team's permission. Violation of the rule was punishable by fine, censure, and possibly suspension from activities within the NFL.

Answering the question, Lambeau said in *The Chicago Tribune* that the Cardinals didn't need any clearance from the Packers or the league to enter into negotiations with him because he was not under contract to Green Bay. This was true; he hadn't signed a new contract with the Packers. However, just a few weeks earlier Lambeau had said quite vehemently that the resolution passed at the board of directors meeting on November 30 was as binding as a contract. Apparently, he was mistaken.

When the question was put to Emil Fischer, he refused to make any comments. If he had said that the Packers had given the Cardinals permission to deal with Lambeau, then he couldn't plead surprise at Lambeau's move, meaning he had no foreknowledge that Lambeau would be leaving the Packers; and if he said that the Packers hadn't given the Cardinals permission to talk to Lambeau, then Bert Bell would be forced into interceding and doing something to punish the Cardinals. By keeping quiet on the subject, Fischer avoided a lot of unnecessary hassle over Lambeau switching teams.

At the time of Lambeau's resignation, a panic nearly erupted among Packer fans. Their worst nightmares appeared to be on the verge of becoming reality. *The Milwaukee Sentinel* reported that the typical thinking in Green Bay was this statement: "Lambeau probably knows what's going on and decided to get out and land another job while the getting is good. Maybe the league is planning to shift the franchise to Buffalo or Houston."

The *Sentinel* writer was pouring gasoline on the fire with that last little tidbit. This was typical of the Milwaukee press at the time because they were sympathetic to Lambeau and definitely opposed to the executive committee.

Lambeau had friends in the press corps all around the country. Oscar Fraley wrote for *United Press International*, and he had a piece to spout on Lambeau's resignation:

"The 'home town pride' which made Earl L. (Curly) Lambeau and the Green Bay Packers sent him packing off today to become coach of the Chicago Cardinals.

"After 31 years as coach of the club which he founded and

made a pro gridiron institution,* Curly was checking out — and with very few regrets either way. Never one to spare the sharp word, *he had committed the unpardonable to Green Bay's civic honor by becoming a Californian in the off season.*

"There were a lot of reasons for the split: Dissension in the ranks and a losing football club being among them. But Green Bay loves its football team and you don't give that town three, six or 11 months of your time. It's all or nothing. So Curly's taking off, yet it leaves a lot of mellow memories."

Fraley failed to obtain the other side of the story from Emil Fischer. If he had, he might have learned that the people of Green Bay didn't object to Lambeau spending the off-season in California; many of them went to Florida and other such warm spots for extended periods to escape Wisconsin's long, cold winters. No, the objection to Lambeau's trips to California was the fact that Lambeau charged many of his expenses to the Packers.

In the early days, Lambeau would go to California on scouting trips because the Rose Bowl was played there and so was the East-West All-Star game. After the games were played, he would work his way back to Green Bay, visiting players at their schools or homes, often signing them to contracts to play the next year in Green Bay. These were legitimate expenses, and no one back in Wisconsin questioned them. Even when Curly began spending the rest of the winter in California, no one cared until someone noticed that his transportation to and from the West Coast was being paid for by the Packers. Besides that, Lambeau claimed that he made several side-trips to Arizona and Texas, allegedly to scout players for the team, and he

---

* **Fraley went on to outline Packer history, getting it all wrong, of course; such as saying that the Acme Packing Company was the team's first sponsor, when it was actually the Indian Packing Corporation that funded the Packers in 1919. Fraley also told the myth about Don Murphy selling his Marmon to loan Lambeau the money to buy the first pro franchise for Green Bay in 1921.**

requested and was given reimbursement for these excursions. When these traveling expenses became excessive during the years immediately after the war, an investigation was begun by Jerry Clifford, and he discovered that Lambeau hadn't made all the trips that he claimed to have made. Word about Lambeau's abuses of his expense account leaked out, and all sorts of rumors followed. The bottom line was simple: Padding an expense account might be acceptable by Hollywood's accounting methods, but it's a crime in Green Bay. Oscar Fraley didn't know that, of course, himself being from a big city.

Also siding with Lambeau was Ollie Kuechle who wrote a lengthy article in *The Milwaukee Journal* about Lambeau leaving the Packers. From its tone, he was obviously sympathetic to Lambeau in the dispute between the "Big Belgian" and the other former members of the "Hungry Five". Wrote Kuechle:

"Whatever the future holds for the Green Bay Packers now that Curly Lambeau has resigned — and speculation ran a wide range Wednesday night — this much is true: The Packers have lost something they can never regain. The romance of the Green Bay story, *the story of Lambeau's original idea in 1919,** (Author's italics) of humble beginnings, of later championships against the big cities, has been tarnished so that it can never be the same.

"Lambeau was the one tie with the very beginning — with the creation of the Packers."* (Author's italics.) Long before Jerry Clifford had an interest in them, or Dr. W.W. Kelly, or Lee Joannes or any of the others who in recent years have fought him in bitter internal fights, and sometimes personal fights, the Packers were Lambeau's baby. They were his. He weaned them. Whatever the Packers now do, they will never recapture what they have lost as the big Belgian leaves.

"The romance of the story has been spoiled."

* Obviously, Kuechle knew as little as Fraley did about the beginnings of the Packers. He was right about one point, though. The Packers were Lambeau's baby — *his adopted child.*

Kuechle's article also quoted Jerry Clifford as saying, "We've had two good breaks in Green Bay in the last two weeks. We lost Rockwood lodge and we lost Lambeau. If Lambeau had stayed here for two more years we would have gone completely busted. We can now go ahead."

At the other extreme, Kuechle quoted Buckets Goldenberg who said, "We're through. I don't see how the Packers can last without him. He was the Packers."

Kuechle went on to describe the troubles between Lambeau and the executive committee. Lambeau fired Dr. Kelly as the Packers' physician because Kelly's health prevented him from making road trips with the team. Joannes resigned as team president because Lambeau had let it be known that he was interested in moving up the corporate ladder. Then Clifford got his resolution passed by the executive committee, limiting Lambeau's authority. According to Kuechle, "Lambeau became general manager in name only and, in some respects, coach in name only. Finances? They were taken out of Lambeau's hands. Player contracts? They were placed in the hands of the contract committee. Selection of players? This was placed in the hands of the league representation and draft committee." This situation was intolerable to Lambeau, but he tried to make the best of it.

The proverbial straw that broke the camel's back came at the winter meeting of the NAFL in Philadelphia that January of 1950. Emil Fischer flew up from Florida with Lambeau's new contract. Curly took one look at it and tossed it back at Fischer. Instead of an extension of his contract, the one written in 1945 under which he had unlimited authority over alomst every aspect of the team, the new document was a reiteration of the power limitations that the executive committee had put on him with Jerry Clifford's resolution.

According to observers at the winter meeting, Lambeau and Fischer had words with each other, then settled into a coldly formal attitude for the rest of the conference. Soon after this, Lambeau put out feelers and found his new job with the Cardinals.

Kuechle was another subscriber to the false story that

Lambeau had given birth to the Packers. Then to add insult to injury, he believed that Lambeau had singlehandedly kept the Packers alive through all their troubles in the '20s and '30s. He completely missed the truth that Andy Turnbull, Lee Joannes, Dr. Kelly, and Jerry Clifford, not to mention dozens of other businessmen in the Green Bay area, had been the real saviors of the Packers during those difficult years, that they had worked behind the scenes to make the organization successful, that they had wisely used Lambeau as the focal point so they could do the real work. Kuechle was blinded to the truth by his admiration for Lambeau.

Kuechle only told Lambeau's side of the story. He neglected to mention why Jerry Clifford and the executive committee passed that resolution that restricted Lambeau's authority. He neglected to mention that it wasn't the firing of Dr. Kelly that was offensive to the doctor and his friends but that it was the sneaky way in which Lambeau had done it. He neglected to mention that Lambeau also fired George Whitney Calhoun from his job as publicity director and let Calhoun learn about his dismissal by reading the wire service story that announced the hiring of George Strickler.* He neglected to mention how Lambeau had abused his expense account. Like Fraley, Kuechle was guilty of irresponsible journalism.

Much to his credit and that of the members of the executive committee, Emil Fischer remained silent about Lambeau and the past. Instead, he went about setting the Packers' house straight by ridding it of everything that smelled of Curly Lambeau, and at the top of his list was George Strickler.

As the Packers publicity director, Strickler was fairly popular with the press, but he was resented by many people because he had replaced Calhoun who was a favorite son in Green Bay. It was thought that he had wormed his way into Lambeau's good graces while he was publicity director of the NFL, then when his job with the league was in jeodpardy, he got Lambeau to hire him to replace Calhoun. The facts were that the hiring of Strickler was all Lambeau's idea, that Lambeau was supposed to tell Calhoun before the story broke but didn't, and that

---

* See Chapter 4.

The Lambeau Years — Part Three

Lambeau let Strickler take the heat for him.

Strickler was given the option of quitting or being fired, although this wasn't made public at the time. The *Press-Gazette* reported: "George Strickler's services as publicity director of the Packers were officially ended as of today. Strickler was notified last fall that his present contract would not be renewed after it expired March 1 of this year. He was given his final paycheck today." This was February 4, 1950.

Three days later Strickler denied that he had been given his notice in the fall. The fact was Lambeau was supposed to tell him that his contract wouldn't be renewed in April, but Curly never did tell Strickler about the executive committee's decision, which was typical of him.

Strickler's dismissal was interpreted by several stockholders who felt that Lambeau was forced to leave Green Bay by Fischer, Clifford, and other members of the executive committee as just another slap at their hero. Talk among these dissidents centered around replacing every director who had been in favor of getting rid of Lambeau, and that probably would have happened if the truth about Lambeau as a double-dealer hadn't come out.

On February 5, the *Press-Gazette* printed a column by Vincent X. Flaherty of *The Los Angeles Examiner*. It was a most revealing piece of journalism:

"Earl 'Curly' Lambeau, coach of the Green Bay Packers for 31 years, signed as head coach of the Chicago Cardinals the other day and some people expressed surprise that this man should sever connections with the pro football team he founded way back in 1919.

"The truth, however, is that Lambeau has been aching to do just that for quite some time.

"Unknown is the fact that Lambeau accepted a job with the Los Angeles Dons more than two years ago. He had repeated conferences with Benjamin F. Lindheimer, chief owner of the Dons. He agreed to terms and sought only one stipulation, which was granted: He wanted to break the news gently to the people back in Green Bay.

"So Lambeau, having agreed to replace Dudley DeGroot as the Dons' head coach, left Los Angeles and returned to Green Bay, where he met with the club's board of directors. He told them he was leaving and that parting was such sweet sorrow and so forth and, in a long distance phone call to Lindheimer in Los Angeles, even repeated his assurances that everything was all set for his switch to the Coast.

"However, the Green Bay board of directors got together, gave Lambeau a boost in salary and the whole picture changed right there. Lambeau stayed on at Green Bay, forgetting all about his verbal agreement with Lindheimer — proving once again that football coaches are worse than women when it comes to changing their minds.

"Lambeau, in his meetings with Lindheimer, expressed grave doubts about Green Bay's future. He was convinced the game had outgrown the little northern Wisconsin town with its population of 46,000 people. He would have moved the franchise to Milwaukee. But the Green Bay club is a community owned proposition and any suggestions about shifting the team were dimly looked upon as treason.

"The miracle of Green Bay, however, is the fact that Lambeau lasted 31 years as head coach. That trick required some extraordinary maneuvering, and Lambeau had to be a top politician, a first-rate glad-hander and baby-kisser as well as a winning football coach.

"But when the football war came along. Green Bay couldn't keep pace. It couldn't afford to go out and buy high-priced talent and the team took a nosedive. Hence, open season was declared on Lambeau, who has had more than his share of hometown critics for many years.

"Green Bay, which has sometimes been called Babbittville on the Bay, came alive with second-guessers and grandstand coaches. The board of directors started shooting at Curly's graying head. Factions started fighting factions and there were resignations and threats of resignations. Curly was in the middle of it all.

"The old grads are the bane of any college football coach's existence — and whenever a bunch of addle-brained alumni begin to howl, it means a football coach's head. Wesley Fesler has been getting it for some time at Ohio State just as a hundred other prominent football coaches have been getting it — or have had it.

"But anything that might have gone on in college football would have to be classified as tame and amateurish compared with what Lambeau had to contend with. Every Green Bay stockholder in town exerted his rights neith (sic) a corner lamp-post at night, telling other fellow stockholders what should be done. Every time Lambeau walked out of the house he ran into stockholders, all of whom had questions to ask and suggestions to offer.

"The only thing that kept Curly's mind in one coordinated mass was his frequent sojourns to his home out here in Malibu. It was his only escape.

"Lambeau had been the strong man of the Green Bay franchise up through the years. He was the guy who held it together. Now that he is gone you can lay odds that it'll fold or, at best, be shifted to a large city — probably Milwaukee, which Lambeau wanted to do in the first place.

"Lambeau wants to live in Los Angeles permanently. He wanted to coach here — and will coach here if he ever gets another chance. Not even Lindheimer knows what happened when Lambeau left Los Angeles a couple of years ago. He never heard from him again.

"How do I know Lambeau wanted to coach the Dons? I contacted him for Lindheimer when Lambeau said he was 'very much interested.' I drove him to Lindheimer's home in Beverly Hills where the two of them hit it off great from the start. What happened when he got back to Green Bay is something only Curly and the Green Bay board of directors can answer."

What happened when Curly got back to Green Bay was Emil Fischer reminded Curly that he had a contract with the Packers and he wasn't about to be let out of it. Lambeau snickered at Fischer's reminder and said he'd walk anyway. Jerry Clifford stepped in and told Curly that the Packers would sue him for breach of contract if he took the job in Los Angeles. Furthermore, the NFL would back the Packers in such a suit. If he didn't believe that, then maybe he should talk to a few of his old buddies around the league. That's exactly what Lambeau did, and every single one of them advised him that if he switched leagues that they would turn on him in a New York minute. But because he was their old friend, they would go to bat for him with Fischer and the executive committee and ask them to ease up on him. Lambeau acquiesced and stayed in Green Bay. Typically, he didn't have the courage to call Lindheimer and tell him about his decision to remain in the NFL.

Flaherty's column was obviously sympathetic to Lambeau, but it served to calm, if not convince, the dissident stockholders that just maybe Curly wasn't the knight in shining armor that they'd been led to believe that he was all these years; just maybe Curly was human after all. At the very least, Flaherty's story about Lambeau and Lindheimer took them by surprise and caused them to take a step backward, allowing Fischer and the executive committee time to resume control of their own destinies as well as the future of the Packers.

§ § §

SUMMARY

Pardon the cliche, but Lambeau's resignation was the end of an era, the like of which will probably never be seen again.

If one man was ever bigger than life, it was Earl L. "Curly" Lambeau. In interviews with those who knew him personally, two words came up continually in descriptions of Lambeau: aggressive and volatile. He approached life like a valiant charger racing into battle, but at the same time, he was susceptible to fits of pique and petulance. He was the sort of man who polarized people; those who knew him either loved him or hated him. Either way, he put people around him into motion, and that is the mark of greatness.

From his earliest days, Lambeau was a focal point; i.e., he was usually the center of attention. He was an outstanding athlete from childhood, and by the time he was in his teens, he was considered to be not just *a* star but *the* star of his high school's football and track teams. As such, he was given the star treatment, and like most youths who receive the accolades of nearly everybody around them, he developed the confidence and cockiness that he could do just about anything.

In 1917, Lambeau was given a good dose of ego leavening when he attended the University of Wisconsin in Madison. He went out for the football team and learned quickly that he wasn't the only high school phenom in the state, that he was only one of dozens, and many of them were in his class at college. Discouraged by this lesson, he quit school and went home to Green Bay.

The following year Curly tried his hand at college again. He attended Notre Dame in South Bend, Indiana, and he adjusted to his new surroundings with the help of his football coach, the immortal Knute Rockne. After a full season running next to the great George Gipp, Fate intervened with Lambeau's life. He came down with tonsillitis and went home for treatment over the Christmas holidays. He never returned to Notre Dame.

Lambeau took a job with the Indian Packing Corporation in 1919, and he courted Marguerite Van Kessel. As the year wore on, Rockne, Marguerite, Curly's father, Marcel Lambeau, urged Curly to return to school, but he chose not to go; he stayed in Green Bay, married Marguerite, and continued to work for the packing company. Why? Marguerite Lambeau provided the answer, although not in these exact words. In Green Bay, Curly had his job, his girl, and his own football team. In South Bend, his work would have been getting an education instead of pulling down a salary of $250 a month on the loading dock of the Indian Packing plant; Marguerite wouldn't have been there and more than likely his social life would have been rather uneventful considering the semi-monastic living conditions at the Catholic university in those days; and he might have been *a* star in Rockne's backfield, but probably he wouldn't have been *the* star. At Notre Dame, he would only be another big jock, a little bluegill in the Lake-of-the-Woods. In Green Bay, he would be a superstar, a giant salmon in the city by the bay. His ego might not get the strokes in Indiana that it was accustomed to receiving in Wisconsin. Returning to Notre Dame was risky for Curly; he had security in Green Bay. Above all, staying at home was what *he* wanted to do.

Once Curly's decision was made, Nate Abrams, who had run the Green Bay town football team in 1918 when Curly was at Notre Dame, stepped aside and turned over the reins of leadership to Lambeau. Curly was elected captain of the team. In those days, the captain was actually a coach on the field; he was the one man that the players expected to lead them to victory. The real coach might direct the team during practice; he might give the players a pep-talk before the game; but once the referee blew the opening whistle, he wasn't much more than a spectator until halftime when he could lecture his charges on what they were doing wrong or he could praise them for what they were doing right.

Bill Ryan was the coach of the 1919 Green Bay team that was called the Packers. Joe Hoeffel was the coach of the 1921 Green Bay Packers in the American Professional Football Association. Cub Buck coached the linemen in 1921, and the Packers had other coaches in those early years. Even so, Curly Lambeau was the man that everybody — fans, journalists, players — saw as the leader of the Green Bay football team.

In 1920, Lambeau recognized the opportunity to expand his horizons with the birth of the APFA. He talked to his boss, John Clair, about joining the new circuit, but they were too late to get the team into the league that season. Clair and his brother Emmett did get the Packers into the APFA in 1921, but Curly's ego took them down the road to destruction in the latter part of the year when he employed college players in a pro game, a definite no–no in the fledgling APFA.

Every intentional rule–breaker has the cocky attitude that he won't get caught, but more often than not, they are found out and punished. Lambeau's penalty for breaking the rules was the expulsion of his team from the league. This was tantamount to taking a toy away from a child. Lambeau threw a fit and went into a panic. Having the team thrown out of the APFA didn't hurt nearly as much as the embarrassment of being caught with his hand in the cookie jar and being publicly punished. In an effort to redeem himself in the eyes of his adoring public, Lambeau applied for a new franchise in the league and was awarded one on the condition that he pay $1,000 into the circuit's Guarantee Fund. This was something Curly couldn't do, not on his own.

Fortunately for Lambeau, he had friends who were susceptible to his natural charm for one reason or another. Joe Ordens was a pencil–pusher who admired Curly for his athletic prowess. Nate Abrams was short and not exactly a handsome guy who envied Curly for his height and good looks. George Whitney Calhoun suffered from arthritis so severe that he was unable to walk unaided and he was unable to straighten the fingers on both hands. Like a lot of people who can't perform in life in the way they want, these three men associated themselves with a man through whom they could reach for fulfillment.

With the backing of his friends, Lambeau met the conditions of the now National Football League, and he received his franchise on August 21, 1922 to redeem himself from the previous year's embarrassment.

Lambeau's success was short–lived. By the middle of the

season, his team was in trouble on the field and off. He was staring total destruction straight in the eye, but he was able to avoid it once again with the help of friends.

Andy Turnbull saw Lambeau for what he was: a catalyst, a focal point, a star. But unlike Curly's buddies, Turnbull knew what to do with him; he knew how to harness Lambeau and all of his attributes for the common good. Turnbull obtained the aid of several friends, and together they gave Lambeau the firm support that was necessary for him to be a success where it counted the most: on the field.

Lambeau matured under the direction of Turnbull and his friends. He made the transition from superstar to a team player under their tutelage; and with the help of such greats as Cal Hubbard, Mike Michalske, and Red Dunn, although their efforts were unrequested, Curly made the switch from player to coach. The evidence of Lambeau's growth materialized in the won–loss columns of the NFL standings as his teams captured three successive championships.

Then Curly heard the call of the Siren known as Hollywood, and all of those good works began to dissipate.

California has always been an expensive proposition, even from the days of the missions and the Spanish rancheros. Nothing came cheap. The Gold Rush only added to the cost of living in the sunny climes. The development of the oil fields pushed inflationary levels yet higher, but Hollywood, with all of its glamour and bright lights, sent prices beyond reasonable limits.

Despite the exhorbitant financial demands, some people become as addicted to the "Land of Dreams" as any poor soul who innocently delves into using heroin or cocaine becomes hooked on narcotics, and once they do become addicted to all the glitz of "Movieland" they will do just about anything to maintain their California high, including lying and stealing.

Lambeau was one of these addicts. He met his first Hollywood starlet on a boat going to exotic Hawaii in December 1932, then he took a walk on the Sunset Strip a month later. The hollow flattery ever floating around Tinseltown was more than his smalltown ego could handle. He sucked it all up like a thirsty kid with two straws in a nickel Coke.

In the beginning, Curly was able to keep his affairs in California out of his life in Wisconsin. His scouting trips to the West Coast were solitary jaunts, and no one back home in Green Bay really cared. No one except his wife, that is. She divorced him, and life went on.

It may seem like a coincidence, but the Packers suffered their first losing record the campaign after Lambeau made his first trip to California. Their mark wasn't much better the following year of 1934, but after his affection for starlets became public knowledge with the end of his marriage, Green Bay improved to 8-4-0 and a close second place finish in their division. Could it be that once he quit concentrating on hiding his private life that he was able to concentrate on succeeding in his public life?

In all fairness, the point must be made that Lambeau had more than his personal life on his mind in 1933. The corporation was forced into bankruptcy,* which threatened the very existence of the team. This little episode must have had an effect on Lambeau's performance as coach and on the Packers' won–loss record, too.

Gradually, more power was given to Lambeau by the stockholders of the Green Bay Packers, Inc. As the saying goes, power has a tendency to corrupt, and while he was under the spell of Hollywood, Curly was susceptible to corruption. With each year after he became an officer in the corporation, he took a little more of the business of running the organization unto himself without consulting the executive committee, but nobody seemed to care because the Packers were winning games and titles with fairly decent regularity.

Then Curly went too far. Abusing his expense account was sinful, but it wasn't reason enough for anyone to grumble too loudly. Firing Dr. Kelly as team physician was, and so was firing George Whitney Calhoun. So was hiring George Strickler. These were the steps that led Lambeau to the termination of his relationship with his team.

Lambeau made these moves because he felt he was bigger than the organization behind him. He was guilty of reading and

* **See Chapter 2 of** *The History of the Green Bay Packers: The Lambeau Years — Part Two.*

believing all those press clippings and Arch Ward's book on the Packers that said he was the founder of the Packers, that said there would be no Packers without Earl L. "Curly" Lambeau. He actually came to believe that the Packers would fold up and blow away in the winds of the football war without him. He learned a hard lesson. It never dawned upon him that he was only the figurehead, the display window, the focal point for the public; that the real power in the Green Bay Packers, Inc., was held and wielded by the executive committee and their authority came from all those other people who worked behind the scenes to insure the survival of professional football in Green Bay, Wisconsin. He had forgotten that all those people — the stockholders, the ticketsellers, the fans — supported him and had been supporting him since his high school days. Without them, he was just another guy with a good build and a lot of unrealized potential.

Francis X. Flaherty wrote: "Lambeau had been the strong man of the Green Bay franchise up through the years. He was the guy who held it together." Flaherty was wrong. However, Ollie Kuechle was right, although not for the reason he thought, when he wrote: "Without Curly Lambeau, there would be no Green Bay Packers."

Lambeau said it himself: "I am not a brilliant man." He was so right. But he was one helluva catalyst, and his place in Packer history, in professional football history, and in sports history is forever guaranteed.

This portion of The History of the Green Bay Packers concludes here because the Packers were entering a new era in 1950. For the first time since 1918, Earl L. "Curly" Lambeau would not be with the team. Also, the National Football League was moving into a new age as the National-American Football League. As in 1933 when the NFL began divisional play and in 1945 when the AAC went to war with the NFL, pro football history was presented with a natural break in time as the war between the two circuits was finally brought to a halt with their merger.

§ § §

APPENDIX A
The All-Time Packers of '46

Early in the 1946 season *The Green Bay Press-Gazette* started a fan poll to name the "All-Time Packers" team. The results of the voting were announced weekly in the newspaper as if they were conducting a horse race. Various past players and officials of Packerdom were asked to name their "All-Time" team, and their choices were periodically printed in the paper to spur the fans to vote. Less than 2,000 voters cast ballots in spite of all the prodding. The final tally was published in the November 19 issue, but it contained few surprises.

Don Hutson received the most votes of any player, which was only natural since no one else could come close to him when comparing his impact on the team to theirs. At the other end position was Lavvie Dilweg who played eight years for Green Bay before going into politics. A distant third was Milt Gantenbein, which surprised many who were in the know. Gantenbein played 10 years for the Packers, four with Dilweg and six with Hutson. Local experts felt Milt was better than Hutson on defense and better than Dilweg on offense. To them, Gantenbein was the more complete player, whereas Hutson was strong on offense and Dilweg was tough on defense. Actually, Hutson's offensive prowess was so great that his defensive ability was overshadowed. The same was said about Dilweg's defense being so prominent that his offensive contributions were frequently overlooked. If the "All-Time" team was divided into defensive and offensive units, Gantenbein would have been chosen both ways, whereas Hutson would have been selected on offense only and Dilweg on defense only.

At the tackle positions, the fans chose Cal Hubbard and Cub Buck. Hubbard's selection was almost a foregone conclusion, the same as Hutson's had been. But the choice of Buck was a surprise in that he was an early player who had played in the days when most of the NFL was comprised of local elevens from more than two dozen small towns across mid-America. Ernie Smith finished third, but he was remembered more for his placekicking talent than his blocking and tackling. Elmer Sleight from the '30 and '31 title teams came in a close fourth, and eight-year veteran Baby Ray was fifth. The vote counts for both of these men was surprising in that Sleight only played for the Packers those two years and Ray had been named to several all-league teams over his career to date.

The fans chose Mike Michalske and Buckets Goldenberg as the guards. Oddly, each man received the same number of votes, 1,738. Russ Letlow was a distant third with 251. The impressive fact about Goldenberg being chosen as a guard was he had spent the first half of his career in the backfield as the blocking back in Lambeau's offensive scheme. Being a Wisconsin lad also played in Goldenberg's favor. Letlow was the better choice, but the war cut short his career by three years.

Charley Brock was the popular choice for center on the team. As a center on offense and a linebacker on defense, Brock was as good as they came in the NFL of that period. Jug Earpe was the runnerup, but he was only a center on offense. On defense, the Jugger played tackle.

The "All-Time" backfield had Arnie Herber at quarterback, Verne Lewellen and Johnny Blood at halfbacks, and Clarke Hinkle at fullback. Hinkle received only nine fewer votes than Hutson, which proved how much the fans of the day thought of him. Herber was named as the QB because he was a home town boy and because of his legendary passing skills. Actually, Herber was a halfback most of the time. Lewellen was one of the few men of his day who could do it all: run, pass, catch, kick, block, and tackle. He was the complete football player. Blood was much like Lewellen in that he could do it all. His kicking and blocking weren't as good as Lewellen's, but his pass receiving and pass defending were better than Lewellen's. Furthermore, he was more colorful. Besides picking up 981 votes as quarterback, Herber also garnered 383 for halfback. Cecil Isbell polled 325 at half and 13 as QB. Red Dunn was named as the QB on 669 ballots.

The *Press-Gazette* poll was really unfair to the fans because it was asking them to pick the best players for *only* 11 positions. It would have better served Art Daley's purpose if he had realized that the Packers with Red Dunn and the Packers of all other years were two different animals. With Dunn at QB, Lambeau used the old Notre Dame "Box" formation, where the QB lined up a yard behind the center and took a *pass* from the lineman instead of a *snap*. After Dunn retired, Lambeau went to his own variation of the single-wing and double-wing attacks where the QB was actually a blocker who lined up a yard back of the space between the tackle and guard and who didn't handle the ball very much at all.

As a field general, Dunn was superior to any man who wore a Packer uniform to that time. For a blocking back, the choice would have to be made between Buckets Goldenberg and Larry Craig. For a passer, Cecil Isbell had the edge on Herber in that he was the better short and medium range passer, whereas Herber stood all alone as the best long passer in the history of the game.

For pure running backs, Lewellen, Blood, and Hinkle were the best in terms of service and production. Isbell was also a topnotch runner, and Tony Canadeo and Ted Fritsch were still showing their stuff. Andy Uram, Bobby Monnett, and Hank Bruder were three men whose contributions were somewhat overlooked by the voters.

Under Lambeau's usual defense, the Packers employed a six-man line with two or three men backing them and two halfbacks and a safety behind them. The lineup depended on who was in the game. Michalske and Russ Letlow were probably the two best defensive guards, Hubbard and Earpe the best defensive tackles, and Gantenbein and Dilweg the best defensive ends. For linebackers, Charley Brock and Clarke Hinkle were superior to all the rest. In the secondary, Blood, Lewellen, and Joe Laws — had they played together in their primes — would have been an incredible trio.

For kicking specialists, Cub Buck was the best dropkicker, Verne Lewellen the best punter, and Paul "Tiny" Engebretsen the best placekicker.

All the members of the "All-Time" team except Cal Hubbard attended the "homecoming game" with the Cardinals in Green Bay as guests of the management, and joining them were the members of the 1919 Indian Packing Corporation football team. Art Daley called them the "first Green Bay Packer squad" in his *Sports Cocktails* column in the *Press-Gazette*. He wrote:

"It was composed of 20 young men, 19 of whom played football. The other gent was George W. Calhoun, present public relations chief who, at the time, handled the club's business affairs, passed the hat, counted the receipts and what not. The players were organized by Lambeau who wanted to play football so badly that he got backing from a local parking (sic) concern to buy the boys uniforms. How Curly got the club rolling and the headaches that developed are interesting indeed but for the sake of brevity tonight, let's discuss that first team which will be seated on the right of the Packer bench during the game."

Daley went on to update his readers on the whereabouts of the men who made up that team. The sports editor was personally acquainted with some of these men, which was evident by the little extra remarks he made about them in the column. One that he didn't know was Nate Abrams, of whom Daley wrote: " . . . one, Nate Abrams, died here several years ago." Nothing else was written about Abrams. Why? Daley couldn't remember why when he was interviewed for this book. Besides the lack of words about Abrams, the other oddity was Daley's use of the word "several" in reference to the length of time since Abrams's death. Why? Especially why, since Abrams had passed away only a five years before in 1941. Again, Daley couldn't recall a reason when he was interviewed.

Besides the typographical error that read "parking" instead of packing, the most curious line in the column was "How Curly got the club rolling . . . " As stated in the first volume of this history on the Green Bay Packers, Lambeau *didn't* get "the club rolling" in the sense that Daley meant it. The team was already in place when Lambeau joined it in 1919. To reiterate earlier statements in this history, Lambeau pushed to have the annual team organizational meeting moved up because he was getting married and he didn't want to miss the meeting. When his teammates made him captain of the squad, he took it upon himself to arrange games for the team, using the occasion of his honeymoon to accomplish this. Daley never knew this, of course, because neither Lambeau nor Calhoun or any of the others who were around in 1919 told him. All Daley knew at the time was the Packers were founded and coached by Earl L. "Curly" Lambeau in 1919 and that Lambeau's first team would be honored guests at the last home game of the 1946 season.

APPENDIX B

A Picture Is Worth A Thousand Words - Sometimes

On August 3, 1948, a cartoon by Erwin L. Hess appeared in the sports pages of *The Green Bay Press-Gazette*. Accompanying the illustration, which appears in the picture section of this book, was an article explaining the picture.

I wish I had seen this article and cartoon while I was writing the first book in this series,* but since I didn't, I'll clear up the episode of that day once and for all now. The article stated:

"On Thanksgiving Day of that year (1922) A. B. Turnbull, general manager of the Press-Gazette, chanced to drop in at the office and there he found three officials of the Packers club in troubled conference. They were Coach Curly Lambeau, G. W. Calhoun, sports editor of the Press-Gazette, and Joseph Ordens. A heavy rain was falling and it looked like the game scheduled with the Duluth Eskimos for that afternoon would be washed out. The club was in no position to stand such a financial loss.

"The three representatives of the Packer management told their story to Mr. Turnbull and asked for advice. He suggested the play rain or shine policy which has been followed ever since. It was at this meeting that Mr. Turnbull became interested in the fortunes of the Packers. He recognized the team as a civic asset and from that date on for many months he gave his best efforts to the business of saving the team for Green Bay.

"Before the next season rolled around he had enlisted the

---

* See Chapter 6 of *The History of the Green Bay Packers: The Lambeau Years — Part One.*

support of a number of Green Bay businessmen who in turn organized a non-profit corporation to finance and manage the team. Mr. Turnbull served as the first president of the corporation and has been active in its affairs ever since.

"The cold, rainy Thanksgiving Day, Nov. 30, 1922, which Erwin Hess selected for his drawing is probably the darkest day in Packer history, but the conference and the dramatic decision is also the crucial point in the team's history. From that time on the fortunes of the Packers have been moving onward and upward."

The writer had his facts straight except for one minor point: the Packers' opponent that day was the Duluth Kellys; the Duluth team wasn't given the name of Eskimos until 1926 when Ernie Nevers was hired to run the team. And he had one major piece of information missing: the fourth man in the club's management, Nate Abrams, was also present.

This article did make the point that Ordens was a party to the conference that decided the Packers fate that day. To the best of my knowledge, only one other story, cited below, has ever stated that Joe Ordens was there. I wonder, why? I can only speculate that it was probably due to Lambeau's faulty and self-serving memory to omit Ordens from the scene. I can also only speculate that Ordens being mentioned in the cartoon story was probably due to George Whitney Calhoun as the following information indicates.

A year later Andy Turnbull resigned from the executive committee and the board of directors of the Green Bay Packers, Inc.* In an un-bylined article about Turnbull's contributions to the organization dated August 10, 1949 in the *Press-Gazette*, the writer summed up that fateful meeting that took place in 1922 in three paragraphs:

"It was a driving rain storm midway in the 1922 season that brought the executives of the club into consultation in the office of the Press-Gazette. Gathered for this dreary conference were Coach Curly Lambeau, G.W. Calhoun, Joseph Ordens and

---

* See Chapter 10.

Nathan Abrams. (Author's italics.) It is reported that they were considering calling the game off, and it must be admitted that some felt that (the) end of professional football in Green Bay was near at hand.

1,300 Fans In Stands
"Mr. Turnbull, general manager of the Press–Gazette, chanced to visit the office of the newspaper that Sunday morning and the troubled quartet eagerly called him into the huddle. He heard the story: The Duluth Eskimos were in Green Bay ready to play and must be paid their guarantee whether the game went on or not. He advised them to play the game, if they wanted to put professional football over in Green Bay, and thus established the policy of playing rain or shine which the Packers have followed ever since.

"There were only 1,300 hardy fans in the stands, but the Packers had won more than a ball game that day. They had won the attention and active interest of Mr. Turnbull and no one will deny that that has been one of their greatest assets during the past 27 years."

The writer stated that he had obtained this information from "George W. Calhoun, former sports editor of the Press–Gazette, who has been a sort of Boswell of the Packers since their beginning in 1919," and that Calhoun wrote this tale "in a history of the club published in the Packer program of Sept. 29, 1946."

The use of the term "a sort of Boswell" was the mark of a man with a real education, and the only man at the *Press-Gazette* in those days with that sort of learning was John B. Torinus, Sr., the man who replaced Turnbull on the executive committee of the Green Bay Packers, Inc. It's possible that someone else might have written the article but not likely because no one at the newspaper was closer to Turnbull than Torinus. (Also, this author can personally attest to the fact that the writing style is nearly exactly that of Torinus, and as my credential for making that claim, I present the fact that I worked with him as his editor and publisher on the three books that he authored during the last years of his life.)

Beyond the authorship of the article was the curious mention of Nathan "Nate" Abrams being a party to this historical moment. No other author or writer has ever mentioned Abrams's presence prior to this story in the newspaper with the exception of Calhoun who stated this fact, according to the article, in his history of the club published in a Packer game program. Calhoun's so-called history was flawed in that he wrote that the game was in mid-season (instead of late November), on a Sunday (instead of Thanksgiving Day), and against the Eskimos (instead of the Kellys), but those mistakes are acceptable because: (1) How often does it rain cats-and-dogs on the last Thursday in November in Green Bay, Wisconsin? (2) Don't most holidays seem like Sundays? (3) And who wouldn't remember the Duluth Eskimos more than the Duluth Kellys? It's also possible that Calhoun was confusing some details of the Duluth game with another contest. The Packers faced another rainy day dilemma of whether to play or not on November 5 that season when Joe Carr's Columbus Panhandles came to town.*

Calhoun's memory might have been a bit faulty about those facts, but it's not likely that he forgot who was at that meeting in the offices of the *Press-Gazette*. The fact that he included Abrams in the conference states — no, shouts! — through the distance of time that Abrams must have been very important to Lambeau and the Packers in 1922. Exactly how important was detailed in the first volume of this series.

---

* **See Chapter 6** of *The History of the Green Bay Packers: The Lambeau Years — Part One.*

APPENDIX C
A Good Yarn

In his August 6, 1948 column, *Sports Cocktails*, in the Green Bay *Press-Gazette*, Art Daley wrote the following:

" . . . When Hutson came up from Alabama in 1935, the Packers had only four ends under contract and only 27 players in all . . . Compare this with 1948 . . . There are nine ends and 49 candidates in all . . . Hutson was fighting with Milt Gantenbein, Al Rose, and Bob Tenner for a starting position. . . . It didn't take him long to earn it. . . . On the first play of the opening league game against the Bears, Hutson caught an 80-yard pass from Arnie Herber for a 7-0 victory. . . . Hutson outlasted two passers and a third, Irv Comp, is still with the squad. . . . Herber was Hutson's first pitcher and the former West High star helped "lead" Don on many a long aerial. . . . Hutson set most of his marks with Cecil Isbell on the throwing end in the early 1940's."

Mr. Daley was guilty of re-writing history again. As it was explained in the second volume in this series, *The Lambeau Years — Part Two*, Chapter 8, page 86, Hutson's first game was the week before the game with the Bears, and Hutson dropped the first pass thrown to him in the NFL.

Because he wrote the same story again, Daley has to be declared guilty of perpetrating the myth about Hutson, then perpetuating it. Good for him, though! Everyone likes a good yarn, and good fiction is harder to write than the truth.

APPENDIX D
The Packers' First Coach

In the first volume of this series, it was pointed out that Curly Lambeau was not the first coach of the Packers but that other so-called historians gave him credit for being the first coach.

This myth was still being propogated on October 27, 1948. On that day, an article appeared in *The Green Bay Press-Gazette* written by Lee Remmel in which he quoted a 1919 story in the same publication about the officiating in the Packers' game with the Fairbanks-Morse team from Beloit. Remmel's article stated that the 1919 piece was written by George Whitney Calhoun, then sports editor of the newspaper. In reviewing Calhoun's story from 1919, Remmel wrote:

"The ire of the Packers and club officials was expressed in three statements, in bold-faced type, which appeared above the game story, written by G.W. Calhoun, then Press-Gazette sports editor. Two of the opinions are reprinted here:

"Most Deliberate Steal"
"C.N. Murphy, official of the Green Bay club, was quoted thusly, 'I wish to go on record as saying that it was the most deliberate steal I have ever seen. Green Bay had the ball over the line for clear touchdowns on three different occasions, and each time home officials ruled offside. It was a cut and dried deal to give Green Bay the worst of it, and they succeeded one hundred per cent.'

"*W.J. Ryan, the Packers' coach*, said, 'I talked to a business man from Janesville. He said, "I was over to the robbery this afternoon."' This expresses the sentiment of everyone from Green Bay that saw the game, as well as a number of people from

Janesville who were neutral. The boys displayed wonderful fighting ability, but it was simply too much Zabel. One of the players put it well when he said: 'Beloit had the game won before the team stepped upon the gridiron.'

"The lead paragraph of the game story was mild enough, but in the second, Calhoun began to to (sic) tell how the Packers were 'robbed.'

" '*Capt. Lambeau*'s team was robbed of victory by Referee Zabel of Beloit. . . . ' "

Remmel's 1948 article continued to quote Calhoun's 1919 report, telling how the Packers were robbed of a win by Baldy Zabel, the referee.

Please note that I have italicized two important parts of Remmel's quote of Calhoun's article. One stated that W.J. Ryan was the team's coach, and the other referred to Lambeau as being the team's captain. In another paragraph of Calhoun's article as quoted by Remmel, Lambeau was again so designated: "Capt. Lambeau bucked the line . . . " and "Capt. Lambeau warned every man on the Packers . . . " Not in one single place did Calhoun refer to Lambeau as the coach; he was the captain and only the captain. Bill Ryan was the Packers' coach.

The Lambeau mythology at that time, 1948, was so virile that this article by Remmel failed to change anything. To the Packers and their followers, Lambeau was the head coach then just the same as he had been since the team's mythical founding in 1919.

Adding more to the Lambeau myth, Art Daley's article of December 1, 1949 contained the following:

"Lambeau organized the Packers as a sandlot team in 1919 after a year at Notre Dame where he played fullback on Knute Rockne's 1918 squad. The now–defunct Acme Packing company put up $500 to outfit the team after agreeing with Lambeau that the word 'packers' would be placed on the jerseys. Though the Packing company went out of business, the name held on.

"Lambeau received the first franchise for Green Bay in the

National Football league on June 24, 1922 — practically the same day the NFL was born. Lambeau served as player–coach through 1928. After that season he retired to coaching and won three straight league championships in 1929, 1930, and 1931. The three in a row still stands as a league record."

Dissecting Daley's story, the Acme Packing Company was yet to be in 1919. It was the Indian Packing Corporation that put up $500 for jerseys for the city team. It's possible that the word "packers" was supposed to be on the uniforms, and one account I read did indicate that the word was to appear on the back of the jerseys, which would explain why the team picture shows no sign of the word. However, I have yet to see the word on the back of any player in any game photographs from that year or the next year, but the name Acme Packers does appear on the uniforms of the players posing in the 1921 team photo.

It seems unlikely if the team was required to have "packers" on the back of their jerseys in 1919 that Lambeau or the Clairs would put "Acme Packers" on the front of the uniforms in 1921. I am inclined to believe that the so-called deal that Curly made with his employer to put the word "packers" on the back of the uniforms was just another story that he told to support his claim to be the Packers' sole founder.

Art Daley must not have been too acquainted with NFL history in 1949. If he had been, he would have known that the NFL was founded in 1920 as the American Professional Football Association. Also, he should have known and made mention of the fact that the Packers were in the league in 1921 when the Clair brothers owned the franchise. He didn't, however. I wonder if it was because Lambeau had caused the Clairs to lose their franchise by employing illegal players and it would have embarrassed Lambeau in 1949 to bring up that faux pas of 1921.

Finally, Lambeau's playing career lasted until the 1930 season. Of course, he only played in one game that year, but he did play. And he played the whole season in 1929. In fact, a story told by Cal Hubbard said a lot about Lambeau as a leader of those great teams that won three straight titles in 1929, 1930, and 1931. Paraphrasing Hubbard, he said:

"Curly came into the game fit to be tied because we weren't moving the ball against the Bears. Those Bears weren't girls. They were tough. He said to give him the ball and he'd show us how to gain some yards. The ball was snapped to him, and we stepped aside and let the Bears pour through at him. He stumbled off the field and let us get on with the game and never shot his mouth off like that again."

Ken Keuper, the former Packer player, spoke of the Packers and Coach Curly Lambeau at an Elks banquet honoring the football Braves of Manitowoc in mid–December 1949. Keuper said that the type of game coached by Lambeau had been "outmoded by four or five years. After playing three years for the Packers, I was traded to New York and came west with the Giants to play Green Bay in Milwaukee last season. Playing as line backer on defense, I naturally expected that Lambeau would be smart enough to change his offensive signals against us, rather than use the same ones with which I was thoroughly familiar. But no, there came the Packers up to the line with the quarterback calling the same signals that had been used the past four years — and perhaps longer. Naturally, I was able to tip off the Giants on most of the Green Bay plays, giving us great advantage."

These remarks by Keuper and the story by Hubbard are only two examples of former players taking parting shots at Lambeau as a football strategist. The list of those who felt Curly wasn't all that great as a coach is long and it features such Pro Football Hall–of–Famers as Mike Michalske, Clark Hinkle, and Johnny Blood.

All of this considered, it's amazing how well the mythology about Lambeau has been kept up through the years.

APPENDIX E
"The Green Bay Story"

In the May 15, 1948 issue of *The Green Bay Press-Gazette*, Curly Lambeau announced that a movie about the Packers would be made in Green Bay.

"The movie, now rated Class A, will be based on the history of the Green Bay Packers football team and will contain a 'plot'.

"Professional actors and actresses are now being selected in Hollywood to play the various parts of persons in the Packer organizations. Some of the film will be made in Hollywood, while the remainder will be taken in Green Bay.

"Lambeau said that the film company, to be named later, will move into Green Bay about the middle of July and continue until early in August, taking scenes for background. The main actors and actresses also will be here where they can be filmed with the 'real' Green Bay background.

"The professionals, including the director, may be announced next week. Lambeau has been conferring with movie people on the coast for several months on arrangements.

"This will be the first full-length film on the Packers — probably the most novel organization in the world in that they represent a city of 50,000 persons in competition with cities many times its size. A number of movie 'shorts' have been taken on the Packers, one of which was filmed in Hollywood in the 1930's when Green Bay played a team of All-Stars there.

"The Packers have been 'written up' many times in national magazines and big city newspapers."

This was pretty heady stuff for the folks of little Green Bay. Excitement raced through the town. Green Bay was going to be in a movie. Wow! Green Bayers couldn't wait for the cameras to start rolling, but they had to wait . . . and wait . . . and wait.

Two months later another story about the proposed film appeared in the newspaper. Lambeau announced that officials from the Packer corporation would be going around town and asking various individuals to sign releases so their faces and places of business could be used in the movie and its publicity. The story also included the name of the screenwriter, Bob N. Lee, who was supposed to have worked on such epics as *Captain Kidd* and *70,000 Witnesses*, to mention a few. Representatives of the Monogram Company, the motion picture company, were due in town in August to make some preliminary studies of the town. They would return in October to do the serious shots.

Tony Owen, the man who was supposed to be the producer of *The Green Bay Story*, arrived in town on August 16. Art Daley featured an interview with Owen in his column of August 18.

From Daley's tone, Owen's remarks were packed with enthusiasm. Daley said the producer "bubbled with ideas" and that he "exploded" when he said, "Why, it will be a great inspiration to every small town in America; that they can succeed in the face of big–city odds." Owen said that Dennis Morgan and Dennis O'Keefe were being considered to play the lead.

Daley lacked experience with Owen's sort. What he was spouting was "Hollywood hype". In the Midwest, that sort of stuff is used to fertilize cornfields.

One more mention of the movie–that–never–was–filmed appeared in the newspaper on November 23 that year. Filming of *The Green Bay Story* would start in February '49 and John Hodiak was being considered for the lead role. The name of the leading character? Why, Curly Lambeau, of course.

APPENDIX F
The Alumni Association

The one thing that separated Green Bay from the big cities of professional football was the high school/collegiate spirit that the fans displayed with pride at Packer games, whether those contests were played in Green Bay, Milwaukee, Chicago, or any other NFL city. In the early years of the National Football League, the press corps of the big cities made sport of Green Bayers, pointing fingers and hiding snickers whenever the folks from Wisconsin came around. Packer players took offense at these better–than–thou attitudes of the big city boys because the people having fun poked at them were their friends and neighbors. As a way of sticking up for their supporters, the Packers kicked the butts of the big city teams and copped a trio of NFL titles from 1929 thru 1931. This brought respect for Green Bay, the Packers and their fans.

The earliest Packers were Green Bayers before they were football players. It was only natural that they should remain in Green Bay after their playing days were completed. But what of those boys who came to Green Bay from all parts of the country to play for the Packers? Many of them settled in Green Bay once their playing careers were finished. In a way, they were graduates of "Packer U."

Recognizing this fact, Fee Klaus, the big center from those earliest of teams, quietly called on a couple dozen former Packers from that era and asked them if they would be interested in forming an alumni organization. Those who were interested were asked to attend a meeting at the Silver Rail, a local pub, on the night of February 7, 1949. Much to Klaus's surprise, 20 former players turned out.

The business of that first meeting was to get organized and to establish a purpose for the group's existence. A three–man nominating committee composed of Lyle Sturgeon, a tackle from the late 1930s; Wuert Englemann, a halfback from the early '30s; and Joe Laws, the recently retired halfback who played on the '36, '39 and '44 title teams, was chosen to select a slate of candidates for the usual offices. This alumni association's primary purpose was to support the current players in whatever ways necessary to make their experience as Packers a good one.

Originally, Klaus thought only 20 or so former players were living in Green Bay, but the number turned out to be closer to 40. Several dozen more were living in Milwaukee and other parts of Wisconsin. Membership was opened up to all of them as well.

The first official meeting of the Green Bay Packers Alumni Association was held a month later on March 7, 1949. Klaus was elected president; Carl Zoll, vice-president; and Dave Zuidmulder, secretary-treasurer. The initial membership was around 40.

At the second meeting, Curly Lambeau was invited to speak to the group, and as the representative of the Green Bay Packers, Inc., he was made aware of the club's purpose which was clearly spelled out in article 2 of its bylaws:

"The purpose of this organization shall be to aid and assist the Green Bay Packers, Inc., in their endeavors to bring to Green Bay professional football of the highest calibre, and to this end, to promote morale and fighting spirit in the team personnel; by bringing to the attention of the Packer management, outstanding football players, and assist the Packer management in contacting and contracting such players; to promote and assist in developing community spirit by sponsoring or assisting in the holding of pep rallies, Monday quarterback clubs, providing speakers for or the showing of Packer football game pictures to civic and other organizations in Green Bay and surrounding areas; and by any other endeavors that will bring about our avowed purpose."

The Alumni Association scheduled its August meeting to be held at Rockwood Lodge so they could meet with the new players. Jug Earpe was selected to be the speaker. At this meeting, as their bylaws allowed them, the Alumni Association organized a Men's Quarterback Club in Green Bay. Membership in this new organization would be open to anyone but would be limited to 750 members. This was due to the fact that the meeting place, the Vocational school auditorium, seated only 750. Earpe was elected "chief" quarterback of the Men's Quarterback Club.

Besides the Alumni Association and the Men's Quarterback Club, Green Bay also had the Minute Men, a group of civic and sports minded Green Bay citizens who had come together in 1948 just before the Bears game. Businessman Jerry Atkinson chaired this organization that met in August 1949 at the Beaumont Hotel for the purpose of seeing what could be done about filling City Stadium, or at least drawing 20,000 fans, for the exhibition game with the Eagles.

These three groups symbolized the major difference between the Green Bay Packers and every other team in the NFL.

APPENDIX G
The Fans to the Rescue

Once again Packer fans proved there are no other fans like them in the world. On the afternoon of November 14, 1949, the feature story on front page of *The Green Bay Press-Gazette* read:

> Open $50,000 Drive To Save Packers
> Play Intra-Squad Tilt
> On Thanksgiving Day
> 500 Workers Will Sell Tickets;
> Club's Financial Plight Explained

By Art Daley

A campaign to raise $50,000 to keep the Packers in Green Bay was launched at a breakfast meeting of 100 "Packer Backers" at the Northland hotel this morning.

As a means of raising the money, the Packers will play an All-Star game at City stadium Thanksgiving day. The contest will feature the new Packers against the old, with Jug Girard quarterbacking the veterans and Stan Heath the newcomers.

Emil R. Fischer, president of Green Bay Packers, Inc., told the meeting that the Packers face a possible $90,000 loss this year. However, Fischer explained that this was the "most pessimistic figure" possible, and that this deficit might be reduced if attendance at remaining games is better than currently estimated.

Could Break Even

Fischer went on to say that "if your $50,000 drive is a success we stand a chance of breaking even." He explained that the

Packers have some assets, and that by applying these assets plus what is raised on this drive they could end the year even or better.

The campaign, climaxing two successive, money-losing seasons, will embrace all of Green Bay and De Pere. In addition, contacts will be made throughout the Fox river valley and other cities in the state.

Approximately 500 individuals, representing every branch of Green Bay industry and commerce, will work in the all-out campaign. The 100 Backers, or captains, who attended the meeting today will enlist the services of over 400 additional workers to make more than 2,000 contacts in Green Bay alone.

The captains are headed by seven majors — Charley Mathys, Oscar Beilefeldt, Jim Stathas, Sam Cohen, Elmer Stone, Ed Wolf, and Heraly McDonald.

Jerry Atkinson, a comparative newcomer in Green Bay who already has headed many campaigns here, is chairman of the Packer "push".

Other Groups Pitch In

Many organizations in Green Bay quickly came to the rescue over the week end, volunteering their assistance. The Brown County Tavern League will cover every tavern in this area; the Green Bay Quarterback club, with Jug Earp at the helm, will organize its own section of ticket sellers; the police department will cooperate in distributing tickets; the service clubs, private groups — everybody will boom it.

Tickets for the game will sell for $3.60 (the two middle sections on each side of the field), $2.40 (to the goal line) and $1.20.

Though the Packers Backers realize they are asking near-top prices for what amounts to an intra-squad game, hundreds of other special sidelights will be added to make the afternoon an entertaining one. Most of the added entertainment will be presented between halves and is now being worked out.

Put Cards On Table

The meeting this morning was an enthusiastic one as the Packers placed their cards on the table for everyone — including the team's legion of fans — to see.

The consensus of opinion wa that the Packers have reached the cross roads, as they did in 1933, and the spontaneous enthusiasm on the part of the more than 100 captains indicated that a step in the right direction was being taken. Advance drive feelers gave the Backers every right to be optimistic. Less than 20 contacts netted $7,000 in tickets.

One reason for arranging a drive of this type, it was pointed out, is that employers who purchase blocks of tickets to give to employees or customers can deduct them as business costs.

The National Football league is even "contributing" to the campaign. Commissioner Bert Bell has announced that the league will waive its usual two per cent on gate receipts of all league attractions. The only "expense" will be the federal tax.

Atkinson Sounds Keynote

Atkinson sounded the keynote with this:

"We have no angels in Green Bay; we've got to get out and work to keep the Packers here."

E.L. Lambeau, the Packers' general manager and advisory coach, launched the meeting by reviewing the war between the National Football league and All–America conference, declaring that "it would not be necessary to hold a meeting of this kind if things were normal."

The player–price war between the two circuits, started in 1946, shot salaries "entirely out of line. A well–known coach in the other circuit came into Green Bay in 1946 and offered to double the salaries of every Packer player," Lambeau said.

The Packer mentor expressed optimism that the war would end after the present season for this reason: "To (sic) many of the rich owners in the other circuit are fed up with taking tremendous losses and are anxious to get out of the game," he pointed out.

Fischer, speaking straight from the shoulder, followed with

The Lambeau Years — Part Three

his important words. Though salaries are high, the Packer president stated that "our biggest losses naturally resulted form smaller attendance. Our losses last year amounted to $33,000, but we had resources to cover it."

Danger of Losing Packers

Fischer, revealing the possible $90,000 deficit, stated bluntly that "there is danger of losing the Packers if your goal is not reached."

H.J. Wintgens, chairman of the Packer finance committee, advanced the possibility that "our budgeted $90,000 deficit could be reduced to $75,000 or $80,000 if we get a break on attendance at our games in Milwaukee (against Pittsburgh next Sunday) and Washington. However, we budgeted $65,000 for yesterday's game (Giants at City stadium) and came with $50,000."

Wintgens stated that its costs approximately $31,000 to put the Packers on the field for each game.

Bill Servotte, a member of the Packer executive committee, reiterated Fischer's statements and emphasized that the "future of the Packers rest on this drive."

Jug Earp, an all-time Packer center who is chief quarterback of the Quarterback club, said that the club (sponsored by the Green Bay Packer Alumni association) would "spread the gospel. We understand the predicament the Packers are in and every one of our 850 members is willing to pitch in." He said drive plans will be presented at next Thursday night's meeting at Vocational school.

Borgenson Explains Mechanics

John A. Borgenson, executive secretary of the Association of Commerce, explained the mechanics of the drive.

More than 2,000 cards, with names of industries, business establishments and many other organizations, were distributed in packs of 20 to the 100 captains. Borgenson said that the police department will deliver tickets to the buyers as soon as the check or cash is received by the worker and turned in to the Packer ticket office.

Six committees have been formed from some of the Packer Backers to work out details of the campaign and game. Headed by Chairman Atkinson, the committees follow:

Publicity — John Torinus, chairman, Bidwell Gage, Don Fairbairn, Claire Stone, Earl Gillespie, Ben Laird, Art Daley, Bob Savage, George Strickler.

Entertainment — Bob Meyer, chairman, Russ Leddy, Haydn Evans, Russ Petreat, Bill Burke, Verne Lewallen, Jug Earp, Herb Nichols.

Tickets — Frank Jonet.

Ticket Distribution — H.J. Bero.

Prizes — Bob Meyer, chairman, F.M. Cooper, Marlowe Baxter, Max Baier, Jim Boex, Bill Clancy, Carl Janssen.

Program — Bob Turek, chairman, Frank Jonet.

In an effort to spur the fans to respond quickly, the newspaper appealed to their hearts by printing a letter from Ralph W. Kluge, a Black Creek, Wisconsin, student who was attending college in St. Louis, dated October 19. In part it read:

"I am a young man from Black Creek who has been a Packer fan for years. The past several seasons I have been a student down here at St. Louis and thus have been unable to attend the games. This season the only game I can plan on is the Packer-Cardinal game in Chicago during the Thanksgiving recess. Since then I shall give the price of the tickets to the rival club, please accept this postal note as a token of the faithfulness of a Packer fan."

Enclosed was a postal note (money order) for $5.

Just as George Whitney Calhoun had done in the early years of the Packers' history, Art Daley pushed the community to support the team. His headline in the *Press-Gazette* on November 16 read:

Packer Drive Hits $7,000 Mark;
Governor To Fly Here for AllStar Tilt

In the opening article, Daley had stated that pledges of $7,000 had already been taken, but no one noticed his faux pas.

In response to an *Associated Press* story that said the Packers were in such dire straits that they were forced to play exhibitions between their own players and charge their fans for the privilege of watching a practice, Emil Fischer replied that "the Thanksgiving day game is a civic undertaking sponsored by Packer fans in Green Bay and came entirely unsolicited by the Packer organization. Green Bay will remain permanently in the National Football league."

Daley considered the success of the Thanksgiving Day fete so important that he put headlines about the progress of the fund-raising campaign over the results of the Packers' game with Pittsburgh. It was just as well because the Steelers won the game, and only 5,483 fans turned out to watch the contest played in Milwaukee. The drive was now up to $25,535.

Approximately 15,000 fans turned out on a snowy Thanksgiving Day to watch the intrasquad game. Enough tickets were sold to raise $42,174 and pledges for $7,826 were made to help Atkinson's group reach its goal of $50,000.

The game featured the Jug Girard led Veterans wearing the blue uniforms and Stan Heath leading the Newcomers clad in gold. The Vets won, 35-31. The "guest" coaches, chosen by drawing from the audience and allowed to sit on the benches with the players were Jo Ann Brazier and Sheila Edelbeck, both 16 and from Green Bay, and 13-year-old Jerry Zablocki from Pulaski, Wisconsin. Cub Buck was unable to make it to the game because of the snowstorm in the southern part of the state. Special attention was given to Jimmy Choles, a factory worker and former shoeshine boy who donated $100 to the Packers; but the shy Choles declined to accept an invitation to sit on the bench with the players. When he was summoned to the sidelines by field announcer Jimmy Coffeen between halves, he left in haste when asked to have his picture taken with the players.

Once again the fans saved the Packers from oblivion.

Appendix H
Who Really Owned the Packers?

In the photo section of this book are pictures of three documents that are supposed to represent the same basic thing; i.e., a certificate of membership in the National Football League. Two are for the Green Bay Packers, while the other is for the Philadelphia Eagles. At a glance, one can easily see that two of the documents bare very little resemblance to the third. That is because those two are real, while the other is a very poor attempt at forgery.

The odd certificate for the Packers was copied from the sports pages of the November 9, 1945 issue of *The Green Bay Press-Gazette*. The real certificate for the Eagles was photocopied from the original which is in the library of the Professional Football Hall of Fame in Canton, Ohio. The real certificate for the Packers was photocopied from a photocopy on file at the same library.

The caption under the bogus Packer certificate read:

"Did you ever see this before? It is the franchise of the Green Bay Packers in the National Football League. It was issued in July 1935 and represents the transfer from the Green Bay Football corporation to the Green Bay Packers, Inc. Its value has been estimated by sports writers around the country from $100,000 to $250,000. Lee Joannes, president of the Green Bay Packers, Inc., declines to estimate its value. He says: 'What is the difference how much it's worth, it's not for sale and it is owned by a non-profit corporation. It cannot be transferred without a majority vote of the 461 shares of stock owned by 104 stockholders which would be practically impossible to obtain because a comparatively small number of the shareholders own more than one or two shares and these are mostly manufacturing and mercantile business concerns. It doesn't seem that any of these would vote to send the Packers away from Green Bay."

On February 2, 1950, while cleaning out his office at Packer headquarters, Curly Lambeau was photographed removing the certificate that granted him a franchise in the National Football League from a file cabinet drawer. The caption said that the document was dated June 24, 1922. Lambeau was quoted. He said jokingly, "Say, I never did get my fifty dollars for that."

Following Lambeau's remark in the *Press-Gazette* was this enclosed statement: "(The franchise was later turned over to the corporation when the Packers were reorganized.)" Now why did Art Daley go to all the trouble to make this point? Was there truth to the rumor that Lambeau still owned the franchise?

Let's go back to 1921 and examine the facts.

The American Professional Football Association was begun in 1920 at a meeting in Canton, Ohio of managers and owners of professional teams. On August 27, 1921, the APFA granted a franchise to John and Emmett Clair of the Acme Packing Company to field a professional football team in Green Bay, Wisconsin. In a late season game, the Packers employed three college players in a game. When this was discovered and brought to the attention of Joe Carr, the APFA president, a cry for blood went up. Emmett Clair attended the league meeting in January 1922. He made an apology for using the college players, and he voluntarily surrendered the franchise for Green Bay.

Unwilling to give up on professional football in Green Bay, Curly Lambeau attended the first APFA meeting held during the summer of 1922. He applied for a new franchise for Green Bay and was told he could have one providing he could come up with the fee for the franchise and pay $1,000 into the Guarantee Fund before September 1. Curly went back to Green Bay and found a backer, Nathan Abrams, who put up the money for the Guarantee Fund. Once the money was received by Joe Carr he issued a franchise certificate to E.L. Lambeau to operate a professional football team in Green Bay, Wisconsin. The certificate was signed at Dayton, Ohio on August 21, 1922. It was signed by Carl L.H. Storck, and Joe F. Carr, secretary and president of the NFL, respectively.

Now that he had his franchise Lambeau and three friends, George Whitney Calhoun, Joe Ordens, and Nate Abrams, founded the Green Bay Football Club on September 8, 1922. They filed their incorporation papers with the secretary of state of Wisconsin on September 13, 1922, then registered them in Brown county on September 14, 1922. (Certified copies of these papers are still on file at the Brown County Courthouse and at the corporation division of the secretary of state's office in Madison.)

Now that they were in business they had stationery printed up that had some very interesting items on the letterhead.*

At the top of the letterhead was the rejoinder:

WISCONSIN PROFESSIONAL CHAMPIONS SINCE 1917

Note that (1) it didn't state that they were Wisconsin's *amateur* champions since 1917; (2) it didn't state that they were Wisconsin's professional champions *since 1919*, the mythical year that Curly Lambeau allegedly founded the Packers.

Below the credibility statement was the title of the business:

Green Bay Football Club

And beneath the title was another interesting item in small type and in parentheses:

Formerly Packers

This was Lambeau's attempt to disassociate his new franchise with the one that Emmett Clair had surrendered back in January. Because they were playing in blue and gold uniforms and because Calhoun had called them "the Big Bay Blues" in

---

* See photo section for letter from Lambeau to Art Schmaehl.

His column on occasion, Lambeau had opted to call his team the Green Bay Blues. The fans wouldn't let this name stick, however, because they knew Curly and most of the boys on the squad as the Packers.

To the left of the title, the executives were listed. Odd, but their offices weren't listed with the names of E.L. Lambeau, Nathan Abrams, and G.W. Calhoun. The text of the letter might hold a clue as to why they were listed without their official capacities. (Please note that I have not corrected Lambeau's spelling typos, but I have corrected the typewriter typos where words were run together. Also, I have italicized a few important parts of the letter.)

Sept. 17, 1922
Dear Friend Art:
We have a good team and are practicing every day. Buck, Murray, Moose Gardner, Owens, Nadolney constitutes our line with Dunnigan and Faye on ends. Our backfield is composed of Regnier of the Manines, Taugher and Cronin of Marquette, Davis and Chas. Mathys.

With exception of Mathys these fellows are playing for forty and fifty per game and living here. Now Art I want you to play here if possible. *I haven't it all to say* but I know I can get you 65 a game for you. If these figures are satisfactory please let me know at once. The management will not pay your transportation from Detroit.

There is a business man in town furnishing us all the money and he is the man that decides every money problem. He wants his name Kept out of Athletics or it would be made public.

Our first game is the 24th so we will have to rush things along.

With kindest personal regards,
(Signed) *Curly*

Curly stated that he wasn't in complete charge of things, and he wrote that a businessman in town was backing the team. The questions are simple: Who, besides Lambeau, had a say in running the team? Who was this businessman who wanted his name kept out of athletics?

Obvisouly, Abrams and Calhoun had a say in the business of the Green Bay Football Club. So did Joe Ordens, as attested by the article written by Calhoun for a game program in 1946 that stated Ordens was part of the decision-making process when the management of the Packers was trying to decide whether to play the Thanksgiving Day game against the Duluth Kellys in 1922. The question is: Which of these three was the businessman that Lambeau mentioned in his letter to Art Schmaehl? Certainly not Calhoun the journalist. Possibly Ordens but not likely because he was a pencil pusher, not a financier. That only leaves Abrams who had been a businessman since he had started buying and selling cattle for a living at the age of 15. It was Abrams who helped Lambeau get his job with the Indian Packing Corporation in 1919, and it was Abrams who did a considerable amount of business with Lambeau's employer. Of the four incorporators of the Green Bay Football Club, Abrams was the only one who had the means to support the team.

The Packers played the 1922 season. Some really horrible weather and a lousy record kept the crowds down, and this hurt the club financially because they were bound by NFL rules to pay each visiting team a guarantee of $1,500 or 40% of the gate receipts (after stadium rental was deducted), depending on which figure was higher. If Lambeau's letter to Schmaehl is to be believed, the club was paying its players a total of about $1,000 per game. Other expenses mounted to the neighborhood of $1,000 per game. Just to break even on a home game, the club had to take in $3,500 in ticket sales. To do that, they had to sell all 2,000 tickets for prime seats at $1.65 each and an additional 500 tickets for end zone seats at $1.10 each. They failed to draw this many fans more than twice during the season.*

The Green Bay Football Club was deep in debt when the 1922 season ended, but it wasn't out of business yet. The club, a legal entity itself, borrowed $3,000 from Nate Abrams to pay its bills. Abrams was given the franchise to hold as collateral.

Lambeau attended the January 1923 meeting of the NFL and

---

* **See Chapter 6 of** *The History of the Green Bay Packers: The Lambeau Years — Part One.*

had the name Green Bay Football Club placed over his name on his franchise certificate. As far as the NFL was concerned, he was still in business. He attended the summer meetings in July under the same pretext.

During the ensuing year, a new corporation was formed in Green Bay. The Green Bay Football Corporation was organized officially on August 14, 1923. Its incorporation papers were filed with the secretary of state on August 23, 1923. (Certified copies of these papers are still on file at the Brown County Courthouse and at the corporation division of the secretary of state's office in Madison.) In time, this new organization paid off the loan from Abrams, and he returned the franchise to Lambeau who gave his tacit approval to the Green Bay Football Corporation to handle the franchise. From this time forward, the National Football League franchise for the city of Green Bay, Wisconsin has been *operated* by this corporation and its re-organized successor.

During the mid-1940s, rumors began to crop up that the Packers would be moved to a big city. Word had it that Lambeau still owned the franchise and that he planned to move it to Los Angeles or some other big city, possibly San Francisco. In an effort to squelch these tales, Ray Pagel, sports editor of the *Press-Gazette* was given a photograph of a phony franchise certificate by someone,* which he printed in the newspaper, thinking nothing was wrong with it. The importance of the photo wasn't so much the certificate but the caption which attempted to convince readers that the Packers couldn't be shifted to another city without permission of the stockholders and that wasn't likely to happen. The picture of the certificate was meant to reinforce the denial that Lambeau still had the franchise in his possession.

* **Most likely this someone was Andy Turnbull, top man at the *Press-Gazette*. Lee Remmel, who was a reporter for the newspaper at that time, related that Turnbull had a policy of printing nothing derogatory about Lambeau or the Packers' management. Turnbull was still the big power behind Lambeau and the Packers until his retirement from the Packers' corporation in 1948.**

The photo of the certificate was published on November 9, 1945. This was a Friday. Lambeau was out of town with the team and on the way to Cleveland by the time the newspaper hit the newsstands. Could it be that Pagel deliberately waited until Lambeau was out of town and was unlikely to see the picture at all, especially since he would be absent from Green Bay for more than three weeks? Yes.

To silence the chatter once and for all, Lambeau was given a new contract after the Cleveland game on November 11, 1945.* All was quiet for a couple of years before the series of events that led to Lambeau's resignation began.

When push came to shove between Lambeau and the executive committee again in 1949, the rumors flew anew. The most prominent of these had Lambeau and Vic McCormick preparing to take over the corporation and re-organizing it into a profit-sharing business. Lambeau even made this proposition public before that fateful board of directors meeting in late November. To divert Lambeau once again from making a move on the franchise, the board voted to renew Lambeau's contract for two years.

Lambeau felt that he had won the battle with Jerry Clifford and discarded his plans to gain control of the corporation and re-organize it. Then Emil Fischer met him at the winter meeting in Philadelphia and presented him with a contract that was unacceptable. Instead of renewing the fight, Lambeau packed up and left Green Bay for the Chicago Cardinals, taking the franchise certificate with him.

Although Lambeau was gone, the question of whether he still owned the franchise persisted in popping up. That point became moot in 1963 when Lambeau turned over the franchise certificate to the Green Bay Packers, Inc.

More than one person who knew personally Lambeau related that he was a known liar; "an inveterate liar," said one; "an incorrigible liar," said another. But he did tell the truth on occasion, such as those times when he was quoted more than once as saying that he didn't own the franchise. He did own a

---

* See Chapter 18, page 231 of *The History of the Green Bay Packers, The Lambeau Years Part Two*.

franchise certificate of membership in the NFL, but that certificate only granted him the right to field a team in Green Bay, Wisconsin to play in the NFL for the 1922 season.

All of this business of who owned the franchise was actually superfluous. On the day that Lambeau gave his permission for the Green Bay Football Club to operate his franchise, he began to surrender any claim to ownership of the Green Bay Packers football team. To complicate matters further, the Green Bay Football Club then allowed the Green Bay Football Corporation to operate the franchise in 1923, and it passed the baton to its successor, the Green Bay Packers, Inc., in 1935. None of these changes of command were registered with the NFL, but they took place all the same. These unofficial transfers of the franchise made each corporation that operated the team after Lambeau was granted a franchise de facto owners of the Green Bay Packers.

Who owns the Packers? The fans, who else?

Index

— A —

Aberson, Cliff - 39, 62
Abrams, Nathan (Nate) - 12, 60, 190, 191, 198, 201-203, 221-224
Agase, Alex - 57, 79
Agase, Lou - 79
Akron, Ohio - 22
Alabama, Univ. of - 88, 93, 95, 204
Alabama Polytechnic Institute - 23
Alger, Horatio - 159
All-America Football Conference (AAC) - 23-27, 29-31, 37, 38, 42, 47-49, 53-57, 64, 77-80, 82-89, 92, 93, 95, 108-115, 121-123, 125, 133, 136-140, 142, 151, 156, 158-166, 170, 194, 216
Ameche, Don - 24, 26, 30
American Association (baseball) - 29, 52
American Football Association (AFA) - 28, 29, 52, 88
American Football League (AFL) - 21-23, 28, 35, 109
American Professional Football Association (APFA) - 190, 191, 207, 221
Ammon, Ralph E. - 37, 50, 51
Andrews, Nathan (also Abrams, Nathan) - 12
Arizona State University - 133
Arkansas, Univ. of - 39, 90
Arnold, Benedict - 159, 160
Associated Press - 51, 59, 81, 114, 121, 122, 151, 158, 166, 176, 219
Atkinson, Dr. H.S. - 96, 127
Atkinson, Jerry - 105, 116, 150, 213, 215, 216, 219
Auburn University - 101

-B-

Baier, Max - 218
Baldwin, Burr - 57
Baltimore, Md. - 21, 27, 46, 47, 54, 84, 114, 115, 163, 164
Baltimore Colts (AAC) - 84, 85, 88, 109, 113, 114, 122, 123, 138, 140, 163, 175
Baltimore Touchdown Club - 53
Barnett, Bubo - 40
Barnett, Mrs. Colleen - 12
Baugh, Sammy - 35, 67, 101
Baxter, Lloyd - 93, 95
Baxter, Marlowe - 218
Baylor University - 39
Bednarik, Chuck - 121
Beilefeldt, Oscar - 215
Bell, Alexander Graham - 30
Bell, Bert - 29, 31, 32, 42, 46-48, 52-54, 64, 83-87, 93, 110-113, 115, 121, 136-139, 156, 158-160, 164, 165, 180, 216

Bell, Ed - 65, 93, 126
Bellevue Park (Green Bay, Wis.) - 29
Beloit, Wis. - 205
Bennett, Jug - 39
Bennigsen, Ray C. - 86, 177, 179
Bentley, William - 24
Bernard, E.B. - 102, 116
Bero, H.J. - 64, 148, 218
Bertelli, Angelo - 26
Beverly Hills, Calif. - 187
Bidwill, Charles - 32, 52, 170
Bidwill, Mrs. Violet M. - 170
Bierman, Bernie - 81, 120
Biggers, Charles - 90, 95
Birmingham, Alab. - 96
Black Creek, Wis. - 218
Blanda, George - 121
Blood, Johnny - 143, 196, 197, 208
Boex, Jim - 218
Boex, Milan J. - 63, 64, 148
Bogda, Russell W. - 63, 64, 148
Booth, John Wilkes - 146
Borgenson, John A. - 217
Boston, Mass. - 21, 54, 96, 103, 163
Boston Yanks (NFL) - 27, 32, 65, 70, 72, 82, 88, 93-96, 100, 109, 112, 114, 115, 129, 163
Boyle, Maj. Gen. Leo M. - 108
Brazier, Jo Ann - 219
Breuil, James - 113
Brickner, F.J. - 22
Brock, Charley - 40, 41, 65, 82, 90, 94, 123, 124, 131, 132, 151, 196, 197
Brogan, Hugh - 50-52
Brogan, John J. - 49-52, 84, 108
Brooklyn, N.Y. - 27
Brooklyn Dodgers (AAC) - 31, 32, 88, 109, 114, 115, 163, 166
Brooklyn Dodgers (baseball) - 86
Brooklyn Tigers (NFL) - 22, 24, 25, 27, 30, 31, 34, 100
Brown, Howard - 93
Brown, Paul - 23, 24, 26
Bruder, Hank - 197
Buck, Cub - 190, 195, 219, 223
Buffalo, N.Y. - 22, 54, 114, 115, 139, 140, 180
Buffalo Bisons (AAC) - 23, 24, 32
Buffalo Bills (AAC) *(see also Buffalo Bisons)* - 112-114, 123, 138-140, 163
Bunyan, Paul - 159
Burke, Bill - 218
Burris, Paul - 123, 125
Bush, Albert J. "Jack" - 126
Butler, Walker - 108

-C-

Calhoun, George Whitney - 41, 44, 58-60, 146, 147, 168, 174, 184, 191, 193, 198-203, 205, 206, 218, 222-224
Callahan, James - 57
Canada, Bud - 129
Canadeo, Tony - 39, 56, 65-67, 78, 90-93, 98, 102-104, 107, 126, 127, 130, 132, 134, 135, 197
Canton, Ohio - 167, 220
Carr, Joe - 203, 221, 222
Case, Ernie - 57
Catawba College - 90
Chicago, Illinois - 15, 22-24, 26, 27, 30, 31, 39, 43, 49, 50, 52, 54, 70, 77, 85, 88, 89, 105, 108, 109, 111, 113-115, 125, 127, 137, 158, 159, 163, 166, 167, 169, 171, 177, 211, 218
Chicago, Univ. of - 37, 39
Chicago Bears (NFL) - 14, 26, 32, 33, 35, 36, 41-44, 48, 52, 63, 65-74, 78, 87, 88, 97-100, 102-105, 108, 109, 111, 113, 117, 129, 130, 133, 134, 140, 163, 164, 171, 204, 208
Chicago Cardinals (NFL) - 32, 34, 43-45, 49, 52, 53, 61, 63, 66-69, 71-74, 86-88, 94, 95, 98-104, 106, 109, 111, 113, 133-135, 140, 152, 154, 157, 163, 164, 167, 170, 176, 177, 179, 180, 183, 185, 218, 226
Chicago Cubs - 62
Chicago Herald-Examiner, The - 59
Chicago Hornets (AAC) *(see also Chicago Rockets)* - 113, 114, 115, 123, 139, 141, 151, 163, 166
Chicago Rockets (AAC) - 23, 24, 32, 37, 49-53, 84, 88, 93, 108, 109, 113-115, 123, 125, 151
Chicago Stadium - 59
Chicago Tribune, The - 46, 59, 85, 86, 95, 179
Chicago Tribune Charities - 86, 95
Choles, Jimmy - 219
Christman, Paul - 66, 67, 98
Church, Norman W. - 26
Cifers, Bob - 128, 132, 135
Cincinnati, Ohio - 22, 77, 137
Ciraolo, Frank - 52
Clair, Emmett - 60, 191, 207, 221, 222
Clair, John - 60, 191, 207, 221
Clancy, Bill - 218
Clemens, Ray - 65, 94
Clement, Frank - 82
Cleveland, Ohio - 54, 115, 226
Cleveland Browns (AAC) - 23-26, 32, 37, 38, 49, 54, 109, 112-115, 136-140, 163
Cleveland Panthers - *(see Cleveland Browns)*
Cleveland Rams *(see also Los Angeles Rams)* - 32-34, 42, 125
Clifford, Gerald F. - 12, 63, 64, 81, 143, 146-148, 168, 171, 174, 178, 182-185, 187, 226
Cody, Ed - 57, 65, 68, 93, 104, 126, 128, 129
Coffeen, Jimmy - 219

Cohen, Sam - 215
Coliseum, The (Los Angeles, Calif.) - 32, 106
Collins, Ted - 21, 138, 139
Columbia University - 23, 88
Columbus Panhandles (NFL) - 203
Comiskey Park (Chicago) - 71
Comp, Irv - 38, 40, 45, 65, 66, 70, 93, 96, 126, 128, 129, 132, 134, 204
Compton (Calif.) Junior College - 126
Connerly, Charley - 88, 134
Connor, George - 88
Conrad, Bob - 81
Conzelman, Jimmy - 43, 44, 61, 66, 120
Cook, Ted - 93, 101, 126, 135
Cooper, F.M. - 218
Cooper, Gary - 127
Cordovano, Sam - 23, 24
Cowboy Quarterback, The - 14
Craig, Larry - 40, 62, 65, 93, 97, 104, 126, 127, 129, 132, 139, 197
Cremer, Ted - 101
Crimmins, Bernie - 36
Croft, Tiny - 40, 43, 65, 78, 94
Cronin - 223
Crosby, Bing - 26
Cross, Hugh W. - 108
Crowley, James - 23, 26, 27, 47, 49, 51-54, 84, 108
Cruice, Wally - 68
Cuff, Ward - 60, 61, 65, 67, 70-72, 74
Cunz, Bob - 90

-D-

Daily Georgian and Sunday American (Atlanta, Ga.) - 59
Daley, Art - 12, 41, 42, 45, 50, 57, 60, 62, 68, 70-72, 84, 85, 100-103, 105, 135, 153, 156, 157, 167, 171, 172, 197-199, 204, 206, 207, 210, 214, 218, 219, 221
Dallas, Texas - 22, 46, 77, 84, 85, 139
Davis, Paul - 223
Davis, Ralph - 65, 93, 126, 129
Dayton, Ohio - 222
Deeks, Don - 93, 94, 104, 126
DeGroot, Dudley - 185
De Moss, Bob - 121
Dempsey, Jack - 59
Denver, Colo. - 40
De Pere, Wis. - 46, 215
Detroit, Mich. - 22, 44, 54, 103, 135
Detroit Lions (NFL) - 26, 30, 32, 33, 42, 44, 61, 63, 68, 70, 73, 87, 88, 93, 98, 100-103, 111, 121, 133-135, 140, 153, 158, 164
Detroit Panthers (NFL) - 44
Devine, Paul W. "Andy" - 125
Dicker, Edward T. - 139
Dilweg, Lavvie - 195, 197
Dixie League (DL) - 29
Dorais, Gus - 61, 158
Dudley, Bill - 68, 98
Duluth Eskimos (NFL) - 200-203
Duluth Kellys - 201, 203, 224

Dunn, Red - 192, 196, 197
Dunnigan - 223
Dworsky, Dan - 122
Dyer, Braven - 160, 165

-E-

Earhart, Ralph - 80, 90, 94, 96, 100, 124, 126, 129
Earpe, Jug - 196, 197, 213, 215, 217, 218
Eason, Roger - 128
East Lansing, Mich. - 61
Ecklund, Brad - 122, 123
Edelbeck, Sheila - 219
Engebretsen, Paul "Tiny" - 197
Englemann, Wuert - 212
Etheridge, Joe - 125
Evans, Haydn - 218
Evanston, Ill. - 123

-F-

Fairbairn, Don - 218
Fairbanks-Morse football team, Beloit, Wis. - 205, 206
Fairchild, O.W. "Shutout" - 103
Faunce, Everett - 122
Faye, Allen "Doc" - 223
Fears, Tom - 124, 132
Fennimore, Bob - 49, 87
Ferraro, John - 57
Ferry, Lou - 125, 132
Fesler, Wesley - 186
Fife, Lyle - 87
Filchock, Frank - 48, 53
Fischer, Emil R. - 63, 64, 77, 78, 94, 96, 127, 131, 147, 148, 160, 161, 164, 166, 169, 170, 172, 175-177, 179, 180, 183-185, 187, 188, 214, 216, 217, 219, 226
Flagstead, Melvin - 175, 176
Flaherty, Ray - 27, 80
Flaherty, Vincent X. - 185, 188, 194
Flowers, Bob - 39, 65, 93, 95, 101, 104, 126, 130
Football Writers Association - 136
Ford, Jim - 126
Fordham University - 23
Fort Worth, Texas - 22
Forte, Al - 65
Forte, Bob - 39, 63, 65, 67, 71, 93, 104, 126, 127
Fraley, Oscar - 26, 180-184
Frankowski, Bob - 38
Fritsch, Ted - 38, 40-44, 56, 63, 65-68, 71, 72, 74, 93, 100, 103, 126, 145, 197
Fullerton, Hugh - 122, 151

-G-

Gage, Bidwell - 218
Gagne, Verne - 129
Gallagher, James T. - 62
Gallery, Thomas - 24
Gantenbein, Milt - 34, 195, 197, 204

Gardner, Moose - 223
Garn, R.E. - 108
Gatewood, Lester "Buddy" - 39, 65
Georgia, Univ. of - 39, 49, 121, 126
Giesler, Jerry - 22
Gillespie, Earl "The Lip" - 82, 110, 218
Gillette, Jim - 65, 70, 93
Gilmer, Harry - 88, 95, 96
Gipp, George - 189
Girard, Mrs. Ann - 81
Girard, Earl "Jug" - 79-81, 88, 90, 94, 106, 126, 128, 219
Goldenberg, Buckets - 120, 183, 196, 197
Goodman, Jim - 129
Goodnight, Clyde - 40, 41, 56, 65, 68, 78, 93, 105, 106, 124-126, 130
Grange, Harold E. "Red" - 22, 25, 27, 28
Great Depression, The - 31, 62
Green Bay Blues - 223
Green Bay Football Club, Inc. - 12, 94, 97, 222, 224, 225, 227
Green Bay Football Corporation - 15, 225, 227
Green Bay Packers, Inc. - 16, 36, 118, 142, 143, 167, 169, 193, 194, 212, 214, 220, 226, 227
Green Bay Press-Gazette - 13, 41, 42, 44, 48, 50, 51, 56-58, 60, 68, 69, 76, 77, 81, 84, 91, 94, 97, 100-103, 106, 110, 116, 119, 122, 130, 138, 148, 153, 174, 176, 179, 185, 195, 197, 198, 200, 201, 203-205, 209, 210, 214, 218, 220, 221, 225
Green Bay Whales - 60
Gregg, Forrest - 11
Grimes, Charles - 24

-H-

Hagemeister Park (Green Bay, Wis.) - 29
Halas, George - 29, 30, 49, 52, 65, 70, 71, 85, 97, 112-114, 120, 137, 138, 160-162, 164, 169, 171
Hanley, Richard - 23, 123
Hansen, Carl J. - 169
Hansen, L. F. - 97, 98
Hapes, Merle - 48, 53
Harmon, Tom - 136
Hardin-Simmons College - 26, 39
Harding, Roger - 134
Hartley, Howard - 101
Haskell Institute - 123
Heath, Stan - 80, 121, 124, 128, 129, 133, 219
Heidelberg College - 125
Heiss, Bob - 94
Hemingway, Ernest - 119
Hennigan, Charley - 35
Herber, Arnie - 40, 61, 145, 196, 197, 204
Herber, Mrs. Arnie - 145
Hess, Erwin L. - 200, 201
Hester, Harvey - 24
Hinkle, Clarke - 46, 196, 197, 208
Hirsch, Elroy " Crazy Legs" - 125, 132
Hodiak, John - 210

The Lambeau Years — Part Three

Hoeffel, Joe - 190
Hollywood, Calif. - 14, 15, 57, 92, 143, 182, 192, 193, 209
Honolulu, Hawaii - 22
Honolulu Bears (USFL) - 22
Hope, Bob - 170
Horton, Orman "Red" - 93
Houston, Texas - 139, 140, 180
Houston Oilers (NFL) - 35
Hubbard, Cal - 192, 195, 197, 198, 207, 208
Hutson, Don - 16, 33-36, 39, 40, 62, 63, 92, 94, 106, 123, 124, 132, 173, 195, 204

-I-

Illinois, Univ. of - 57, 79, 85, 90, 94
Indiana University - 59, 65, 121, 144
Ingram, Admiral Jonas W. - 53, 54, 83, 113, 136
International News Service - 59
Iron Mountain, Mich. - 171
Iron Mountain News, The - 171
Iowa, Univ. of - 39
Isbell, Cecil - 35, 40, 84, 123, 163, 175, 196, 197, 204

-J-

Jacobs, Jack - 57, 62, 63, 65-67, 69-71, 74, 78, 93, 95-98, 100, 101, 104, 105, 107, 124, 126, 128, 129, 134
Jacunski, Harry - 34
Janesville, Wis. - 205, 206
Janssen, Carl - 218
Joannes, Leland - 32, 36, 37, 40, 62, 63, 142-144, 146, 147, 171, 182, 184, 220
Johnson, Clyde - 93
Johnson, Glen - 133
Johnson, Van - 92
Jones, Biff - 123
Jonet, Frank - 40, 94, 127, 142, 143, 146, 176, 218

-K-

Kalosh, Mike - 93, 95
Kaukauna, Wis. - 169
Keeshin, John L. - 23, 24, 49
Kekeris, Jim - 95, 126
Kelley, Edward A. - 126
Kelley, William "Wild Bill" - 125
Kelly, Dr. W.W. - 146, 147, 168, 170, 171, 174, 182-184, 193
Kennedy, Myrna - 143
Kenosha, Wis. - 154
Kentucky, Univ. of - 79, 90, 93, 121
Kercheval, Ralph - 100
Kessing, O.O. "Scrappy" - 136, 138, 139
Keuper, Ken - 40, 41, 62, 65, 93, 208
Kezar Stadium (San Francisco, Calif.) - 32
Kiesling, Walt - 39, 40, 62, 94, 122, 123, 151
King, Joe - 112, 136
Kirby, Jack - 133
Klaus, Fee - 211, 212

Klawans, J. Rufus - 87
Kluge, Ralph W. - 218
Kranz, Ken - 125, 127, 132
Kovatch, John - 65
Kuechle, Oliver - 51, 52, 166, 182-184, 194
Kupcinet, Irv - 137
Kuusisto, Bill - 40

-L-

LaCrosse State Teachers College - 93
Lafayette College - 61
Laird, Ben - 218
Lambeau, Marcel - 190
Lambeau, Marguerite - 144, 190, 193
Lang, James W. - 169
Lansing, Hal - 75
Larson, Lloyd - 76, 77, 112, 116, 119, 120, 123
Lawler, Allen - 104
Lawrence College - 39
Laws, Joe - 36, 197, 212
Lawton, Mich. - 50
Layden, Elmer - 24, 26, 27, 31, 59
Layne, Bobby - 88, 104, 140
Leahy, Frank - 77, 165
Leddy, Russ - 218
Lee, Bill - 39
Lee, Bob N. - 210
Leicht, Fred - 64
Letlow, Russ - 39, 196, 197
Lewellen, Verne - 196, 197, 218
Lewis, Floyd - 129
Lewis, Glenn - 125, 127, 129
Lhost, Harvey - 63, 64, 148
Lincoln, Abraham - 146
Lindheimer, Ben - 26, 113-115, 161, 166, 185-188
Lipp, Joseph J. - 108
Lipscomb, Paul - 40, 65, 78, 93, 126
Lombardi, Vince - 107
Los Angeles, Calif. - 22, 32, 54, 77, 80, 81, 89, 100, 113-115, 143, 144, 159, 160, 163, 165, 166, 173, 186, 187, 225
Los Angeles Dons (AAC) - 24, 26, 32, 38, 54, 77-79, 81, 82, 112-115, 136, 139, 141, 159, 165, 166, 185, 186
Los Angeles Examiner, The - 185
Los Angeles Rams (NFL) - 32-34, 38, 41-45, 57, 63, 66-69, 73, 77, 88, 93, 99, 100, 102, 106, 111, 113, 114, 123-125, 128, 132-134, 136, 139, 140, 160, 170, 172, 173, 176
Luckman, Sid - 35, 67, 70
Luhn, Nolan - 40, 56, 65-67, 69, 78, 93, 101, 104, 124, 126
Lujack, Johnny - 87, 97, 130
Lynch, R.G. - 133, 151

-M-

Madison, Wis. - 51, 60, 189, 222, 225
Magnani, Dante - 43
Majkowski, Don - 13
Maley, Howie "Red" - 95

Malibu, Calif. - 187
Mandel, Fred - 26, 61, 87
Manhattan College - 22
Manitowoc, Wis. - 208
Mara, Tim - 25, 27, 31, 111, 137, 138, 160, 161, 166
Marinette, Wis. - 79, 80, 128
Marquette University - 37, 61, 109, 123, 171
Marshall, George Preston - 22-24, 29, 30, 85-87, 95, 101, 114, 137, 138, 140, 158, 160, 161, 163
Mastrangeli, John - 129
Mathys, Charley - 215, 223
Mayer, Louis B. - 26
Maznicki, Frank - 43
McAdams, Dean - 22, 23
McArdle, Mickey - 57
McBride, Arthur "Mickey" - 24, 138
McCarthy, Glenn - 139
McCormick, Vic - 127, 168, 172, 174, 175, 226
McDonald, Heraly - 215
McDougal, Bob - 60, 61, 65
McGeary, Clarence - 79
McKay, Roy - 40, 41, 65, 93
McLean, Ray "Scooter" - 108
McNally, Johnny - *(see Johnny Blood)*
McWilliams, Shorty - 121
Mead, Jack - 93, 96
Meagher, Jack - 23
Meehan, Chick - 22, 25
Menominee River - 79
Menomonee Falls, Wis. - 121
Meyer, Bob - 218
Miami (Fla.), Univ. of - 61
Miami Seahawks (AAC) - 23, 24, 26, 32, 47, 49
Michaelosen, Johnny - 95
Michalske, Mike - 192, 196, 197, 208
Michigan, Univ. of - 39, 61, 122
Miller, Hank - 39
Milton, Wis. - 59
Milwaukee, Wis. - 37, 40, 42, 44, 47, 50-52, 58, 61, 66-69, 77, 84, 88, 94, 98, 102, 109-111, 121, 133, 134, 152-157, 162-164, 166-168, 170, 171, 180, 186, 187, 208, 211, 212, 217, 219
Milwaukee Badgers (NFL) - 44, 109
Milwaukee Braves (baseball) - 109
Milwaukee Brewers (baseball) - 110
Milwaukee Chiefs (AFL) - 109
Milwaukee Journal, The - 82, 133, 151, 166, 168, 172, 174, 182
Milwaukee Sentinal, The - 76, 112, 116, 117, 120, 123, 180
Milwaukee Teachers College - 125
Minneapolis, Minn. - 94
Minnesota, Univ. of - 39, 79, 81, 90, 120, 122
Mississippi, Univ. of - 88
Mississippi State University - 121
Missouri, Univ. of - 93, 95
Mitchell, Charley - 39
Molenda, Bo - 61, 62, 123, 151

Moncrief, Monte - 57
Mongin, Arthur H. - 169
Monk, Art - 35
Monnett, Bobby - 197
Montana, Univ. of - 65
Morabito, Tony - 24
Morgan, Dennis - 210
Mosely, Russ - 40
Moss, Perry - 80, 90, 94, 102, 116, 126
Mraz, Carl - 39, 98
Mulleneaux, Carl - 34, 40, 66
Mullins, Noah - 97
Murphy, C.N. - 205
Murray, Jab - 223
Muscatine, Iowa - 49
Musso, George - 108

-N-

Nadolney, Romanus "Peaches" - 223
Nagurski, Bronko - 92
National-American Football League (NAFL) - 139, 140, 170, 177, 183, 194
Neal, Ed - 40, 65, 66, 93, 126, 128
Nevada, Univ. of (Reno) - 80, 121, 125
Nevers, Ernie - 23, 201
New Orleans, La. - 22, 84, 85, 139
New York, N.Y. - 21, 22, 25, 26, 29, 36, 40, 46, 48, 54, 72, 77, 89, 105, 110, 112, 113, 115, 121, 132, 136, 137, 140, 159, 163, 166
New York Bulldogs (see Boston Yanks) - 129, 132, 135, 138, 140
New York Daily News, The - 165
New York Giants (NFL) - 14, 32-34, 40, 41, 43, 48, 61, 64, 72, 73, 88, 93, 94, 100, 105, 110-112, 126, 128, 132, 134, 139, 140, 155-157, 208, 217
New York Giants (baseball) - 76
New York Yankees (AAC) - 24, 25, 32, 49, 54, 79, 80, 109, 110, 112-115, 122, 133, 137, 139, 140, 163, 166
New York Yankees (baseball) - 27
Nichols, Herb - 218
Norbertine Brothers - 38
Northwestern University - 23, 123
Notre Dame box formation - 36, 197
Notre Dame, Univ. of - 23, 26, 36, 57, 59, 60, 65, 77, 79, 85, 88, 93, 121, 123, 125, 165, 189, 190, 206
Nussbaumer, Bob - 39, 41, 57

-O-

O'Brien, Margaret - 127
O'Brien, Pat - 26
Oconto, Wis. - 60
Odson, Urban - 39, 65, 69, 78, 93, 126
Ohio State University - 23, 186
Ojai, Calif. - 106
O'Keefe, Dennis - 210
Oklahoma A&M (State) University - 49, 93
Oklahoma University - 62, 123, 124, 125, 128
Olsen, Ralph - 125, 134

The Lambeau Years — Part Three

Olsonoski, Larry - 79, 80, 90, 94, 98, 104, 126, 128, 132
Omaha University - 82
Oorang Indians (NFL) - 38
Ordens, Joe - 191, 200, 201, 222, 224
Oregon, Univ. of - 122
Orlich, Dan - 125
Oshkosh, Wis. - 97
Oshkosh All-Stars (basketball) - 152
Owen, Steve - 61
Owen, Tony - 210
Owens - 223

-P-

Pacific Coast League (PCL) - 29, 52, 87, 93
Packer Legend, The: An Inside Look - 14, 59
Packer Report, The - 13
Pagel, Ray - 225, 226
Panelli, John - 79
Paris, Alvin J. - 48
Payne, Roland Donald - 21, 22
Pearl Harbor, Hawaii - 21
Petreat, Russ - 218
Pennsylvania, Univ. of - 121
Peshtigo, Wis. - 80
Philadelphia, Pa. - 21, 42, 47, 54, 111, 113, 139, 175, 183, 226
Philadelphia Eagles (NFL) - 31, 32, 40, 42, 67-74, 78, 83, 88, 95, 97, 100, 102, 103, 106, 110, 112, 113, 124, 127, 128, 133, 134, 140, 158, 170, 220
Pihos, Pete - 124
Piotrowski, Ray - 93, 94
Pittsburgh, Pa. - 21, 54, 79, 128, 158, 161, 217
Pittsburgh Pirates - (*see Pittsburgh Steelers*)
Pittsburgh Steelers (NFL) - 31, 32, 42, 65, 68, 69, 71-74, 88, 89, 95, 100, 104, 121, 122, 128, 134, 140, 153, 219
Poillon, Dick - 101
Polo Grounds (New York) - 132
Pool, Hampton - 26, 49
Poole, Barney - 88
Poole, James - 26
Portland, Ore. - 22
Portland Rockets (PCL) - 93
Pregulman, Merv - 39, 61
Prell, Edward - 46, 47
Prescott, Hal - 39
Pritko, Steve - 132
Professional Football Hall of Fame - 132, 220
Providence Steamrollers (NFL) - 44
Provo, Fred - 80, 90, 96, 126
Pulaski, Wis. - 219
Purdue University - 57, 65, 121
Pyle, C.C. - 22

-Q-R-

Racine, Wis. - 154
Ratterman, George - 85, 86, 138
Rausch, John - 121

Ray, Buford "Baby" - 40, 65, 69, 78, 93, 105, 126, 196
Reeves, Dan - 32, 57, 160, 161, 172
Regnier - 223
Remmel, Lee - 41, 42, 69, 205, 206, 225
Rennebohm, Bob - 90, 93
Reynolds, Jim - 93
Rhodemyre, Jay - 79, 80, 82, 90, 94, 95, 97, 98, 104, 126
Rice, Daniel F. - 26, 108
Rice, Jerry - 35
Rice Institute - 79
Richards, Don - 90, 94
Rickey, Branch - 86
Riddick, Ray - 39
Ripon, Wis. - 108
Rock Island, Ill. - 129
Rock Island Independents (NFL) - 44
Rockne, Knute - 59, 189, 190, 206
Rockwood Lodge - 38, 64, 105, 116-120, 150, 167, 169, 175, 176, 183, 212
Rodenberg, Bob - 84
Rohrig, Herman - 39, 65, 94
Ronzani, Gene - 171
Rooney, Art - 160
Rose, Al - 204
Rosentover, Joseph - 28
Roskie, Ken - 93, 102
Rozelle, Pete - 136
Ruth, George "Babe" - 35
Ryan, William J. - 190, 205, 206
Rymkus, Lou - 26

-S-

Sainsbury, Ed - 121
St. Anselm's College - 108
St. Louis, Mo. - 22, 77, 137, 153, 218
St. Louis Browns (baseball) - 43, 152
Salt Lake City, Utah - 93
San Diego, Calif. - 22, 87, 161
San Diego Bombers (PCL) - 36
San Diego Navala Base - 61
San Francisco, Calif. - 22, 32, 37, 46, 54, 77, 85, 87, 114, 161, 225
San Francisco Clippers (PCL) - 52, 87
San Francisco 49ers (AAC) - 23, 24, 32, 37, 49, 54, 93, 109, 112-115, 136-138, 163
San Francisco 49ers (NFL) - 35, 140
Santa Clara University - 23
Savage, Bob - 218
Scalla, Howard - 126
Schlinkman, Walt - 39, 41, 56, 65, 66, 78, 93, 95, 96, 100, 104, 126, 130
Schmaehl, Art - 222-224
Schroeder, Bill - 125, 129
Seattle, Wash. - 22, 87
Seattle Bombers (AFL) - 23
Seno, Frank - 129
Servotte, William J. - 63, 64, 148, 217
Shannon, Harold T.I. - 75
Sharpe, Sterling - 13
Shaughnessy, Clark - 99, 100, 176
Shaw, Buck - 23

Shea, Dinny - 30
Sheboygan, Wis. - 125
Sherby, Daniel - 139
Sinkwich, Frankie - 30
Skoglund, Bob - 57, 65, 70, 93, 96, 123
Sleight, Elmer - 196
Smith, Bruce - 40, 41, 63, 65, 66, 81, 90, 93, 96, 97, 99, 100
Smith, Ernie - 39, 196
Smith, O. Ed - 79, 80, 90, 105, 126, 127, 129, 132
Snyder, Bob - 99, 123-125, 131-133, 151, 175
Soldier Field (Chicago, Ill.) - 23, 85
South Bend, Ind. - 59, 189, 190
South Bend Tribune - 59
South Carolina, Univ. of - 93
Southern California, Univ. of - 57, 102
Southern Methodist University - 57, 65, 93, 95, 121, 125
Southwestern University - 93
Sparlis, Al - 39
Spitz, Leo - 26
Sport magazine - 111
Sports Illustrated - 85
Sprinkle, Ed - 43, 104
Stahas, Jim - 215
State Fair Park (Milwaukee, Wis.) - 37, 50-52, 99, 109, 119, 133, 152, 153
Steuber, Bob - 26
Stevens, Mal - 24
Stidham, Tom - 123, 124, 131, 132, 151, 175
Stone, Claire - 218
Stone, Elmer - 215
Storck, Carl L.H. - 222
Strickler, George - 58-60, 79, 82, 119, 120, 146, 167, 184, 185, 193, 218
Strzykalski, John - 36, 37
Sturgeon Bay, Wis. - 99
Sturgeon, Lyle - 212
Stydahar, Joe - 125
Summerhays, Bob - 125, 128
Sutherland, John "Jock" - 89, 95
Swiacki, Bill - 88
Syracuse, N.Y. - 128
Syzmanski, Frank - 93, 95

-T-

Taliaferro, George - 121
Tassos, Damon - 60, 61, 65, 93, 104, 126, 129
Tatom, Charley - 129
Taugher, Claude - 223
Tenner, Bob - 204
Texas, Univ. of - 93, 126
Texas A&I College - 93
Texas A&M University - 57, 61
Texas College of Mines - 79, 90
Texas Technical Institute - 39, 90, 125
Thomason, Bobby - 121
Thompson, Alexis - 83, 87, 110-112, 158
Thorpe, Jim - 38
Titanic, S.S. - 83

Tollefson, Charley - 40
Toohey, William S. - 49, 50, 84, 108
Topping, Dan - 27, 30, 31, 110, 111, 115, 121, 123
Torinus, John, Sr. - 14, 59, 94, 127, 168, 202, 218
Touchback, The - 24
Trans-America Football League - 22, 25
Triboro Municipal Stadium (New York, N.Y.) - 25
Trippi, Charley - 49, 66, 87
Tripucka, Frank - 121
Tulsa University - 39, 90, 126
Tunney, Gene - 59
Turek, Bob - 218
Turnbull, Andrew V. - 64, 127, 148, 171, 179, 184, 192, 200-202, 225
Turner, Clyde "Bulldog" - 26
Two Rivers, Wis. - 54

-U-

UCLA - 38, 39, 57
United Press International - 26, 111, 180
United States Football League - 21, 22, 25, 136
Uram, Andy - 64, 197
Utah, Univ. of - 125

-V-

Van Brocklin, Norm - 132
Van Kessel, Marguerite - *(see Marguerite Lambeau)*
Vant Hull, Fred - 64, 93
Villanova University - 125, 133
Virginia Military Institute - 121
Vogds, Evan "Red" - 93, 106, 126, 128

-W-

Walker, Doak - 121
Walmsley, George - 79
Walsh, Charles "Chili" - 38
Walsh, Christy - 24, 26
Ward, Arch - 85, 86, 95, 194
Washington, D.C. - 54, 137, 217
Washington, George - 160
Washington, Kenny - 38, 99
Washington, Univ. of - 38, 90, 93
Washington Redskins (NFL) - 14, 22, 23, 26, 32, 33, 35, 40, 45, 53, 57, 62, 65, 67, 68, 70, 72, 73, 85, 88, 93, 95, 96, 100-103, 111, 112, 129, 133, 135, 136, 140, 158
Waterfield, Bob - 67, 100, 132
Watertown, Wis. - 102, 116
Wayne, John - 92
Weiss, Seymour - 139
Wells, Don - 39, 65, 93, 96, 126, 132
West, Bob - 93, 94
West, Pat - 102, 126
WHBY-radio (Green Bay) - 75
Wildung, Dick - 39, 65, 93, 103, 104, 123, 126, 132

Williams, Frank - 129
Wilson, Gene - 57, 63, 65, 93, 126
Winnie, Russ - 75
Wintgens, H.G. - 64, 217
Wisconsin, Univ. of - 60, 65, 79, 90, 93, 125, 189
WJPG-radio (Green Bay) - 76, 82, 94, 110
Wojciehowicz, Alex - 128
Wolf, Ed - 215
World War I - 49
World War II - 15, 16, 21, 22, 29, 31, 33, 36, 38, 39, 58, 69, 76, 109, 143, 145
Wrigley Field (Chicago) - 134
WTMJ-radio (Milwaukee) - 75, 76, 94

-XYZ-

Yankee Stadium (New York, N.Y.) - 25, 31, 110, 139
Young, Claude "Buddy" - 85, 86
Zabel, Baldy - 206
Zablocki, Jerry - 219
Zeller, Joe - 143, 144
Zoll, Carl - 212
Zuidmulder, Dave - 212
Zupek, Al - 39

Bibliography

Books

The Baseball Encyclopedia, Sixth Edition, Revised, Updated & Expanded, edited by Joseph L. Reichler, Macmillan Publishing Co., Inc., 1985

George Halas and the Chicago Bears, George Vass, Henry Regnery Company, 1971

The Green Bay Packers, Pro Football's Pioneer Team, Chuck Johnson, Thomas Nelson & Sons, 1961.

The Green Bay Packers, The Story of Professional Football, Arch Ward, G.P. Putnam's Sons, 1946.

Halas on Halas, George Halas with Gwen Morgan and Arthur Veysey, McGraw–Hill Book Co., 1979

History of American Football, Allison Danzig, Prentice–Hall, Inc., 1956.

The NFL's Official Encyclopedic History of Professional Football, Macmillan Publishing Co., Inc., 1973

Official 1985 National Football League Record & Fact Book.

The Packer Legend: An Inside Look, John B. Torinus, Sr., Laranmark Press, 1982

The Pro Football Digest, edited by Robert Billings, Digest Books, Inc., 1978

The Scrapbook History of Pro Football, Richard M. Cohen, Jordan A. Deutsch, Roland T. Johnson, and David S. Neft, The Bobbs–Merrill Company, 1977.

Newspapers and Periodicals

The Chicago Tribune.
The Green Bay Gazette.
Green Bay Packers Media Guide, 1987.
The Green Bay Press–Gazette.
The Milwaukee Journal.
The Milwaukee Sentinel.
The New York Times.
Collier's
Time
The Chicago Sun
The Chicago Daily News
The Los Angeles Times
The Chicago Herald–Examiner
Daily Georgian and Sunday American
The Iron Mountain News
The Los Angeles Examiner
The New York Daily News
The South Bend Tribune
Sport magazine
Sports Illustrated
The Touchback
The Packer Report

Green Bay Packer Media Guide, 1986
Green Bay Packer Media Guide, 1987
Green Bay Packer Media Guide, 1988
Green Bay Packer Media Guide, 1989